D. H. LAWRENCE
His Life and Works

D. H. LAWRENCE
His Life and Works

Harry T. Moore

SOUTHERN ILLINOIS UNIVERSITY

TWAYNE PUBLISHERS, INC.

New York

To Beatrice

FOREWORD TO THE SECOND EDITION

IN REVISING THIS BOOK I HAVE MADE EXTENSIVE corrections and additions and have also taken out some of the material that appeared in the original edition (1951), principally an appendix now obsolete.

This book is essentially a study of D. H. Lawrence's work. The biographical data serve mostly as background to the comments on Lawrence's writings. This volume should not be confused with another which I have written about Lawrence, *The Intelligent Heart*. First published in 1955 and now available in paperback editions in England and America, that book is essentially a biography. Further information about Lawrence's life may be found in my edition of his *Collected Letters* (1962), which also contains important commentaries he made on his own work. Once again, the present volume—although it provides some biographical information—is mainly a study of Lawrence's writings and, of course, of the thought behind them.

Since this book first appeared, the Lawrence situation has greatly changed. As Lawrence's antagonist and champion, the late John Middleton Murry, said in 1956, "his significance is no longer in debate." Lawrence now stands high among all writers of our time. Part of the reason for this was also noted in 1956 by Murry: "Lawrence was alone in the depth of his prescience of the crisis of humanity which has developed since his death." This continues to be true, but we must also remember the power of Lawrence's expression; the present book contains many examples of this, for in it I attempted to fulfill my deepest obligation to both reader and subject by letting Lawrence, as often as possible, speak for himself.

HARRY T. MOORE

Taos, New Mexico
July 21, 1963

7

ACKNOWLEDGMENTS

THE AUTHOR IS INDEBTED ABOVE ALL TO THE LATE Mrs. Frieda Lawrence Ravagli, particularly for her generosity in permitting extensive quotations from Lawrence's work and, for similar reasons, to Lawrence's good friend Mr. Laurence Pollinger.

Among others who have kindly assisted the author in connection with the original as well as the revised edition of this book, are: the late Benedict Abramson; the late Richard Aldington; Miss Ruth Bailey, formerly Librarian, Babson Institute; Professor Angelo P. Bertocci, Boston University; Mr. E. Coulston Bonner, Headmaster, Davidson Secondary Modern School, Croydon, South London; Professor Gerald Warner Brace, Boston University; the late Catherine Carswell; Mr. John Ciardi; Mr. Edward Clarke, Ripley, Derby, and his late wife, the former Ada Lawrence; *Ing.* Guido Comboni, Gargnano, Lago di Garda; Miss Helen Corke; Mrs. Caresse Crosby; Mr. John Davenport; Signorina Laura Falorni, Rome; Mr. A. S. Frere; Mr. David Garnett; Mr. Duncan Gray, City Librarian, Nottingham; Mr. Phil Heald, photographer, Worcester, Mass.; the late County Councillor William E. Hopkin, Eastwood, Notts; Frau Dr. Else Jaffe-Richthofen, Heidelberg; Mr. Jan Juta; Mr. George Lawrence, Nottingham; Mr. Ralph Lewis, U. S. Department of State; Mr. J. Wesley Littlefield, University of Toledo, Ohio; Sir Compton Mackenzie; Professor Emeritus Fred B. Millett, Wesleyan University; the late John Middleton Murry; Miss Anaïs Nin; the late Edward J. O'Brien; Mr. Hedley Pickbourne, Registrar, Nottingham University College; Sir Richard Rees; Professor F. Warren Roberts; Miss Frances Steloff, Gotham Book Mart, New York City; Mr. W. Scorer, Division Educational Officer, Ilkeston, Derby; Professor Mark Schorer; Mr.

9

Irwin Swerdlow; the Reverend J. R. Thomas, Sneinton Vicarage, Nottingham; Mr. Frank E. Turner, Press Association, Ltd., London; Dame Rebecca West.

Lawrence's American publishers, the Viking Press and Alfred A. Knopf, have been extremely generous in permitting quotations of Lawrence material. The Viking Press publishes the following books of Lawrence's which have been quoted from in this volume:

Aaron's Rod	*The Lovely Lady*
Amores	*A Modern Lover*
Apocalypse	*New Poems*
The Boy in the Bush	*Phoenix*
The Captain's Doll	*The Prussian Officer*
Collected Poems	*Psychoanalysis of the*
England, My England	*Unconscious*
Etruscan Places	*The Rainbow*
Fantasia of the Unconscious	*Sea and Sardinia*
Kangaroo	*Sons and Lovers*
Last Poems	*Studies in Classical American*
Letters	*Literature*
Look! We Have Come	*Touch and Go*
Through!	*Twilight in Italy*
The Lost Girl	*The Widowing of Mrs. Holroyd*
Love Among the Haystacks	*Women in Love*

Viking also publishes Frieda Lawrence's *Not I, But the Wind*.

Alfred A. Knopf publishes the following books of Lawrence's which have been quoted from:

Assorted Articles	*The Plumed Serpent*
David	*Pornography and Obscenity*
The Man Who Died	*St. Mawr*
Mornings in Mexico	*The Woman Who Rode Away*
Pansies	*The Virgin and the Gipsy*

Knopf also publishes *Lorenzo in Taos*, by Mabel Dodge Luhan.

CONTENTS

11

PROLOGUE

THE NINETEENTH CENTURY HAD COME TO SEEM an eternal achievement: the long Tennysonian dream did not end with the last page of the century's calendar, or even with the death of the age's supreme symbol, Queen Victoria, but rather with the Germans' march into Belgium. It was then that Grey of Fallodon pronounced the epitaph of the nineteenth century: "The lamps are going out all over Europe; we shall not see them lit again in our lifetime."

The years of D. H. Lawrence, 1885 to 1930, crossed this period of frightening change from a world of apparent order and contentment to a world of chaos and sick nerves.

His writings were not popular or commercially successful during his lifetime. A few readers found in this work a strange and compelling beauty, but Lawrence was known to the wide public only as the author of "indecent" books that were from time to time suppressed. He had written boldly of sexual matters because he felt that too much repression and intellectualization were destroying the instinctual part of man's nature: Lawrence stressed passion not because he believed in passion exclusively but because he believed it should be brought into balance with intellect. This is his central message. He repeated it in various ways, and in combination with other ideas, through most of his work.

His writing career was a brief one: it lasted only twenty

years. And though he was often ill during that time, and now and then at the edge of death, he produced about fifty volumes and left material for about twenty more, some of it among the finest literature of its time.

This twenty-year writing period of Lawrence's had four phases, determined by events in his life and in his writings: 1909-1912, 1913-1919, 1920-1925, 1926-1930.

His first professional appearance in print under his own name was in 1909, when an English magazine published a group of his poems. By the end of 1912 Lawrence, then in Italy, had completed his third novel, *Sons and Lovers*. This first phase of his writing was concerned chiefly with recording his youth in poetry, stories, and novels.

In Italy for the second time in 1913-1914, Lawrence worked on the material that was to become *The Rainbow* and *Women in Love*, the two novels of his second period, books which he subsequently completed in England. With these novels and the poems in *Look! We Have Come Through!*, Lawrence went in a new direction creatively: he wrote intensely of modern love experience, and he made important psychological explorations into the emotional consciousness. This period ended in despair over the prolongation of the First World War, at the end of which Lawrence went into voluntary exile.

After his arrival in Italy in 1919, he began his wander-years and a new phase of his work. Travelling around the Mediterranean and then going to India and Australia and America, Lawrence in the years following the war wrote some of his finest poems and travel books as well as the three novels concerned with problems of mystical-political leadership: *Aaron's Rod*, *Kangaroo*, and *The Plumed Serpent*. What he called his "savage pilgrimage" was a quest for social certainty, expressed imaginatively in his writings of this period, which are more scattered, less cohesive, than most of his other work, though more richly colored than any of the rest.

When Lawrence went back to Europe from America late in 1925, he once more began a new phase of his writing coincident with a return to Italy. As in his second period, when he grew beyond the experiences of his youth, Lawrence in his fourth period again went beyond the interests of his preceding phase.

In *Lady Chatterley's Lover*, the only full-length novel written at this time, Lawrence abandoned political and leadership ideas and returned to sexual themes. He was frequently ill during these last years, and much of his work was bitter; this is particularly true of his poems, which also indicate an awareness of death and, finally, an acceptance of it. Religious themes underlie Lawrence's short novel, *The Escaped Cock*, and his last philosophical book, *Apocalypse*.

Lawrence was forty-four years old when he died in southern France in the spring of 1930. For a while after his death there was a false-dawn of interest in his work: the bizarre early memoirs of his campfollowers attracted a host of new readers to Lawrence's books, but because these books were literature rather than gossip, the interest passed. Also, the more serious type of reader was at this time deflected from work such as Lawrence's, by the world-wide financial crisis, which induced a quite different kind of reading; later, the Second World War hammered people's attention to still another kind of book. But since the war there has been a revival of interest in Lawrence, marked by the steady reprinting of his work, and by a more tolerant attitude toward it on the part of those who write about literature.

Such a change in attitude as that manifested by Professor William York Tindall is typical of the newer approach to Lawrence. Tindall was one of the most caustic critics of Lawrence in 1939, in *D. H. Lawrence and Susan His Cow*, which particularly made fun of Lawrence's mystical side. But in 1947, Tindall's *Forces in Modern British Literature: 1885–1946* took a modified, post-Hiroshima view of Lawrence, whose crusade against science "preached by allegory and symbol seems less absurd today than it used to seem. . . . About to be decomposed, we can turn with understanding," Tindall suggested, toward such prophets as Lawrence, perhaps even accept some of their religious pronouncements.

Not all of Lawrence's readers will agree with all of his philosophy, with his remedies for the social illnesses he so effectively diagnosed; they may nevertheless find some important areas of agreement. In any event there is always a reward for readers in Lawrence's expressional power: his writing, just as writing, provides one of the richest reading experiences of our time.

PART ONE

$\mathbf{T}$HE TRACING OF FAMILY CONNECTIONS BEGINS
with Lawrence's paternal heritage. According to one family tradition, his grandfather John Lawrence was a Frenchman, the
son of a man who had fought at Waterloo. D. H. Lawrence
once wrote that John Lawrence had come from the south of
England, but Lawrence's surviving brother, George, has told the
author of the present book that their grandfather was from the
city of Nottingham. He was a noted athlete, and his son Arthur
used to say that his father had once got the better of Ben Caunt,
the British boxing champion, in an informal fight. John Lawrence learned the art of tailoring from his stepfather, and after
marrying the daughter of a Nottingham lace-maker became company tailor at Brinsley colliery near Eastwood.

This village, in 1086 mentioned in the Domesday Book as East-
wic, is about eight miles north of the city of Nottingham. Eastwood is in the Midland coalfields which have been exploited for
centuries; its true growth as an industrial town began in
Victorian times, when between 1861 and 1881 its population
increased from 1,860 to 3,566. By 1891, six years after the birth
of D. H. Lawrence, 4,363 people lived in the town. Most of
them were miners and their families, with shopkeepers moving
in as the community spread out. Among them all, Lawrence
found many types for his novels and stories.

17

When he was a child, the company stopped supplying the miners with pit-clothes, but he could always remember his grandfather's shop at Brinsley with its great rolls of flannel for the thick vests, "and the strange old sewing-machine, like nothing else on earth, which sewed the massive pit-trousers." Lawrence's sister Ada recalls her grandfather in his eighties as "a big, shambling, generous-hearted man whose waistcoat front was always powdered with snuff. He was very deaf and didn't talk much, but he never forgot to ask, 'Would you like some apples, my duckies?'" His deafness protected him from the shrill complaints of his wife, who used the front room of their cottage as a shop. Her drapery business had once flourished, but it was declining in the days when the Lawrence children used to walk the mile across the fields from Eastwood to Old Brinsley on visits to their grandparents.

The name of John Lawrence's son—father of the poet—is sometimes given as John Arthur, though on official documents it is Arthur John. In childhood he went for a time to one of the dame schools which were so common in the Victorian period. D. H. Lawrence later said that his father had barely learned to write his name at Mrs. Eite's. "As for his feelings, they had escaped her clutches entirely: as they escaped the clutches of his mother." He "rackapelted with his own gang. And to the end of his days his idea of life was to escape over the fringe of virtue and drink beer and perhaps poach an occasional rabbit."

Arthur Lawrence went to work in the pits in his childhood, dressed in the flannel singlet and moleskin trousers his father made. And although he remained a miner until he was an old man, he never became anything more than a butty—foreman of a section of the coal-face, with three or four men under his direction—the industrial equivalent of a corporalship.

He was a grumbler who prevented his own advancement by continually wrangling with his immediate superiors. Outside the pit, he was popular with his fellow-workers. He had a good voice and for some years sang in the choir at Brinsley church. His daughter Ada remembers him as a handsome, ruddy-faced man with dark, flashing eyes and a beard; "he boasted that a razor had never touched his face." Her mother, who had never been near a mining town, "met him at a party at Nottingham, and was attracted by his graceful dancing, his musical voice, his gallant manner and his overflowing humor and good spirits."

Arthur Lawrence is portrayed in his son's novel, *Sons and Lovers*, as a brutal drunkard. In later years Lawrence felt that he had not understood his father because he had, in childhood and youth, seen him through the prejudiced eyes of his mother. Less than ten years after he completed *Sons and Lovers*, Lawrence expressed the wish that he could rewrite it in fairness to his father; friends report his saying that he and his brothers and sisters "had accepted the dictum of their mother that their father was a drunkard, therefore contemptible, but that as Lawrence had grown older he had come to see him in a different light; to see his unquenchable fire and relish for living."

Tolerance was something Mrs. Lawrence did not possess. Lydia Beardsall was a member of a proud Nottingham family that had lost its money in her grandfather's time; for a while in her youth she was a schoolteacher. When she married the gay and vital collier, after having been jilted by a refined young man, she had little idea of what it was like to be a coal miner's wife. But she learned as soon as her husband took her to his native town of Brinsley. It is safe to assume that the disappointment of Gertrude Morel in *Sons and Lovers* is an accurate record of the disappointment of Lydia Lawrence, as she had described it to her son.

The local mining operators—Barber, Walker, and Company—had with the recent growth of the town built squares of barracks-like dwellings for the colliers' families at the north end of Eastwood and in the valley below. This environment of illiteracy and ugly brick seen through a veil of soot was far different from what Lydia had known in the Peashill Rise district of Nottingham and during her years of school teaching at Sheerness.

As an ancestral voice, her father must have been an important contributor to D. H. Lawrence's emotional make-up. For this grandfather was a prophetic, evangelistic man.

George Beardsall was by profession an engineer—he became foreman at Sheerness dockyard, off the coast of Kent—but by inclination he was an evangelist. He was known in Nottingham religious circles for the stubbornness of his piety and the ferocity of his quarrels. In one altercation, Beardsall's opponent was the chemist-shop magnate Jessie Boot, later Sir Jessie and eventually Lord Trent. "My mother's father and this grand-duke of drugs quarrelled and had a long war as to which of them should govern a chapel in Sneinton, in Nottingham. My grandfather won."

This chapel was probably the Wesleyan church in Sneinton, since Boot was a Wesleyan. Some of the Beardsalls, however, seem to have been members of the Church of England in that parish, for it was in the Established Church there that Lydia Beardsall married Arthur Lawrence on December 27, 1875.

George Beardsall seems also to have quarreled with another famous native of that city, whose name resembles that of Boot: "General" William E. Booth. The founder of the Salvation Army was born a few yards from the Established Church at Sneinton, in which he was baptized in 1829. David Garnett has reported that Lawrence told him that his grandfather "was the earliest friend, collaborator, and inspirer of William Booth, and that he broke off with the 'General' over their joint plans for formation of what turned into the Salvation Army."

The similarity of the names Boot and Booth might suggest that there is some confusion in regard to George Beardsall's quarrels. Lawrence himself is on record as to the Boot episode, but that George Beardsall also wrangled with another famous local citizen of almost identical name might seem too coincidental to be actually true. But Frieda Lawrence has attested, in a letter of May 16, 1950, that her husband had also spoken of his grandfather's quarrel with Booth: "Grandfather Beardsall was a friend of General Booth and they separated—L told me Beardsall was a very pious man and would say after lunch: Now I will have an hour with 'Paul,' you know the apostle Paul."

We have a fuller picture, now, of Lawrence's heritage, with this Pauline figure in the background. Lawrence in his essay "Hymns in a Man's Life" told how the songs he sang in childhood in the Congregational chapel in Eastwood remained important to him all his life; but he was susceptible to such influence, having the mother and grandfather that he had. And Lawrence's great-grandfather, John Newton (1802-1886), was a famous hymn-writer. (He should not be confused with an earlier hymn-writer of the same name, Cowper's collaborator.) A Nottingham lace-maker whose daughter married George Beardsall, this John Newton wrote what remains one of the most popular chapel hymns in England, "Sovereignty."

As we shall see, Lawrence's father figures importantly in his background too. For beyond the portrait of him in *Sons and Lovers*, which at the realistic level perhaps helped Lawrence exorcise the father-image, there seems to be a lingering influence of the father in the son's later worship of earth-men, and even in the value he places upon darkness in many of his poetic passages: this was probably a development of the image of mine-darkness which must have always haunted him.

These three men, the collier father and the hymn-writing and hymn-singing grandfathers, should be remembered as standing behind Lawrence ancestrally. The father in his bearded virility became, for the most part unconsciously perhaps, a kind of ideal to Lawrence, though except in conversation he would rarely have good words for his father as an individual: the deflected praise was symbolic, the worship of earth-bound peasant and simple Indian. The Beardsall grandfather and the Newton great-grandfather perhaps make their most important hereditary contribution in the hymns of one of Lawrence's last novels, *The Plumed Serpent*, and in his last long essay, *Apocalypse*.

But his mother was the strongest influence on D. H. Lawrence. As he shows in his most famous novel, she turned, after the disappointment of her marriage, to her sons as lovers.

She had three sons altogether—George Arthur, William Ernest, and David Herbert—and two daughters, Emily and Lettice Ada. David Herbert Richards Lawrence, the next-to-youngest child, was born in the tenth year of his parents' marriage, on September 11, 1885, in a mean brick house on slanting Victoria Street. Before the children came, Mrs. Lawrence had, like her querulous mother-in-law, used the front room of her house as a shop where she sold lace caps, linens, and aprons. She was thus able to add slightly to her husband's irregular and uncertain salary in those days before trams and buses took local shoppers conveniently into Nottingham.

When Lawrence was about two years old, the family moved to The Breach, a hollow below the north end of the town, where blocks of houses had been erected by the mine owners for their workers. A battered corner of nature existed there: currant bushes and hawthorn hedges and a brook with a mill that still ground the local corn. Mrs. Lawrence, who associated but little with the other miners' wives, had an end house with a garden of its own, but she hated The Breach: the houses backed onto clamorous alleys full of ash heaps. After five years the family moved to Number 3 Walker Street, on the hill above the miners' tenements, and the landscape of the Lawrence Country spread out below them: "Underwood in front, the hills of Derbyshire on the left, and the woods and hills of Annesley on the right . . . I lived in that house from 6 to 18, and I know that view better than any in the world."

An ash tree that stood near the Walker Street house appears in *Sons and Lovers:* the children in the story, sleepless and frightened in their beds on nights when their father comes home drunk, hear the wind-blown tree crying out above the noise of their parents' quarrelling. This situation also occurs in one of Lawrence's early poems, "Discord in Childhood," which ends:

Within the house, two voices rose in anger, a slender lash
Whistling delirious rage, and the dreadful sound
Of a thick lash booming and bruising, while it drowned
The other voice in a silence of blood, 'neath the noise of the ash.

In a poem written toward the end of his life, Lawrence speaks of the parental oppositions in a sociological sense. The mother, in carrying her warfare to the father, was purity against bestiality, decency against drunkenness, education against ignorance, but above everything she was Victorian bourgeoise against industrial proletarian: the continuing battle was really class warfare, and in one of the irascible and not very poetic *Pansies* poems, "Red-Herring," Lawrence says in part:

My father was a working man
    and a collier was he,
at six in the morning they turned him down
    and they turned him up for tea.

My mother was a superior soul
a superior soul was she,
cut out to play a superior rôle
in the god-damn bourgeoisie.

We children were the in-betweens
little non-descripts were we,
indoors we called each other *you*
outside it was *tha* and *thee*.

But time has fled, our parents are dead
we've risen in the world all three;
but still we are in-betweens, we tread
between the devil and the deep cold sea.

The clear distinctions between the different branches of Lawrence's family were not actually so strong as he rather dramatically saw them. The father was the first member of the family to become a part of the working proletariat. His wife had little reason to look down on him socially, for the Lawrences and the Beardsalls had been related by marriage even before Arthur Lawrence had met Lydia Beardsall: his aunt Alice had married Lydia's uncle John (son of the hymn-writer), and it was at the house of these younger Newtons, in the Basford section of the city of Nottingham, that the parents of D. H. Lawrence met. Arthur courted her for at least a year before they entered upon the marriage that Lawrence later wrote of as a series of bitter quarrels.

One of the issues the parents battled over was the childrens' future. Mrs. Lawrence wanted to have her daughters marry above the working class, and she wanted to keep her sons out of the mines. She was at the last successful in having her wishes granted.

When her son David Herbert was a child, she was particularly happy over his school career, for although he was not so brilliant in his studies as his older brother Ernest, whose promising London business career was cut short by an early death, the younger boy was a good student. After several years at the local Board School, D. H. Lawrence won a scholarship to the Nottingham High School. The fifteen pounds a year which the award provided could not cover the cost of daily transportation between Eastwood and Nottingham and of the lunches the boy had to eat in the city, but the mother's stubborn self-sacrificing made it possible for him to attend the high school and remain there for three years.

A friend who shared many of Lawrence's school experiences at both Eastwood and Nottingham, and later at Ilkeston, has given a somewhat full picture of Lawrence's youth. George H. Neville says that he and Lawrence had to leave home at seven every morning, returning twelve hours later "with always a pile of lessons to do." Lawrence even then "had that little, troublesome, hacking cough that used to bring his left hand so sharply to his mouth—a cough and an action that he never lost."

The school, which was in existence as long ago as 1289, is by Act of Parliament known as "the Nottingham High School of the Foundation of Dame Agnes Mellers." When Lawrence left he was in the Modern Sixth Form, which was the highest reached by those not taking Classics, Mathematics, or Science. The present headmaster, C. L. Reynolds, wrote in a letter to the author of this volume:

He won a town prize in 1900 and two mathematical set prizes, in 1899 and 1900 respectively, but there is no evidence that he distinguished himself at school in any way. Nobody now living and connected with the school has any recollection of him but some years ago I enquired of a retired schoolmaster who had taught him. He described Lawrence as a quiet, shy boy, not prominent in any way and showing no sign of his future distinction or of the fires that burned within him.

Lawrence withdrew in the summer of his sixteenth year, as the record shows; Mr. Reynolds says that this was the normal age at which boys left the school. Lawrence subsequently found a job at Haywood's, a firm of surgical goods manufacturers in Nottingham, where his salary was thirteen shillings a week.

It was in the summer of 1901, shortly after leaving school, that Lawrence met Jessie Chambers, the girl he was to write of as Miriam in *Sons and Lovers*. Her father had rented The Haggs, a quaint gabled farm two miles north of Eastwood; like Paul in that novel Lawrence often walked or cycled out to the farm.

The family there was about the size of his own, with a father and mother and several boys and girls, but tempermentally these were quite different people.

At harvest time, when Jessie's father and brothers went to work in the fields at Greasley, a mile to the east of town, Lawrence went with them, happy in the comradeship and activity. Mr. Chambers told his wife, "Work goes like fun when Bert's there."

But it was Jessie with whom Lawrence spent most of his time, reading romantic poetry and novels with her in a corner of the farm kitchen, and walking with her across the fields to Annesley, where Byron had courted Mary Chaworth, or through the surviving fragments of Sherwood Forest. It was a tortured, Congregational-young-British love affair, under intense fire from village publicity and from Lawrence's mother.

Jessie Chambers' account of this experience is found in the memoir she published in 1935, nine years before her death—*D. H. Lawrence: A Personal Record*, by E. T. This book is her version of the *Sons and Lovers* story, and there are frequent resemblances of incident and detail between the two books. Yet there are many dissimilarities both of fact and of interpretation. Paul in the novel feels that Miriam is too possessive and clutching; the original of Miriam says she was never really able to get close to Lawrence because of his mother. In *Sons and Lovers*, Paul seduces Miriam; in Jessie Chambers' memoir there is no hint of even the possibility of a seduction. She shows the young Lawrence as a Puritan, afraid of sex, disturbed by the difference he felt to exist between physical and spiritual love. Jessie Chambers implies that her attitude was more sensible and natural, yet her own fundamental Puritanism keeps revealing itself in the narrative, as when she tells of being scolded by Lawrence because she was unable to read aloud a passage from Ibsen about "keeping mistresses."

Other parts of her story are self-contradictory, yet her memoir is of pronounced biographical value, particularly because it mentions some of the books Lawrence read in his youth. The first novel he brought Jessie was *Little Women*, the kind of story he later abominated; but at the time he said they were Laurie and Jo. Together they read Longfellow, Scott, Dickens, Cooper, and Stevenson: after Lawrence went to college they read Carlyle and Schopenhauer and other philosophers, and finally Huxley and Haeckel, who had begun to shake the Congregationalism out of Lawrence. He taught Jessie to read French, and they went through Baudelaire and Hugo and Verlaine. Often in his walks through the fields, Lawrence carried with him a copy of *The Golden Treasury*, and he read Jessie the poems in this book. Perhaps the favorite author of their youth was George Eliot, who wrote of nearby Derbyshire; her influence is strong in *The White Peacock*.

Lawrence learned to paint, and copied pictures from magazines and from the *Studio* series of British water-colorists. He apparently did not paint Midland landscapes directly, though his copying of other men's work doubtless increased his perception and helped make his natural descriptions more vital.

Jessie encouraged his self-expression. She was a dreamy girl who thought of herself as a Walter Scott heroine; another woman who knew Lawrence has suggested that the dark-eyed and dark-haired Jessie was like a Murillo madonna. A year younger than Lawrence, Jessie worshiped him and praised his manuscripts and paintings. He afterward said it was at her farm that he got his first incentive to write.

He resumed his education not long after meeting Jessie. He had become seriously ill with pneumonia during his first winter of work at Haywood's, and after his convalescence had been offered a chance to become a pupil-teacher at the British School in his home town. This was a form of apprenticeship in which uncertificated teachers received training by instructing classes; they were in turn instructed by older teachers, generally before classes began in the morning. Some of Lawrence's experiences at this time were given to Ursula in *The Rainbow:* like Ursula, he had to teach in a huge room where other classes were also held, and there was much battling between groups. Lawrence later referred to his "three years' savage teaching of collier lads." Actually, the experience lasted through four school years, from the autumn of 1902 till the spring of 1906.

In 1903, Lawrence with other Nottinghamshire students was transferred to the Ilkeston Pupil-Teacher Centre in the Wilmot Street Schoolroom, and for two years he commuted to this

Derbyshire town. Jessie Chambers says that he was happier during this phase of the work than he was at Eastwood. She was then going to Ilkeston as a student teacher also, along with Ada Lawrence, George Neville, and other Eastwood young people, who were collectively known as "the Pagans."

In December 1904, Lawrence took the King's Scholarship Examination for uncertificated teachers and, according to a report from the Derbyshire Local Education Authority, "secured a first-class in Division I, being bracketed top in the country." Lawrence later said that after he led the entire country in the King's Scholarship Examination, he was "considered clever." But he lacked the hundred pounds required in advance for matriculation at training college, and had to continue teaching. By the time he was twenty-one, however, he was able to enroll in the Teachers' Training Department of Nottingham University College, which did not become the University of Nottingham until 1948. During his two years there, from September 1906 to June 1908, Lawrence took what was known in those days as the "normal course." This course, which qualified students for the Board of Education Teacher's Certificate, comprised both academic study and practical teaching.

Academically, Lawrence did not perform so brilliantly as might have been expected from one who had distinguished himself in scholarship examinations. His record was not, however, bad, though he received only one "A" grade—in Reading. His work in Teaching, Drawing, and Music was no higher than "B."

In addition to this required work, Lawrence took two optional subjects. One of these was Botany, for which he had a pronounced aptitude; from earliest childhood he had been fascinated by the flowers that, growing in the fields outside Eastwood, had flaunted their bright colors against the drabness of the mining town—and flowers figure importantly through all of Lawrence's work.

The other optional subject he took at Nottingham was French. He studied this under Professor Ernest Weekley, the etymologist. A few years after he left school, Lawrence and Professor Weekley were to become involved in a strange relationship; at the time Lawrence was an undergraduate, the teacher encouraged the young man but remained personally and socially aloof.

Lawrence later wrote that college to him "had meant mere disillusionment, instead of the contact of living men." He was a year or two older than most of the other students, with several years' teaching experience behind him, and he resented being "treated like a school kid." He was particularly angered by the teachers' red-ink notations and corrections on his class papers. One instructor objected to the appearance, in an essay, of the word stallion: "My boy, that's a word we don't use," this teacher explained to the future author of "St. Mawr," that classic of stallion worship.

Lawrence's bitterness toward the college lasted throughout his life. In one of the poems in the *Pansies* volume in 1929, "Nottingham's New University—," he speaks of Nottingham as "that dismal town/where I went to school and college," and refers to the new buildings being put up by Sir Jesse Boot (Lord Trent):

> Little I thought, when I was a lad
> and turned my modest penny
> over on Boot's Cash Chemist's counter,
> that Jesse, by turning many
>
> millions of similar honest pence
> over, would make a pile
> that would rise at last and blossom out
> in grand and cakey style
>
> into a university
> where smart men would dispense
> doses of smart cash-chemistry
> in language of common-sense!

After Lawrence escaped from what he felt were the repressions and pedantries of the college, he spent some time trying to find an instructorship that would pay him suitably. Jessie Chambers says that he refused to work for the customary salary of ninety pounds, and that when the 1908 fall term began in September, he had no job. His recommendation from the Teachers' Training Department at Nottingham, while not specifically unfavorable, was full of reservation clauses and *if's* and *how-*

ever's. Here is what Lawrence's supervisor wrote of his teaching practice:

Well-read, scholarly and refined, Mr. Lawrence will make an excellent teacher if he gets into the right place. His work at present is uneven according to the ordinary standard owing to his lack of experience of the elementary schoolboy and his management. He would be quite unsuitable for a large class of boys in a rough district; he would not have sufficient persistence and enthusiasm but would become disgusted.

Mr. Lawrence's strong bias is towards the humanistic subjects and at times boys' interest in such lessons is intense. Intelligence, however, is cultivated in lessons on all subjects by the treatment, especially the questions, the defect being a want of that persistent driving home and recapitulation which are necessary—like many intelligent teachers, Mr. Lawrence tends to teach the best pupils exclusively. Though very fluent, he sometimes has an obvious difficulty in finding words suitably simple. He is emphatically a teacher of upper classes.

Mr. Lawrence is fastidious in taste, and while working splendidly at anything that interests him would perhaps easily tire amid the tedium and discouragements of the average class-room. With an upper class in a good school or in a higher school he could do work quite unusually good, especially if allowed a very free hand.

In October 1908 Lawrence accepted a job and began teaching "an upper class in a good school": the Davidson Road School at Croydon, South London, which had opened just a year before. Lawrence said in his "Autobiographical Sketch" that his salary was one hundred pounds a year.

The Davidson Road School, now the Davidson Secondary Modern School, was one of the largest and most fully equipped buildings of its kind in the South London area. Lawrence wrote of it, "From the big new red school where I taught, we could look north and see the Crystal Palace: to me, who saw it for the first time, in lovely autumn weather, beautiful and softly blue on its hills to the north. And past the school, on an embankment, the trains rushed south to Brighton or to Kent. And round the school the country was still only just being built over, and the elms of Surrey stood tall and noble. It was different from the Midlands."

A different Lawrence had begun to grow in this new environment: Lawrence the writer. Lawrence the teacher changed and improved, and Lawrence the man became more assured, though many of his most agonizing problems remained with him. But his personal development and experiences will be discussed further on; it is time to look at his beginning literary career.

✦ ✦ ✦ ✦

Lawrence was first published professionally in 1909, when the November issue of the *English Review* printed a group of his poems under the general title of "A Still Afternoon." Jessie Chambers had sent them to the editor, Ford Madox Hueffer (later Ford Madox Ford). As Lawrence said later, "The girl had launched me so easily, on my literary career, like a princess cutting a thread, launching a ship."

It was also in 1909 that Lawrence completed *The White Peacock* "after four or five years' spasmodic effort." The novel was accepted by the first publishing firm to which it was submitted, William Heinemann, Ltd., which brought it out on January 20, 1911.

The White Peacock attracted favorable attention in London literary circles and, for the most part, in the British press. The few unfriendly reviews and the antagonism of people in the Midlands disturbed Lawrence, who told an admirer that the book had brought him "very little but bitterness." Some reviews in the United States were rather harsh, but not sufficiently so to justify Lawrence's sweeping statement that "all America" was hostile to him. This exaggeration indicates that his first brush with fame had left him a bit dizzy. He had been enthusiastically sponsored at the start by two prominent writers who were soon to drop him: Hueffer and Violet Hunt, both of whom had grown up in Pre-Raphaelite circles. Miss Hunt, who had carried the manuscript of *The White Peacock* to the publishers', later wrote almost as exaggeratedly of the book as Lawrence had done; in a reminiscence some years afterward she said that the novel "took the town." This statement is more subjective than accurate, but it reflects what many writers had felt at the time.

Francis Brett Young, remembering in 1925 how *The White Peacock* had delighted him when it appeared, called it "the most astonishing first novel of the last half-century."

The White Peacock is a first-person story, narrated by a sensitive and rather flaccid young man named Cyril Beardsall. Most of the action concerns his friend George Saxton, who comes from a farming family. George loves Cyril's sister Lettie. After flirting with George for years, Lettie marries a wealthy young man, Leslie Tempest. The disappointed George, after some successes as a horsetrader, as a man of property, and as a dabbler in politics, falls at last into a condition of physical and spiritual decay.

Earlier drafts of *The White Peacock*, which Lawrence originally planned to call *Nethermere* after the lake in the story, were quite different from the final version. Jessie Chambers reports in her memoir that, in the first draft of the story, George was a noble young farmer who married a socially unattainable Lettie after she had been seduced by a young man of still higher social status. All this was thickly sentimentalized, "though something in the atmosphere was alive."

And it is Lawrence's use of atmosphere that gives the final, published version of the book its strength. Francis Brett Young, in the essay previously referred to, said that *The White Peacock* invests the landscape of the Midlands "with a light that no other writer, living or dead, has ever cast upon it." Although he had never reread the book, Young said that its setting remained as poignantly real to him as landscapes remembered from childhood, "and bloomed with the same magic."

One of the finest passages in *The White Peacock* is that describing autumn in Nottinghamshire and the development of the friendship between George and Cyril:

I was born in September, and love it best of all the months. There is no heat, no hurry, no thirst and weariness in corn harvest as there is in the hay. If the season is late, as is usual with us, then mid-September sees the corn still standing in stook. The mornings come slowly. The earth is like a woman married and fading; she does not leap up with a laugh for the first fresh kiss of dawn, but slowly, quietly, unexpectedly lies watching the waking of each new day. The blue mist, like memory in the eyes of a neglected wife, never goes from the wooded hill, and only at noon creeps from the near hedges. There is no bird to put a song in the throat of morning; only the crow's voice speaks during the day. Perhaps there is the regular breathing hush of the scythe—even the fretful jar of the mowing machine. But next day, in the morning, all is still again. The lying corn is wet, and when you have bound it, and lift the heavy sheaf to make the stook, the tresses of oats wreathe round each other and droop mournfully.

As I worked with my friend through the still mornings we talked endlessly. I would give him the gist of what I knew of chemistry, and botany, and psychology. Day after day I told him what the professors had told me; of life, of sex and its origins; of Schopenhauer and William James. We had been friends for years, and he was accustomed to my talk. But this autumn fruited the first crop of intimacy between us. I talked a great deal of poetry to him, and of rudimentary metaphysics. He was very good stuff. He had hardly a single dogma, save that of pleasing himself. Religion was nothing to him. So he heard all I had to say with an open mind, and understood the drift of things very rapidly, and quickly made these ideas part of himself.

We tramped down to dinner with only the clinging warmth of the sunshine for a coat. In this still, enfolding weather a quiet companionship is very grateful. Autumn creeps through everything. The little damsons in the pudding taste of September, and are fragrant with memory. The voices of those at table are softer and more reminiscent than at haytime.

Afternoon is all warm and golden. Oat sheaves are lighter; they whisper to each other as they freely embrace. The long, stout stubble tinkles as the foot brushes over it; the scent of the straw is sweet. When the poor, bleached sheaves are lifted out of the hedge, a spray of nodding wild raspberries is disclosed, with belated berries ready to drop; among the damp grass lush blackberries may be discovered. Then one notices that the last bell hangs from the ragged spire of fox-glove. The talk is of people, an odd book; of one's hopes—and the future; of Canada, where work is strenuous, but not life; where the plains are wide, and one is not lapped in a soft valley, like an apple that falls in a secluded orchard. The mist steals over the face of the warm afternoon. The tying-up is all finished, and it only remains to rear up the fallen bundles into shocks. The sun sinks into a golden glow in the west. The gold turns to red, the red darkens, like a fire burning low, the sun disappears behind the bank of milky mist, purple like the pale bloom on blue plums, and we put on our coats and go home.

Most of that is simple and fresh, and it is genial, the work of an author who loves the things he is writing about. The occasional patches of awkwardness are those of a young student of composition; the two similes in the first paragraph, "The earth is like a woman married and fading" and "The blue mist, like memory in the eyes of a neglected wife," are too literary, but most of the passage has an assurance, an observational sharpness, and a sense of prose rhythm rarely found in the work of twenty-five-year-old novelists.

But Lawrence could do more at this time than reflect the mood of landscapes; he could also create the effect of life in motion and could do this with vividness and precision, as in the night scene at the pond, another of the remarkable passages in *The White Peacock:*

Suddenly, as we went by the pond-side, we were startled by the great, swishing black shadows that swept just above our heads. The swans were flying up for shelter, now that a cold wind had begun to fret Nethermere. They swung down onto the glassy mill-pond, shaking the moonlight in flecks across the deep shadows; the night rang with the clacking of their wings on the water; the stillness and calm were broken; the moonlight was furrowed and scattered and broken.

This presages the remarkable scene in *Women in Love* where Birkin throws stones into the moonlit pool. That passage is quoted at length in the later discussion of *Women in Love:* a comparison of that passage with the foregoing paragraph will show how Lawrence developed, within a few years, from a writer of promise into a writer of power.

The conversations in *The White Peacock* are, however, less assured. Jessie Chambers reported in her memoir that Lawrence told her that all of what they and their friends said "would go ever so well in a book," and in this first novel he included too much of the small-town intellectuals' type of conversation, stilted and pretentious, as when Cyril says to Emily, "You are like Burne-Jones' damsels. Troublesome shadows are always crowding across your eyes, and you cherish them. You think the flesh of the apple is nothing. You care only for the eternal pips."

Many of the characters in *The White Peacock* are as artificial as their speech. For some of them, Lawrence drew upon members of his own family, but instead of showing them amid the soot of the Nottinghamshire colliery town they really lived in, he put them into a country house suggested by a hunting lodge near the Chamberses' farm. Lawrence moved Jessie Chambers and her family, whom he also used for some of his characters, to an even more idyllic place than in actual life—a picturesque old mill near their farm. Everything is thus pushed out into the country: there are only rare and offstage glimpses of the mines that dirtied the edges of the towns.

The most important difference between actual conditions and those in the book is in the status of the father of the Lawrence family. He and the mother in the story have separated, and the children do not even know him. He is once brought feebly onto the scene, as a derelict, and soon after this he dies in another town. Cyril goes over quietly to this town with his mother to have the father buried; the daughter, Lettie, is not even told of it until sometime later. It is significant that the name used for the Lawrences in *The White Peacock* is Beardsall, in actuality the family-name of Lawrence's mother.

That Lawrence could, however, face the reality of his family situation at the time is shown by the play he wrote during this period, *A Collier's Friday Night*, which was not published until after his death. This play is a first working of the *Sons and Lovers* theme, with sketches of characters and incidents that were to be used later in the novel. In the play and in *Sons and Lovers*, Lawrence wrote of people he knew in life, as he knew them in life; in *The White Peacock* Lawrence took people he knew in life and portrayed them as he did not know them—that is, as they did not exist.

Few of them come out successfully as characters in this first novel. The most believable of them is one in whom the story is centered—George. Lettie in *The White Peacock* is a faint and uncertain outline of Annie, the sister of the leading character in *Sons and Lovers*. In the earlier novel Lettie represents a rather obvious attempt on the author's part to show a kittenish female; it is only rarely that she seems to be as much a living person as Annie does in a far less important rôle in *Sons and Lovers*.

The mother in *The White Peacock* is idealized almost out of existence. Although at one level Mrs. Beardsall seems to be the same sad little woman of *Sons and Lovers*, she lacks the other sides of Mrs. Morel's nature—the harshness, the firmness. She is spared the daily turmoil of the Lawrence-Morel household. With her husband extracted, Mrs. Beardsall of *The White Peacock* has, in her country home with deckchairs on the lawn, a sense of contentment the poet's mother never knew in life. Her daughter Lettie is courted honorably by the son of a wealthy industrialist. Her son Cyril is also an idealized escape from fact; he is really too vapid to arouse admiration, yet he has a certain vitality as a narrator: those natural descriptions that are the best part of the book are presented through his consciousness.

Leslie Tempest is the first of Lawrence's portraits of wealthy young men who inherit industrial interests. Leslie is in social circumstance the immediate ancestor of Gerald Crich of *Women in Love*. He even lives in the same house, which is a place near Lawrence's native town called Lamb Close (Highclose in *The White Peacock*, Shortlands in the later book). Both Leslie and Gerald try to be "enlightened" mine-owners, as their counterpart Gerald Barlow does in the play *Touch and Go:* none of them quite succeeds. Gerald Crich, a full-drawn figure emerging from Lawrence's later experience, is a vital and credible character in a way the papier-mâché Leslie is not.

The thought of a young man born in country-squire circumstances weighed heavily on Lawrence's mind: toward the end of his life he was to present a last phase of Leslie as Clifford Chatterley. In quite another way Lawrence was also, as John Middleton Murry first pointed out, haunted by the idea of gamekeepers, and there is doubtless a connection between Annable of *The White Peacock* and Mellors of *Lady Chatterley's Lover*. As we have seen, Lawrence read the Victorian novels in his youth, and while Jessie Chambers does not mention Kingsley's *Yeast* as being among them, it is possible that Tregarva, the philosophical gamekeeper in that book, was an ideological ancestor of Annable and Mellors.

Aside from all else that Annable and Mellors may stand for in the first and last novels of Lawrence, it must be remembered that the gamekeeper has a particular vocational function. From the first, Lawrence was against that part of civilization which destroyed natural things: the gamekeeper is a man specially committed to protecting wild life.

Annable is not involved in the main plot of *The White Peacock;* he serves as a commentator or chorus. He is antagonistic to the young couples who continually trespass on the preserves he is guarding, and he is barely respectful to Leslie, whose father employs him. But Annable and Cyril become friends, and he tells the young man of his experiences as a student at Cambridge, as a clergyman, and as a husband. Now he is a man of field and forest, who usually speaks in dialect. And although Annable is only a background figure, he comes closest to George as the most believably alive character in *The White Peacock.*

George's sister Emily fails to provide a basis of conflict with Cyril such as her double, Miriam, does in *Sons and Lovers.* Her relationship with Cyril is essentially insipid, largely because of his lack of enthusiasm, but she seems so thinly human that it is difficult to blame him entirely for not being particularly interested in her. Cyril and Emily battle each other with feeble epigrams. And when Emily, after several years of this and several years of Cyril's vaguely explained absence, announces to him during one of his visits home that she plans to marry someone else, all Cyril can do is turn to the husband-to-be and say, "Mr. Renshaw, you have out-manoeuvred me all unawares, quite indecently." Cyril's regret never finds deeper expression than this rhetoric: Emily is justified in taking his protest as a joke.

Her brother George is the first of a gallery of Lawrence's male characters whose virility is gradually undermined. Cyril for all his cleverness would perhaps enjoy being just what George is, the natural man, the farmer, the man whose mind—at the start, at least—has a wholesome simplicity. Yet George is brought down. Cyril's sister Lettie upsets his way of life, leads him on, then drops him. It is his own weakness that is essentially to blame for his downfall, not only because he is susceptible to

Lettie but also because he could have mastered her if he had had the courage. Yet the instrument of his degradation is Lettie.

She is the peacock. Both Lettie and the first wife of Annable are identified with the central symbol in the book. The destructive woman is, to Annable, "all vanity and screech and defilement," and when he speaks of her as the peacock, Cyril adds the adjective *white*. Lawrence does not let this symbol remain a conversational abstraction, but several times introduces it concretely; its most important usage is in the episode in which Cyril meets Annable in the graveyard by the abandoned church. A peacock from the adjoining woodland flaps heavily through the evening air and lights on a stone angel above a tomb. Annable drives the bird away, and it is then that he tells Cyril of his unhappy past, of his marriage to a destructive, will-driven woman with ideals of purity—the kind of woman Lawrence portrayed unsympathetically throughout his work, perhaps in unconscious rejection of his mother's influence.

One other important non-abstract use of the peacock symbol occurs later in the story, after Lettie has married Leslie, and George has married his cousin Meg: Lettie and her mother and Cyril and Leslie are walking near Highclose when they meet George; it is New Year's Eve, and they invite him in for a drink. As they enter the house, Lettie seems in a mood of gloating over the two men who love her; she is wearing a silk cloak of peacock blue: "There she stood, with her white hand upon the peacock of her cloak, where it tumbled against her dull orange dress. She knew her own splendour, and she drew up her throat laughing and brilliant with triumph." Outside, she had asked Leslie to tie her shoelace, and he had dutifully knelt to do so. Now she requests him to take off her shoes, and again he kneels to oblige. Cyril comments a bit later that Leslie has "lost his assertive self-confidence."

The perceptive but ineffectual Cyril has only one human relationship with any profundity in it, and that is the relationship with George; its high moment is reached in the chapter called "A Poem of Friendship." George in this chapter points to a sycamore with the leading shoot broken off and says he will feel like that after Cyril has gone away, but it is Cyril who feels the deeper regret at the departure, and it is Cyril who, later in the story, has the nostalgic remembrances. The homoerotic suggestions in this relationship are most strongly marked in the passage describing Cyril's pleasure in the towel-massage administered by George after the two friends have been swimming. How much of this is mere immaturity and how much is seriously sexual is difficult to judge: the possible significance of such themes in Lawrence's work is discussed later, in relation to *Women in Love*.

The White Peacock, which with its groups of young couples in a rural setting drew much from George Eliot and other traditional novelists, goes to pieces structurally after the "Poem of Friendship" chapter. There is a painful public meeting between George and Lettie, following which the characters are moved about like checkers over the years. Until this point, about three-fifths of the way through, the story has been fairly consistent and even-paced in development, but now there are spasmodic jumps of two years, five years, one year, and so on. The main theme, the deterioration of George, is all that holds the book together, and this is often too fragmentarily presented. The other characters become even vaguer; Cyril, for example, seems to go to France at times, but how or why is never made clear. Too much detail in such matters might prove burdensome, but after the closeness of the circumstantial focus of the first sixty per cent of the book, the shuttling cinema of the last parts is confusing.

George goes through many changes after marrying Meg, who lives with her savage old grandmother at the Ram Inn. In both his failures and successes in business and politics, he is shown to be a better man than Leslie—whom he can even out-argue at the dinner table—a better man than Leslie, in everything except adaptation. The mediocre Leslie fits into existing society. When George becomes a socialist of the bitter kind, his socialism is partly a protest against Leslie's standard of living. But the bored Lettie by her meddling takes even George's socialism away from him, and the full power of the gamekeeper Annable's symbol is realized. Annable is a stronger man, but his life is almost prophetic of George's, and their destinies are importantly connected by the peacock symbol which indicates the power of women over the two most vital men in the story.

George drops socialism, makes money, and becomes unhappy. Cyril comes to see him for the last time in the concluding chapter, "A Prospect Among the Marshes of Lethe." Meg has told him that George is "sick every morning and after almost every meal," and Cyril has heard of a scene between George and one of the children, in which George seemed "demoniacal." After a bad attack of delirium tremens, George has been sent to stay at Emily's farm in the country, and Cyril bicycles out to see him.

It is a far different September from the one described earlier in the book, when Cyril worked in the fields with George and told him about sex and Schopenhauer and William James. It is fifteen years since George's marriage to Meg, who has won "in the marital duel." Cyril finds George in bed in the daytime, with a swollen and discolored face; when they go for a walk—slowly, because George is feeble on his legs—Cyril is horrified to learn that his old friend has become a loud and vulgar monologuist, with lapses into stupidity. They watch Emily's husband and his brother working in the fields, as George used to. George, seeing the men vigorous and quick in the softly beautiful autumn afternoon, says he will soon be out of everybody's way. Afterward, at tea, George sits apart from them all, "like a condemned man." His deterioration is almost complete.

George's great sin was to deny the life-flame. He did this rather obviously; future Lawrencean protagonists who are doomed to a grievous end will do it differently. But the lesson is there from the first.

The book foreshadows much of Lawrence's later work: this is the principal reason it is studied here so closely and at such length. He had not yet found his idiom, but in spite of its ineptitudes, *The White Peacock* has a compelling charm, particularly in its nature passages, a morning-light quality.

✦ ✦ ✦ ✦

The White Peacock and the first three stories appearing in Ford Madox Ford's *English Review* in 1910 and 1911 ("Goose Fair," "Odour of Chrysanthemums," "A Fragment of Stained Glass") mark the published beginning of Lawrence the prose-writer. But the real beginning of Lawrence's prose lies farther back; there was an anonymous prize-winning story in 1907, and some other examples have been presented in the memoir by his sister Ada, who preserved several fragments from an early diary. Here is the earliest, dated August 1906, just before Lawrence was twenty-one, more than four years before *The White Peacock* was published:

Walked to Theddlethorpe—the rushes, reeds and the blue butterfly, the countryside and charming farms and cottages. Fancy trekking thence from Hagg's! The trippers down to Mablethorpe in the haywaggon, and the sheep whose faces and legs gleam white as they trot south. Came at last to Theddlethorpe St. Helens, where the post office is kept by Hepzibah Lingard.

This is hardly a fair prose specimen, since it is merely spontaneous jottings in a diary—Lawrence at his mature best preferably used the spontaneous method, and with success, but in this earlier time he needed to rewrite in order to bring out his best effects. Yet even this diary-fragment gives indications of the Lawrence-to-be. Although the writing is a bit clogged, and generally poor in cadence, the eye of Lawrence is there, noting flora and fauna and significant details of landscape. In his later writing he would have arranged the details more skillfully, and would not have used the banal phrase, "charming cottages." The second sentence is jarring—"Fancy trekking thence from Hagg's"—but this is also a hint of the Lawrence-to-come: in most of his later writing there are awkward or colloquial phrases that occasionally disfigure his work. The better side of the future Lawrence is suggested in "the sheep whose faces and legs gleam white as they trot south"—here is Lawrence's kinetic touch, here is a sentence with a moving image and the rhythm that goes with it. Another attempt to describe action in a later sentence of this diary fails under its own heaviness: "Horses rear and struggle, but are disunited"—the last word, a latinized abstraction, reduces the pictorial value of the first part of the statement. But a more kinetic sentence closes the diary-fragments: "The wind fills the brown sails, and away she glides like a live thing, the sun burning on her red sails." There is some confusion here, and an unskillful repetition, but the statement has a pulsing movement:

it suggests that the young man knows how poetic effects can be used in prose and is trying his strength.

The story "Goose Fair," Lawrence's first prose piece in the *English Review*, effectively suggests the restlessness of Nottingham in Fair time; and Lawrence's descriptive gifts come admirably into play for a picture of a burning factory. The story turns upon a misunderstanding of the heroine's and is therefore an index to her mind. She thinks her young man burned the factory for its insurance; when she discovers that she is wrong and that he has been away reveling, she cruelly mentions that he is suspected:

Lois drew herself up. She had delivered her blow. She drew herself up and for a moment enjoyed her complete revenge. He was despicable, abject in his dishevelled, disfigured, unwashed condition.

"Aye, well, they made a mistake for once," he replied, with a curl of the lip.

Curiously enough, they walked side by side as if they belonged to each other. She was his conscience keeper. She was far from forgiving him, but she was still further from letting him go. And he walked at her side like a boy who has to be punished before he can be exonerated. He submitted. But there was a genuine bitter contempt in the curl of his lip.

This is the end of the story, with the charred ruin of the factory smoking beyond them in the grey October morning. And here, in Lawrence's first published fiction, a theme that runs through much of his work is first announced: the antagonism between men and women who do not separate but find the antagonism a bond.

"Odour of Chrysanthemums" is a good mood-sketch and has some believable characterization. Ford Madox Ford has said it was the first piece of Lawrence's writing to catch his editorial eye: he once wrote that he accepted the story at a glance, for he could tell immediately that the writer was one who knew what he was doing. "Odour of Chrysanthemums" is Lawrence's first story of miners' families, and prefigures his developments along this line: the ending, with the miner brought home dead and the women washing his corpse, strongly resembles Lawrence's later play, *The Widowing of Mrs. Holroyd*.

"A Fragment of Stained Glass" was originally submitted to a story competition in the *Nottinghamshire Guardian* at Christmas 1907, while Lawrence was in college. Lawrence took the contest seriously—the prize was three pounds—and he had Jessie Chambers and another girl also send in stories that he wrote. The rules required entries to be submitted under assumed names; the stories had to deal with a joyful or amusing Christmas, or with a historic building. The one Jessie sent in under the name of Rosalind, entitled "A Prelude," was the winner. In bestowing the prize, the *Guardian* said that "a simple theme was handled with a freshness and simplicity altogether charming," and that rather aptly describes the story, which has recently been dug out of the *Guardian* files and printed as a book. It is not worth so much emphasis; Lawrence once wrote to his bibliographer, McDonald, of "a youthful story in the bad grey print of a provincial newspaper—under a *nom de plume*." He added, "But, thank God, that has gone to glory in the absolute sense." The tale has some of the flavor of *The White Peacock*, and some of its characters are apparently first sketches of people who were to appear in the novel. The two stories that lost in the competition, however, appeared later in the *English Review* and in *The Prussian Officer*. One of these, as we shall see later, was rewritten as "The White Stocking": the other, as already mentioned, is "A Fragment of Stained Glass."

In its original version it was called "Legend." It fulfilled one of the contest conditions in that it was about a historic building: its setting is Beauvale Abbey, outside Eastwood. The story represents one of Lawrence's few attempts at fiction about the past. The *Guardian* referred to it as "a tale of the escape of a serf remarkable for its vivid realism," but the story seems to have been somewhat too grim for the Christmas competition. Lawrence changed it considerably, and expanded it, before it appeared in the *English Review* nearly four years later. "A Fragment of Stained Glass" has in it a feeling of medieval barbarity that comes through strongly to the reader: the story of the maddened serf fleeing into the frozen dark woods with the miller's daughter is one that is projected with imaginative vigor into the deep past of the Lawrence country.

Those two stories are in Lawrence's first collection of tales, *The Prussian Officer*, published in 1914. The other ten stories in that volume, which appeared in magazines after these earliest tales, will be discussed later. At this point the beginnings of Lawrence's poetry should be considered.

His verse apparently antedates his first serious prose—prose, that is, independent of required school essays. In the prefatory note to his *Collected Poems* in 1928, Lawrence spoke of writing his first verses when he was nineteen. "To Guelder-Roses" and "To Campions" might have been written by any young lady, Lawrence says. In a longer introduction to the *Collected* edition, which he did not use (it was published in the posthumous *Phoenix* volume), he spoke of the poems he began writing a year or so later, which haunted him and made him feel guilty, as if the experience of creating them were abnormal:

Then the haunting would get the better of me, and the ghost would suddenly appear, in the shape of a rather usually incoherent poem. Nearly always I shunned the apparition once it had appeared. From the first, I was a little afraid of my real poems—not my "compositions," but the poems that had the ghost in them. They seemed to me to come from somewhere, I didn't quite know where, out of a me whom I didn't know and didn't want to know, and say things I would much rather not have said: for choice. But there they were. I never read them again. Only I gave them to Miriam, and she loved them, or she seemed to. . . . Save for Miriam, I perhaps should have destroyed them all. She encouraged my demon. But alas, it was me, not he, whom she loved. So for her too it was a catastrophe. My demon is not easily loved: whereas the ordinary me is. So poor Miriam was let down. Yet in a sense, she let down my demon, till he howled.

Lawrence here, as in many of his statements, shows how much he had in common with the Romanticists, whose work was often haunted by the demonic—not only in the matter of inspiration but also in regard to descriptions of love and to effects of horror. Wordsworth, for example, felt that he was under the spell of outside forces; in *The Prelude*, describing the high moment when he became "dedicated," on a summer dawn in his nineteenth year, he wrote:

> I made no vows, but vows
> Were made for me; bond unknown to me
> Was given, that I should be, else sinning greatly,
> A dedicated Spirit.

The reader going through the body of Lawrence's poems, indeed of Lawrence's prose also, will observe repeatedly how many other characteristics of the Romanticists can be found in Lawrence. René Wellek has shown that the Romantic Movement was international in scope and character and not a complex of Romanticisms, as Arthur O. Lovejoy has asserted. Professor Wellek mentions three important criteria of Romanticism in general—"imagination for the view of poetry, nature for the view of the world, and symbol and myth for poetic style"—which also figure importantly throughout Lawrence's work. Lawrence did not have so large a conception of imagination as the Romanticists, although in common with them he used the imagination as an important intuitional force; but he did not talk about the imagination in the way the Romanticists did. To them it was perhaps a nobler instrument than it was to Lawrence: with them it was a means of getting in touch with a higher reality; the fulfillment Lawrence came to seek in his "dark gods" was not a higher reality but rather another reality. Yet in the actual working out of ideas, Lawrence often came close to Romanticist imaginative usage: *The Plumed Serpent*, for example, is almost pure Romanticism, full of the elements of mysticism and strangeness which are predominant in the "Gothic" aspects of that movement.

As for the second characteristic mentioned by Wellek, "nature for the view of the world"—Lawrence lived "through" nature as fully as any of the Romantics. As the poems discussed in this chapter—as well as the prose passages quoted throughout the book—will show, Lawrence felt himself deep inside nature, so deep that he could speak contemptuously of the feeling for nature held by Rousseau and Chateaubriand as a kind of misdirected intellectualism. Horace Gregory is perhaps right in calling Lawrence "the last Romantic."

The third criterion Wellek speaks of, "symbol and myth for poetic style," is also applicable to Lawrence. His affinity with the *symbolistes*, who represent a recrudescence and a refinement of the Romantic Movement, is examined in the next chapter. As to mythology, Wellek does not refer to conventional mythology alone—there is a certain amount of this in Lawrence, particularly in relation to Christian figures—but also to created mythology such as Blake's. Again *The Plumed Serpent* will serve as example; and Lawrence's resemblances to Blake are discussed elsewhere in this volume. The important point to remember in the present survey of Lawrence's early poetry is that it was, whether consciously or not, Romantic. And his novels were Romantic too, though they showed the marked influence—as the poems occasionally do—of nineteenth-century Naturalism and twentieth-century Realism. Lawrence, in brief, rises up as a belated Romanticist, strained through the Industrial Revolution, Darwinism, Victorianism, "the triumph of science," Zolaism, and other phenomena that came between him and the principal Romantics.

Throughout the rest of this book, then, Lawrence will be regarded as a latter-day Romantic, although the matter will not be continually hammered into the reader's mind. To call Lawrence such is not to damn him as unoriginal, for even though he had no brilliant solutions to the social problems he came to write of, he was always *artistically* original. But he had the Romantic temperament—anti-intellectualism, the fierce love of nature, the tendency to be "amorous of the far," the belief in individuality, the extreme sensibility, and the other characteristics—and this temperament he carried through twentieth-century experience. And the impact of that experience upon that temperament is first expressed most directly and most strongly in Lawrence's early verse.

The poems of Lawrence's youth were printed in magazines and in his first two books of verse, *Love Poems* (1913) and *Amores* (1916); a few of them were put into *New Poems* (1918). Many of them are changed in the *Collected Poems* because "sometimes the hand of the commonplace youth had been laid on the mouth of the demon. It is not for technique these poems are altered: it is to say the real say." Even more than the fictional material taken from life, the verse is the autobiography of Lawrence's youth.

The poetry he wrote at that time is concerned mainly with seven subjects. With one or two typical examples of each, these are: *nature*, as in "The Wild Common"; *dialect verse*, such as "Whether or Not" ("Dunna thee tell me it's his'n, mother . . ."); *schoolmastering*, as in "Discipline" and "Afternoon in School"; *mystic creation*, as in "Corot" and "Michael Angelo"; *love*, as in "Lightning" and "Kisses in the Train"; and *the death of the mother*, as in "Brooding Grief" and "Troth with the Dead."

Lawrence placed "The Wild Common" first among his *Collected Poems:*

> The quick sparks on the gorse-bushes are leaping
> Little jets of sunlight texture imitating flame.

It is appropriate that the discussion of Lawrence's beginnings as a poet start with these two lines, not only because he put this poem first when he arranged his work chronologically, but also because the quality that is so distinctly Lawrence's is already apparent in these opening lines. They have the uprush of feeling, the bright livingness, and the quick movement of his later verse, and they forecast its types of rhythm and imagery.

Lawrence, who was always to remain somewhat awkward poetically, from the point of view of conventional versification, defended his poetic style in a letter in 1913 to Edward Marsh, who was publishing Lawrence's work in the *Georgian Poetry* anthologies. Lawrence, never awed by a mere editor, called Marsh a "bit of a policeman in poetry" and told him:

I think I read my poetry more by length than by stress—as a matter of movements in space than footsteps hitting the earth. . . . It doesn't depend on the ear, particularly, but on the sensitive soul. And the ear gets a habit, and becomes master, when the ebbing and lifting motion should be master, and the ear the transmitter. If your ear has got stiff and a bit mechanical, don't blame my poetry. That's why you like *Golden Journey to Samarcand*—it fits your habituated ear, and your feeling crouches subservient and a bit pathetic. "It satisfies my ear," you say. Well, I don't write for your ear. This is the constant war, I reckon, between new expression and the habituated, mechanical transmitters and receivers of the human constitution.

Readers of lines such as those quoted from "The Wild Common" should keep this statement in mind. For in such lines Lawrence was writing of the effect upon his consciousness of the unkempt fields with the irregular gorse-bushes touched into little flames by the sun; to express all this, he wanted something more than an instrument of known mathematical measurement such as ordinary iambic. He was not completely successful in those opening lines of "The Wild Common," for the verse trips too fast; the reader is left breathless. A caesura somewhere in either of the lines would have reduced the speed of that enjambment after *leaping*. Yet, aside from their headlong haste, the lines are effective in the quickened sense of life they give. And they point the way to Lawrence's subsequent success with the kinetic line; his best verse has a combination of urgency and vividness that touches the reader's emotions directly. The following poem, "Coldness in Love," is predominantly erotic, yet it has as much scenery in it as most of the nature poems, and atmosphere is perhaps its most important element:

And you remember, in the afternoon
The sea and the sky went grey, as if there had sunk
A flocculent dust on the floor of the world: the festoon
Of the sky sagged dusty as spider cloth,
And coldness clogged the sea, till it ceased to croon.

A dank, sickening scent came up from the grime
Of weed that blackened the shore, so that I recoiled
Feeling the raw cold dun me: and all the time
You leapt about on the slippery rocks, and threw
Me words that rang with a brassy, shallow chime.

And all day long, that raw and ancient cold
Deadened me through, till the grey downs dulled to sleep.
Then I longed for you with your mantle of love to fold
Me over, and drive from out of my body the deep
Cold that had sunk to my soul, and there kept hold.

But still to me all evening long you were cold,
And I was numb with a bitter, deathly ache;
Till old days drew me back into their fold,
And dim hopes crowded me warm with companionship,
And memories clustered me close, and sleep was cajoled.

And I slept till dawn at the window blew in like dust,
Like a linty, raw-cold dust disturbed from the floor
Of the unswept sea; a grey pale light like must
That settled upon my face and hands till it seemed
To flourish there, as pale mould blooms on a crust.

And I rose in fear, needing you fearfully.
For I thought you were warm as a sudden jet of blood.
I thought I could plunge in your living hotness, and be
Clean of the cold and the must. With my hand on the latch
I heard you in your sleep speak strangely to me.

And I dared not enter, feeling suddenly dismayed.
So I went and washed my deadened flesh in the sea
And came back tingling clean, but worn and frayed
With cold, like the shell of the moon; and strange it seems
That my love can dawn in warmth again, unafraid.

That poem has much in common with the verse that other
young Georgian poets were writing. Compare, for example,
Rupert Brooke's "A Memory," written at Waikiki in October
1913 and beginning:

> Somewhile before the dawn I rose, and stept
> Softly along the dim way to your room . . .

In Brooke's sonnet, the poet does not turn away at the girl's door,
but enters for a "poor moment's kindliness, and ease, / And
sleepy mother-comfort!" And the poem ends with the characteristic Brookean turn of mood from light contentment to light
regret. It is smoother and neater than Lawrence's "Coldness in
Love," which has a kind of ugly unhappiness pervading it;
Brooke's music is more dextrous and, throughout the sonnet,
more varied, yet it lacks the force of this poem of Lawrence's
which is not really a first-rate poem. But "Coldness in Love" has

a rude strength beyond the reach of most of the other Georgians except perhaps W. H. Davies; yet Davies, often awkward and often verging on doggerel, can rarely approximate the suggestive power of the nature pictures in "Coldness in Love."

The greyness of the setting and of the recorder's mood is skillfully set in the first stanza, and repeated by suggestion and statement just often enough through the poem to retain its effectiveness without becoming wearisome; the repetitions build toward the startling image of the crust-mould on the lover who has awakened in the dawn "that blew in like dust." Occasionally the mood is jarred by a conventionalized figure, such as "your mantle of love," but in the main the emotion is consistent, and the events leading to the climax of the action develop organically out of that emotion. In the original version in *Love Poems*, the last line had read "That my love had dawned in rose again, like the love of a maid," but Lawrence changed that in the *Collected* edition—one of that volume's improvements by alteration.

The comparison of "Coldness in Love" with the work of some of Lawrence's fellow-contributors to the *Georgian Poetry* collections was made for the purpose of emphasizing Lawrence's individuality. He was not limited to the Georgian mold, nor did he properly belong to that group he aligned himself with under Amy Lowell's banner—the poets whom their former leader, Ezra Pound, called the Amygists.

It has been previously indicated that Lawrence had certain elements in common with the *Georgian Poetry* contributors. Since he lived when he did, most of his early verse came, like theirs, out of nineteenth-century British poetry. But the intensity of his chapel upbringing seems to have made him more susceptible to Biblical language than his contemporaries were. He adapted Biblical rhythms to his own uses, however, as he adapted the English landscape. To most of the Georgian poets, nature was important poetically, but it was something glimpsed beyond the edges of the tennis court; to Lawrence, nature was a part of one's consciousness, virtually a part of one's body—indeed, it might be said of Lawrence that he was a part of all that he had *touched*. This tactual relationship with nature was intensified in him because the landscapes he knew in childhood and youth were an escape from the mining town and the surrounding col-

lieries; and he expressed the effect of nature upon him in an
individualistic manner, as the letter to Marsh indicates. No other
Georgian landscapes assault the reader's consciousness so forcibly
as Lawrence's do.

For these and other considerations, it is somewhat surprising
to find him in the *Georgian Poetry* anthologies; he appeared in
four of the five that were issued, including the last of the volumes
in 1922. He was not given to affiliations with groups or to sup-
port of platforms; and it is particularly surprising to find him in
Marsh's books, which generally excluded the more "daring"
poets.

His presence among the Imagists is less startling, although the
Imagists were a rival clique that was even more exclusive and
pretentious. Ezra Pound did not invite Lawrence to appear in
Des Imagistes in 1914, though Amy Lowell included him in the
three anthologies of *Some Imagist Poets* in 1915, 1916, and 1917,
after Pound and his faction had seceded from the coterie to
become Vorticists. *That* was one contemporary group Lawrence
did not join—and he never enlisted himself in any other association of the kind. In defense of Lawrence's independence, it may
be pointed out that he became a *Georgian Poetry* and *Imagist
Poets* contributor fairly early in his career, and that both these
collections remained hospitable to his work at times when he
found it difficult to be published at all. The pronouncements of
each group were not so ironclad that the individualistic Lawrence could not be reasonably included, and he certainly did not
relinquish any of his independence, as the correspondence with
Marsh (as well as the letters in Damon's biography of Amy
Lowell) proves. Glenn Hughes in *Imagism and the Imagists*
(1931) reports that Lawrence told him in May 1929 that he
had denied being an Imagist when Amy Lowell first approached
him while she was collecting material for the anthologies; she
replied by quoting the opening lines of his "Wedding Morn":
"The morning breaks like a pomegranate/ In a shining crack
of red." Hughes says Lawrence was not fooled by this—images
can "be plucked from the work of any poet"—but he gave Amy
Lowell some poems anyway, though he never took the "movement" seriously. Hughes, who believes Lawrence's poetry was
most strongly influenced by Whitman, says it underwent "no

radical change . . . as a result of his association with the Imagists."

This excursion into Lawrence's associations has been necessary in order to show how Lawrence differed from the other poets who were young when he was, and in order to place him in relation to the literary movements of his time. As a poet he was to develop far beyond the range of the verse of *Love Poems* and *Amores*. This development will be discussed in its proper place: it will not be understood, however, without a somewhat thorough examination of the tendencies and accomplishments of Lawrence's beginnings as a poet.

Lawrence's principal dialect verse, which will be considered next, was written in the earliest phase of his career. He wrote a bit more later, in the *Pansies* period toward the end of his life, but these poems were not serious in the way that the four which appear in *Love Poems* were serious. The later dialect verse employed the vernacular for humorous purposes only, and usually with Lawrence himself as the speaker, as in "Up He Goes!—":

> No, there's nowt in the upper classes
> as far as I can find;
> a worse lot o' jujubey asses
> than the lot I left behind.

This stanza, typical of the others in the poems and in other verses of that phase, is quite different from the four earlier examples of dialect poetry in *Love Poems:* "Violets," "Whether or Not," "A Collier's Wife," and "The Drained Cup." These four pieces are serious stories—often with humorous overtones— in Midland dialect. Three of them are fairly short: "Violets" tells of an unknown girl who comes quietly to the burial of a young man and, standing among women who loved him openly, drops a "pack" of violets into the grave; "A Collier's Wife" contains a situation familiar to readers of *Sons and Lovers* and Lawrence's short stories of mining towns, in which a woman is notified that her husband has been injured in the mine and is being taken to the hospital; "The Drained Cup" is the bitter monologue of a woman addressing a lover who is leaving her for a younger woman.

These verses are a kind of Midland equivalent of the Kailyard School of Scottish poets who had recently had great success with dialect poems of village life and cabbage patches. Ezra Pound once said that Lawrence's dialect poems were his best; Louis Untermeyer says that none of Lawrence's writings, "none of his verse, is more surely projected than the dramatic lyrics in dialect." This statement, like Pound's, seems to overrate Lawrence's vernacular work, though the "more surely projected" phrase has a careful vagueness about it, since there is no guarantee that material less "surely projected" might not, through compensating factors, be more successful totally than what was "more surely projected." Untermeyer is more specific and more accurate when he speaks of "Whether or Not" as "that remarkable sequence which a ruder Browning might have fathered and which is a completely rounded tale, a poignantly condensed novel." In this long poem a young constable has been having an affair with his landlady; when she becomes pregnant, the girl who loves the policeman goes to the forty-five-year-old widow and offers money for the care of the child; then she proceeds to steer the young man toward the altar. In the original version she offered to rear the child if its mother would give it up; this offer is omitted from the story as it appears in the *Collected Poems*. The later version of "Whether or Not" has, however, an additional section, a conclusion in which the young man is allowed to demur; and he wants neither woman:

> I'll say good-bye, Liz, to yer,
>   Yer too much i' th' right for me.
> An' wi' 'er somehow it isn't right.
>   So good-bye, an' let's let be.

Lawrence made various other changes in these dialect poems for the *Collected* volume; occasionally he altered a word, as when he made *railroad* into *reelroad*—perhaps his years of being away from the dialect had made his ear keener for its finer shades, as he remembered them from childhood.

The poems about schoolmastering which Lawrence wrote in his youth describe the red-brick school at Croydon, and the teacher's problem of maintaining order in the classroom and of keeping the students and himself from getting bored. The pic-

torial quality of the poems is often effective, as in these lines
from "The Best of School":

> The blinds are drawn because of the sun,
> And the boys and the room in a colorless gloom
> Of under-water float: bright ripples run
> Across the walls as the blinds are blown
> To let the sunlight in . . .

The poems of mystic creation, "Michael Angelo" and "Corot,"
were considerably changed in the later versions: in each of them
the name of God is dropped and "Life" or an unnamed creative
force substituted. If Lawrence in 1928 wanted to remake his
earlier love poems into products of greater erotic intensity, he
also wanted to make his early religious poems seem less orthodox.
"Michael Angelo," for example, begins in this way in the original
version in *Love Poems:*

> God shook thy roundness in His finger's cup,
> He sunk his hands in firmness down thy sides,
> And drew the circle of His grasp, O Man,
> Along thy limbs delighted, thine, His bride's.
>
> And so thou wert God-shapen: His finger
> Curved thy mouth for thee, and His strong shoulder
> Planted thee upright: art not proud to see
> In the curve of thine exquisite form the joy of the Moulder?

When he rewrote these lines fifteen years after they were first
published, Lawrence retained the archaic language ("thine,"
"art proud," etc.) but changed the thought:

> Who shook thy roundness in his finger's cup?
> Who sunk his hands in firmness down thy sides?
> And drew the circle of his grasp, O man,
> Along thy limbs delighted as a bride's?
>
> How wert thou so strange-shapen? What warm finger
> Curved thy mouth for thee? and what strong shoulder
> Planted thee upright? Art proud to see
> In the curves of thy form the trace of the unknown moulder?

The last stanza in the original version read:

God, lonely, put down his mouth in a kiss of creation,
He kissed thee, O man, in a passion of love, and left
The vivid life of His love in thy mouth and thy nostrils:
Keep then this kiss from the adultress' theft.

This was the work of a young man with a religious imagina-
ion; the stanza had a kind of crude effectiveness. It was afterward changed to this piece of banality:

Whence cometh, whither goeth? still the same
Old question without answer! Strange and fain
Life comes to thee, on which thou hast no claim;
Then leaves thee, and thou canst not but complain!

There are similar, although not so damaging, changes in
"Corot," originally an impressionistic poem suggesting both the
style of that artist ("The trees rise tall and taller, lifted/On a
subtle rush of cool grey flame") and "the luminous purpose of
God." In the later version, *Life* is substituted for *God*. Most of
the changes are of that kind.

Although Lawrence recharged some of the erotic poems, he
fortunately did not meddle with too many of them or with
most of the poems to his mother—the kinds of verse in the last
two categories to be considered.

Few of the love poems were so drastically rewritten as "Virgin
Youth," in which Lawrence tells of the rise of passion in a
young man's body; this lyric was expanded from twenty-three
lines in *Amores* to sixty-two in the *Collected* edition. In the
prefatory note to the later volume, Lawrence said that "Virgin
Youth" was so greatly changed because it had been "struggling
to say something which it takes a man twenty years to be able
to say." This is one of the poems improved by increase: the
version in the *Collected Poems*, which would be spoiled by
partial quotation here, is far more vital than the original.

Many of the early love poems, as previously explained, went
unchanged into the *Collected* edition. Practically all this erotic
verse is set against a natural background. The scenery of these

love poems is sometimes the country south of London and sometimes the Lincolnshire coast, but principally it is the terrain
immediately north of Eastwood, near the Chamberses' farm.

> This is our own still valley,
> Our Eden, our home.

The earliest love poems are to Jessie Chambers, pieces such as
"Cherry Robbers," which ends:

> Under the haystack a girl stands laughing at me,
> With cherries hung round her ears—
> Offering me her scarlet fruit: I will see
> If she has any tears.

This poem had few changes, chiefly punctuative; the same may
be said for another item which also appeared first in *Love
Poems*—"Dog Tired." In this lyric, the poet wishes at sunset
that the girl would come out to him in the fields and take his
head upon her knee:

> I should like to lie still
> As if I was dead—but feeling
> Her hand go stealing
> Over my face and my hair until
> This ache was shed.

Some important changes were made, however, in the later
poem, "Last Words to Miriam," which first appeared in *Amores*.
The changes were in the direction of frankness, and since this
was Lawrence's last full statement about the relationship, here
is the text of "Last Words to Miriam" as it appears in the
Collected Poems:

> Yours is the sullen sorrow,
> The disgrace is also mine;
> Your love was intense and thorough,
> Mine was the love of a growing flower
> For the sunshine.

You had the power to explore me,
    Blossom me stalk by stalk;
You woke my spirit, you bore me
To consciousness, you gave me the dour
    Awareness—then I suffered a balk.

Body to body I could not
    Love you, although I would.
We kissed, we kissed though we should not.
You yielded, we threw the last cast,
    And it was no good.

You only endured, and it broke
    My craftsman's nerve.
No flesh responded to my stroke;
So I failed to give you the last
    Fine torture you did deserve.

You are shapely, you are adorned
    But opaque and null in the flesh;
Who, had I but pierced with the thorned
Full anguish, perhaps had been cast
    In a lovely illumined mesh

Like a painted window; the best
    Fire passed through your flesh,
Undrossed it, and left it blest
In clean new awareness. But now
    Who shall take you afresh?

Now who will burn you free
    From your body's deadness and dross?
Since the fire has failed in me,
What man will stoop in your flesh to plough
    The shrieking cross?

A mute, nearly beautiful thing
    Is your face, that fills me with shame
As I see it hardening;
I should have been cruel enough to bring
    You through the flame.

It is interesting to compare the second and third stanzas of this version with those of the original:

> I was diligent to explore you,
>   Blossom you stalk by stalk,
> Till my fire of creation bore you
> Shrivelling down in the final dour
>   Anguish—then I suffered a balk.

> I knew your pain, and it broke
>   My fine, craftsman's nerve;
> Your body quailed at my stroke,
> And my courage failed to give you the last
>   Fine torture you did deserve.

In the last stanza of the poem, the first three lines are the same in both versions, though the original had a comma rather than a semicolon at the end of the third line. The last two lines of the poem in its first appearance were:

> Warping the perfect image of God,
>   And darkening my eternal fame.

The conflict of mother and son over the girl is expressed in several of the poems; in "Monologue of a Mother" the woman feels that she has finally lost her son, and that there is nothing to do now but wait for death:

Strange he is, my son, whom I have awaited like a lover,
Strange to me like a captive in a foreign country, haunting
The confines and gazing out on the land where the wind is free;
White and gaunt, with wistful eyes that hover
Always on the distance, as if his soul were chaunting
The monotonous weird of departure away from me.

Lawrence's mother became ill with cancer in the summer of 1910. In October, Lawrence told Sydney Pawling of William Heinemann, Ltd., that he wished those who were printing *The White Peacock* would "make haste. Not that I care much myself. But I want my mother to see it while she keeps the live consciousness. She is really horribly ill."

Lawrence was able to put a copy of *The White Peacock* in his mother's hand not long before she died:

She looked at the outside, and then at the title-page, and then at me, with darkening eyes. And though she loved me so much, I think she doubted whether it could be much of a book, since no-one more important than I had written it. Somewhere, in the helpless privacies of her being, she had wistful respect for me. But for me in the face of the world, not much. This David would never get a stone across at Goliath. And why try? Let Goliath alone!—Anyway she was beyond reading my first immortal work. It was put aside, and I never wanted to see it again. She never saw it again.

Lawrence reports his father's reaction to the book:

"And what dun they gi'e thee for that, lad?"

"Fifty pounds, father."

"Fifty pound!" He was dumfounded, and looked at me with shrewd eyes as if I were a swindler. "Fifty pound! An' tha's niver done a hard day's work in thy life."

Mrs. Lawrence died late in 1910, in the brick house in Lynn Croft, Eastwood, where she and her husband had moved after the children had begun to leave home. Lawrence wrote, some eighteen years later, that when his mother died, "the world began to dissolve around me, beautiful, iridescent, but passing away substanceless. Till I almost dissolved away myself, and was very ill: when I was twenty-six." In the poem written soon after his mother's death and called "The End," he wrote:

And oh, my love, as I rock for you to-night,
And have not longer any hope
To heal the suffering, or to make requite
For all your life of asking and despair,
I own that some of me is dead to-night.

And in "The Virgin Mother" he said:

Is the last word now uttered,
Is the farewell said?
Spare me the strength to leave you

Now you are dead.
I must go, but my soul lies helpless
Beside your bed.

These stanzas are typical of the poems Lawrence wrote during this period about the illness and death of his mother. He stayed on teaching at Croydon through most of the year following her death, until his own illness forced him to retire. On November 7, 1911 he wrote to Garnett, "This last fortnight I have felt really rotten—it is the dry heat of the pipes in school, and the strain—and a cold. I must leave school, really." The records at Davidson have Lawrence absent from that day forth.

He had pneumonia again. On December 17, he wrote to Garnett from his lodging at Croydon that the doctor told him he would become consumptive if he returned to school: "I shan't send in my notice, but shall ask for a long leave of absence. Then I can go back if I get broke. The head-master grieves loudly over my prolonged absence. He knows he would scarcely get another man to do for him as I have done." Lawrence stayed on, convalescing, at the Jones house on Addiscombe Road, Croydon; at the end of the year he had neuritis in his left leg. He spent a month at Bournemouth, from early January to early February. Ill and bored, he began writing his novel *The Trespasser* for the second time.

He lived most of February in Eastwood, where he went out to parties, despite his lingering illness. The school records show that Lawrence officially left the service of the Croydon Education Committee on March 9, 1912. From that time forth he lived on his earnings, usually slight, as an author.

The preceding year, 1911, which Lawrence afterward called "the sick year," was the one in which he broke away from several women he had been involved with. It was the time of the end of his association with Jessie Chambers, although he saw her again in 1912 and continued writing to her into 1913. Jessie had often had rivals for Lawrence's interest and affection during his years of study and teaching; the most important of them appear in his writings, particularly Louie Burrows, a Midlands girl to whom he was engaged for a while, and Helen Corke, also a teacher in South London. Friends of Lawrence mention a Mrs.

Davidson with whom he was friendly during the Croydon period, and Jessie Chambers in her memoir says that he was engaged for a while to an auburn-haired fellow-teacher whom she does not name. This was Agnes Holt, who left Croydon and married a schoolmaster on the Isle of Man. Helen Corke, in a conversation with the author in the summer of 1950, said she doubted that Lawrence was ever actually engaged to Agnes Holt. There was also Mrs. Alice Dax in Eastwood, a feminist and socialist who served as one of the models for Clara Dawes in *Sons and Lovers*. But Lawrence could never form a permanent connection while his mother was alive, compelling him by her will to stay in the orbit of her affections; and after her death he wanted to follow her, as the poems—as well as the end of *Sons and Lovers*—indicate. In that bitter year of 1911, Lawrence wrote Helen Corke that "the one beautiful and generous adventure left seemed to be death." And, in the preface he wrote, but did not use, for the *Collected Poems*, Lawrence said "In that year, for me, everything collapsed, save the mystery of death, and the haunting of death in life."

It was about this time that Lawrence, skeptical of religion even while in college, gave up the Congregationalism of his childhood. Although he was for a while interested in Unitarianism, he soon broke away from all orthodox creeds. But he was to remain throughout his life an intensely religious man. He later became absorbed in ancient religions, Druid worship and Etruscan and Aztec theology, and although some readers have felt that his last work of fiction, *The Escaped Cock*, is sacrilegious, it is difficult to imagine a more intrinsically religious story.

In 1911, when Lawrence's sister Ada was also becoming disillusioned with chapel religion, he wrote to her, on April 11:

I am sorry more than I can tell to find you going through the torment of religious unbelief: it is so hard to bear, especially now. However, it seems to me like this: Jehovah is the Jew's idea of God, not ours. Christ was infinitely good, but mortal as we. There still remains a God, but not a personal God: a vast, shimmering impulse which waves on towards some end, I don't know what—taking no regard of the little individual, but taking regard for humanity. . . . I would still go to chapel if it did me any good. I shall go myself, when I am married. Whatever name one gives Him in worship we all strive towards the same God, be we generous hearted: Christians, Buddhists, Mrs. Dax, me, we all stretch our hands in the same direction. What does it matter the name we cry?

Lawrence wrote to Ada again on the 26th of April, telling her that he did not really know what to say to her: "There is nothing to do with life but to let it run, and it's a very bitter thing, but it's also wonderful." He wanted to protect Louie Burrows, to whom he was then engaged, from the realization of how tragic life could be. He was sorry that his father was "proving such a nuisance . . . Let him eat a bit of the bread of humility. It is astonishing how hard and bitter I feel towards him." Louie, when somewhat older, would "be more understanding. Remember, she's seen nothing whatever of the horror of life, and we've been bred up in its presence: with father."

Louie, who with Jessie Chambers and Helen Corke seemed to have become so intimate a part of Lawrence's life, was to be cast off during that "sick year" as the other two were: Lawrence in that unused preface to the *Collected Poems* said that this was the time of "the collapse of Miriam, of Helen, and of the other woman, the woman of 'Kisses in the Train' and 'The Hands of the Betrothed.'"

Like the Miriam poems, those to Helen are full of desperate conflict. "Lilies in the Fire," which Lawrence identifies as one of the Helen poems, is typical of the others. The poet sees the woman as a "stack of lilies, all white and gold," and himself as a sunbeam (*moonbeam* in the later version in the *Collected Poems*) that will warm their "pallor into radiance" and light up their cold white beauty. He is ashamed that the woman does not want him, that she shrinks away from him despite her love:

> 'Tis a degradation deep to me, that my best
> Soul's whitest lightning which should bright attest
> God stepping down to earth in one white stride,
>
> Means only to you a clogged, numb burden of flesh
> Heavy to bear, even heavy to uprear
> Again from earth, like lilies wilted and sere
> Flagged on the floor, that before stood up so fresh.

In the altered version, Lawrence replaced "stepping down to earth" with "stepping through our loins."

"The Appeal" was taken into the *Collected* volume with only slight punctuative changes; here is the original:

> You, Helen, who see the stars
> As mistletoe berries burning in a black tree,
> You surely, seeing I am a bowl of kisses,
> Should put your mouth to mine and drink of me.
>
> Helen, you let my kisses steam
> Wasteful into the night's black nostrils; drink
> Me up I pray; oh you who are Night's Bacchante,
> How can you from my bowl of kisses shrink.

In the same way that "Last Words to Miriam" is a valediction to the Miriam poems, "Passing Visit to Helen" is the end of the Helen poems. Lawrence in the *Collected* edition indicated that "Passing Visit" marked the conclusion of the Helen series, for it was there that he gave it that name; in *New Poems* (1918), "Passing Visit to Helen" had the title of "Intime."

The poem, another of those Lawrence altered slightly, begins with the narrator returning to Helen and finding "her just the same/At just the same old delicate game." She tells him to be his old self, incandescent, but not to come near her with his passion.

> You are lovelier than life itself, till
> Desire comes licking through the bars of your lips,
> And over my face the stray fire slips,
> Leaving a burn and an ugly smart
> That will have the oil of illusion . . .

Most of the poem is her monologue; he listens, watches her "ward away the flame/Yet warm herself at the fire" as she intimates that he should be proud to be her fire-opal.

> It is well
> Since I am here for so short a spell
> Not to interrupt her?—Why should I
> Break in by making any reply!

The poems to "the other woman" Lawrence mentions in his introduction to the *Collected* volumes—"Kisses in the Train" and "Hands of the Betrothed"—have in them less frustration than any of the other love lyrics. "Kisses in the Train," which came out in *Love Poems,* is the account ("I saw the Midlands/Revolve through her hair") of a passionate embrace in a speeding railway carriage. In "Hands of the Betrothed" there is some frustration because the girl is holding off her lover, yet she is not doing so out of terror or frigidity: she wants him physically, passionately, but

>   she's the same
> Betrothed young lady who loves me, and takes care
> Of her womanly virtue and of my good name.

The poem ended this way in *Amores;* in its later appearance, Lawrence for *womanly* substituted *maidenly.*

Jessie Chambers' memoir places "Snap-Dragon," originally in *Amores,* with "Kisses in the Train" and "Hands of the Betrothed" and indicates that they are to be identified with Louie Burrows. "Snap-Dragon" is the first of Lawrence's lyrics to make extensive use of flowers as erotic symbols; a number of his later poems, particularly in *Birds, Beasts and Flowers,* also deal with the phallic aspects of flowers.

The setting of "Snap-Dragon" is the girl's garden; there, "The mellow sunlight stood as in a cup/Between the old grey walls." The atmosphere of this poem is one of confusion, rapid movement, and shifting symbols: this is one of Lawrence's earliest "modern" poems, and it has much in common with *symboliste* verse.

At the beginning of "Snap-Dragon," the poet does not dare to look into the girl's face

> Lest her bright eyes like sparrows should fly in
> My windows of discovery, and shrill "Sin!"

The girl, laughing, turns her flushed face to the poet and asks if he can also make the snap-dragon yawn:

                                                    —I put my hand to the dint
In the flower's throat, and the flower gaped wide with woe.
She watched, she went of a sudden intensely still,
She watched my hand, to see what it would fulfil.

I pressed the wretched, throttled flower between
My fingers, till its head lay back, its fangs
Poised at her. Like a weapon my hand was white and keen,
And I held the choked flower-serpent in its pangs
Of mordant anguish, till she ceased to laugh,
Until her pride's flag, smitten, cleaved down to the staff.

She hid her face, she murmured between her lips
The low word "Don't!"—I let the flower fall,
But held my hand afloat towards the slips
Of blossom she fingered, and my fingers all
Put forth to her: she did not move, nor I,
For my hand like a snake watched hers, that could not fly.

Then I laughed in the dark of my heart, I did exult
Like a sudden chuckling of music. I bade her eyes
Meet mine, I opened her helpless eyes to consult
Their fear, their shame, their joy that underlies
Defeat in such a battle. In the dark of her eyes
My heart was fierce to make her laughter rise.

Till her dark deeps shook with convulsive thrills, and the dark
Of her spirit wavered like water thrilled with light;
And my heart leaped up in longing to plunge its stark
Fervour within the pool of her twilight,
Within her spacious soul, to find delight.

And I do not care, though the large hands of revenge
Shall get my throat at last, shall get it soon,
If the joy that they are lifted to avenge
Have risen red on my night as a harvest moon,
Which even death can only put out for me;
And death, I know, is better than not-to-be.

The mingling of symbols and realistic descriptions, as well as
the violent changes of mood and the shifts of rhythm, fore-
shadow the method used in some of the poems in *Look! We*

Have Come Through!—the principal verse product of Lawrence's next phase. "Snap-Dragon" is, however, somewhat more obscure than most of the *Look!* poems. Technically, "Snap-Dragon" is perhaps less important in the study of the development of Lawrence's poetry than it is in the study of the development of his prose, particularly in the novels of his second period, *The Rainbow* and *Women in Love.* In those books the emotional states of the characters are suggested rather than described—suggested by shuttling images and mixing rhythms, in a manner evolved from the "Snap-Dragon" method.

The quality of technical experimentation in this poem makes it stand out from the other early verse as a more "daring" item, though it does not necessarily stand above the rest in the matter of quality. None of the early love poems markedly does that: consequently it is difficult to say which of them, or which group of them, would be "most representative" for an anthology—and this is why Lawrence usually suffers in such collections. Like most of Lawrence's verse, the love poems should be read in their entirety.

↑ ↑ ↑ ↑

Many of the characteristics of Lawrence's youthful erotic poems are also found in his second novel, *The Trespasser,* which came out in 1912. It often uses the same kind of symbolism that is to be found in the love poems and, like them, almost invariably sets its love scenes against a natural background. And the book is full of such episodes; it is, next to *Lady Chatterley's Lover,* the most thoroughly erotic of all Lawrence's novels.

Begun in 1910 and rewritten for the last time in late 1911 and early 1912, *The Trespasser* grew out of Lawrence's Croydon experiences during those years. The main part of the book was based upon another person's autobiographical narrative—a manuscript by Helen Corke—but Lawrence put a good deal of himself into the adaptation.

A knowledge of what Lawrence was like at the time, and of what he was living through, will contribute toward a fuller understanding of *The Trespasser* as well as of the love poems written in this period.

The previous discussions of Lawrence's experiences in the

Midlands have shown that these years were for him a time of emotional crisis, and that his difficulties were not exclusively erotic. His dissatisfaction with college, for example, was chiefly social and ideological. His scholastic record indicates that he did only reasonably well at Nottingham, but at Croydon he was highly successful as a teacher. The training college's suggestion that Lawrence "could do work quite unusually good, especially if allowed a very free hand" with upper classes in a superior school, was borne out. When Lawrence left Croydon, the headmaster wrote that Lawrence had been a member of the Davidson School staff for two years, during which time he was responsible for the instruction of three upper "Standards." He also supervised the art training and "to a great extent influenced the science training of the whole school"—the latter achievement was a remarkable one indeed, for in another ten years Lawrence had become one of the age's fiercest enemies of science. But he seems, during his Croydon period, to have been not only a likeable teacher but also a well-adjusted one. The headmaster stated, in a report and testimonial:

His methods are wholly modern, and have the great merit that they are particularly adapted to obtain results in face of the limitations imposed by the elementary school curriculum. Mr. Lawrence is thoroughly in sympathy with his pupils, and possesses their entire regard, respect and confidence. Discipline on the highest plane naturally follows, and I am convinced that his genial manners and his well conceived methods of obtaining ready obedience in his class, could be extended with the greatest success to any school placed under his direction. I am sure that any Education Authority could place the greatest confidence in Mr. Lawrence, and that any duties undertaken by him would be fully, faithfully and zealously attempted.

This report is so different from the principal sections of the one from Nottingham College that it indicates a great change in Lawrence, at least in the matter of adjustment to outward conditions. Getting away from the Midlands doubtless helped him a great deal: in South London he was no longer teaching provincial boys and colliers' sons. He had access to the cultural life of London, and as a contributor to the *English Review* and, subsequently, as the author of a much-discussed first novel, he had an entrée into literary circles. When Hueffer and Violet Hunt dropped him, he was picked up by another outstanding discoverer and developer of literary talent, Edward Garnett, the champion of Conrad, Doughty, and Hudson.

The young man gained in confidence; Edward Garnett later spoke of Lawrence as having, in 1911, "loveableness, cheekiness, intensity and pride." This makes him appear somewhat more forceful than his self-portrait as Cecil Byrne in *The Trespasser* and the variants of Cecil Byrne in the short stories written about the Croydon situation, which will be examined later. The young man recurring in these stories is of course Cyril Beardsall of *The White Peacock*, with Cyril's vagueness and indecision. But Lawrence himself was getting beyond being a young man of this kind.

One of the elements in his growing poise and assurance was his ability to hold the interest of groups when he spoke. This is an important point in Lawrence's development, for it leads toward his later assumption of the rôle of prophet. As Lawrence conceived this rôle, it was not entirely dependent upon the written word; the spoken word was also important, as *The Plumed Serpent* shows, with Don Ramón's speeches to the people, and his Quetzlcoatl chants.

During Lawrence's Croydon period he occasionally addressed groups; he was apparently one of the leading figures of a discussion society. One of his early addresses which has been preserved, "Art and the Individual," was, according to his sister Ada, "probably delivered in Croydon," though Jessie Chambers and William E. Hopkin both say it was read at Eastwood—perhaps Lawrence delivered it at both places. In this paper, the young intellectual begins by saying, "These Thursday night meetings are for discussing social problems with a view to advancing a more perfect social state and to our fitting ourselves to be perfect citizens—communists—what not." He then proceeds to discuss "Herbart's classification of interests, adding one that he overlooked." Lawrence speaks of aesthetics at some length, and in a commonplace manner: "If we bend our minds, not so much to things beautiful, as to the beautiful aspect of things, then we gain this refinement of temper which can *feel* a beauti-

ful thing. We are too gross—a crude emotion carries us away—
we cannot feel the beauty of things. It is so in Socialism as in
everything. You must train yourself to appreciate beauty or
Art—refine yourself, or become refined, as Hume puts it. And
what is refinement? It is really delicate sympathy. . ." These
sentences do not sound like the later Lawrence, either stylistically or ideologically, and in themselves they give no suggestion
of an original mind or a potentially important writer. The
material, however, was not intended for publication and is hardly
more than a series of notes for a talk; it is full of questions
("Why is this Art?") and suggestions ("Let us take a book of
socialistic essays for full discussion one evening, someone presiding"). The paper must have been presented fairly early in Lawrence's residence at Croydon, for he seems to have become disillusioned with the discussion group there at least as early as
August 1910, since on the 24th of that month he wrote to William E. Hopkin, in Eastwood: "I seem to have lost touch
altogether with the old 'progressive' clique: in Croydon the
Socialists are so stupid, and the Fabians so flat."

Another of Lawrence's papers also apparently read at Croydon
is one on Rachael Annand Taylor. This is entirely literary, in
no way sociological, and it is so unlike the later Lawrence that
it indicates the extent of the change that took place in him
within the space of only a few years. The Croydon paper on
Mrs. Taylor begins by describing her as "not ripe yet to be
gathered as fruit for lectures and papers"; barely thirty, she
lives in Chelsea, knows Professor Gilbert Murray at Oxford,
and has been abandoned by her husband; she "says strange, ironic
things of many literary people in a plaintive, peculiar fashion."
Lawrence admits that her work "is raw green fruit to offer you,
to be received with suspicion, to be tasted charily and spat out
without much revolving and tasting." Lawrence says that the
fresh, green work of an unknown "must be sun-dried by time
and sunshine of favorable criticism, like muscatels and prunes":
then the eternal flavors of the poetry will come out, "unob-
scured and unpolluted by the temporal." But, whatever the
ultimate quality of the verse, Mrs. Taylor looks like a poet, with
her Rossettian appearance, her "slim, svelte, big beautiful bushes

of reddish hair," her "scarlet, small, shut mouth," and her "long, white, languorous hands of the correct, subtle radiance." Lawrence speaks enthusiastically of Mrs. Taylor's *fin de siècle* poetry, saying that her sonnets "stand apart in an age of 'open road' and Empire thumping verse." Lawrence, who was later to be greatly influenced by Whitman's "open-road" style, praises Mrs. Taylor, in this 1909 lecture, for her orthodoxy in the matter of rhythms and meters: "She allows herself none of the modern looseness." The previously quoted letter from Lawrence to Edward Marsh, attacking orthodoxy and defending "modern looseness," was written only four years later.

Lawrence describes a conversation with Mrs. Taylor, who apparently opened her "scarlet, small, shut mouth" to deliver to him an epigram about love:

"There is nothing more tormenting," I said to her, "than to be loved overmuch."
"Yes, one thing more tormenting," she replied.
"And what's that?" I asked her.
"To love," she said, very quietly.

This amusingly crude exchange sounds like the conversations of the young intellectuals in *The White Peacock* and *The Trespasser*, and it once again shows us the literary-minded Cecil-Cyril young man of those books and of the early stories. He is also the Derek Hamilton of Helen Corke's novel, *Neutral Ground* (1933), and the D. of her reconstructed conversations in *Lawrence and Apocalypse* (1933), in which a D. and H. (not split selves of Lawrence, but David and Helen) wander across the southern edges of Greater London discussing the meaning of the Book of Revelation.

Although Helen Corke's *Neutral Ground* was not published until 1933, most of it was written in 1918. When published, the book contained an Author's Note which said in part:

The autobiographical section of this story (Book III, Section 1) is a revision of papers, written at intervals during 1910, 1911, 1912, upon some of which Lawrence based his novel *The Trespasser*.

Neutral Ground is the life story of one Ellis Brooke, of her childhood and her period of education and her love affair with her music teacher, Angus Raine; she calls him Dominie or, when in a specifically Wagnerian mood, Siegmund; the story ends after his suicide, based on that of Herbert B. MacCartney, violinist of the Carl Rosa Opera Company, in 1909. In both this book and *The Trespasser*, the outlines of the "Siegmund" story are the same: the middle-aged music teacher, who has an embittered wife and several clamoring children, takes a holiday on the Isle of Wight with his girl pupil and, after several days of passionate but not satisfactory love-making, returns to the London suburbs to kill himself.

Neutral Ground is full of novelese extravagances: "guide his soul to the shelter of a House Beautiful"; "antic shadows on her soft, green dress"; "Dear, you may be a saint, or heaven knows what strange being spiritually, but physically you're a woman, of course"; "Her tone cut through the fumes of his passion"; "The jangling voices of the Little Things reach me"—these are a few random examples; similar passages may be found on almost every page. Lawrence, who occasionally took over whole sections of the Corke manuscript with little change, was infected by this type of writing, and the consequence is that *The Trespasser* is the poorest of his novels. It is not altogether bad, and it is much more skillfully put together than *Neutral Ground*—the people in *The Trespasser* are much more real—but it is not good Lawrence. *The White Peacock* had its crudenesses, but that book was at least simply written: the prose of *The Trespasser* is often thick and gummy.

Lawrence was never enthusiastic about *The Trespasser*. In October 1910, he wrote Sydney Pawling of William Heinemann, Ltd., that he was "not in the least anxious to publish that book." He was speaking of the first draft, "the rapid work of three months," which he was willing to let "lie for a few years." He wrote with greater warmth of the book that was to become *Sons and Lovers*—"my third novel, *Paul Morel*, which is plotted out very interestingly (to me), and about one-eighth of which is written. *Paul Morel* will be a novel—not a florid prose poem, or a decorated idyll running to seed in realism." Lawrence at least recognized the weaknesses of *The Trespasser*.

Hueffer disliked the book; Lawrence quotes him as calling it "a rotten work of genius. It has no construction or form—it is all execrably bad art, being all variations on a theme. Also it is erotic—not that I, personally, mind that, but an erotic work *must* be good art, which this is not."

Edward Garnett's "rescue" of Lawrence—after Hueffer, in Lawrence's account, "left me to paddle my own canoe" and "I very nearly wrecked it and did for myself"—has already been mentioned. Garnett, an editor for the house of Gerald Duckworth, Ltd., accepted *The Trespasser* after William Heinemann had offered to publish it although he felt it was too erotic—causing Lawrence to withdraw it. Lawrence revised the book completely in January 1912, while convalescing from the illness that made him give up teaching.

The style of this novel, which came out in May 1912, has been mentioned. Despite Lawrence's assurance to Garnett that he would "wage war on" his adjectives on the proofsheets, the book is hectically overwritten. Many of the faults of *The White Peacock* recur, particularly in the unreal conversations, which are again like that nothing-is-so-tormenting-as-love conversation, previously quoted, with Rachel Annand Taylor. This bit between Cecil Byrne and Helena will serve as an example:

"But I am not a bare tree. All my dead leaves, they hang to me—and go through a kind of *danse macabre*—"
"But you bud underneath—like a beech," he said quickly.
"Really, my friend," she said coldly, "I am—too tired to bud."
"No," he pleaded, "no!"

The natural descriptions are occasionally as literary-false as some of those in the earlier book, but most of them have a turgid and feverish quality not found in *The White Peacock*. Sometimes Lawrence's effects are almost a parody of his later accomplishments, yet now and then in *The Trespasser* there are passages of prose that are already mature:

The lights of the little farmhouse below had vanished, the yellow specks of ships were gone. Only the pier-light, far away, shone in the sea like the broken piece of a star. Overhead was a silver-greyness of stars; below was the velvet blackness of the night and the sea.

The family scenes are, as always in Lawrence, effective: Siegmund's homecoming, with the wife and children bitter against him, is an excellent piece of realistic writing. The passages in which Siegmund lapses into a silent despair are skillfully done, but the episode in which he kills himself is marred by a literary touch—Siegmund's mind twice quotes (actually misquotes) Shakespeare.

There is no flaw, however, in the presentation of Siegmund's motive for the suicide. He feels the social burden of his escapade with Helena, and after his return home he realizes the difficulty of his position. He cannot keep running away from his wife and children, and he is not strong enough to leave them for good. His gross suicide is his choice of a way out. And although he is a negative character he has a positive value in Lawrence's development in that he helps to point out to Lawrence the way his future characters would not take. Here was a man who let himself be hounded to death by society's traditions—this is how the later Lawrence would look at Siegmund. And what good did those traditions ever do Siegmund? They merely made him wretched. Yet he was willingly their victim, emphatically so at the last. While Lawrence was not trying to point a moral, the working out of the Siegmund problem must inevitably have led to certain corollaries which hereafter were to influence both his life and his work.

Helena is the first of the series of intellectualized, will-driven females Lawrence was to write of so bitterly. She is a "dreaming woman" of the kind whose passion only "exhausts itself at the mouth." She rejects the animal in Siegmund, will accept only kisses from him, and these seem to fulfill her. Her type is later most completely delineated in Hermione Roddice in *Women in Love*, though Miriam in *Sons and Lovers* has some of her characteristics. Another version of Helena appears in a short story Lawrence wrote at this time, "The Witch *à la Mode*"; this was not published until after his death, in the volume called *A Modern Lover*.

Lawrence in *The Trespasser* employed symbolism in the usual literary-poetic way, and not after the fashion of the French *symboliste* movement, which used the term in a specialized sense; Lawrence's symbols in this book were not Baudelaire's synaesthetic *correspondances:* rather, they were more conventional and explicit identifications to reinforce theme and meaning. The symbolism in *The Trespasser* is more diffused and less clearly understandable than that in *The White Peacock.* Moonlight figures through most of *The Tresspasser,* but more as a leitmotif drawing certain emotions together than as a coherently worked out symbol. There is a different kind of symbolism in the sunburn on Helena's arms, which is at one level a shrewd psychological presentation: her arms become inflamed during the time she is with Siegmund on the island, and the burn lingers through the winter and into the following summer.

There are various other thematic developments—Siegmund's violin, parts of the Wagnerian mythology and, in an almost accidental sense, the Isle of Wight itself—but there is no effective central symbol such as Lawrence used in *The White Peacock* and was to use in *The Rainbow,* a symbol that illuminates and deepens the understanding of the central action of the story.

↗ ↗ ↗ ↗

Shortly before *The Trespasser* was published, Lawrence met the woman who was to become his wife. She was married to another man and was the mother of three small children, but she and Lawrence immediately took up their life together, leaving England. Lawrence began to free himself from the bondage of his past: his breaking with that past is signalized by the completion of *Sons and Lovers* and by the early poems in the *Look! We Have Come Through!* volume.

The woman with whom Lawrence united himself was the wife of one of his former professors at Nottingham, Ernest Weekley. After Lawrence had left Croydon, he asked Professor Weekley to enquire about educational conditions abroad, for a relative on his mother's side had suggested a lectureship at a German university. Professor Weekley invited the young novelist-poet to lunch at his fine home in the Victoria Crescent section of Nottingham. And there Lawrence met Frieda for the first time. She was the daughter of Baron Friedrich von Richthofen, who

as a young officer in the Franco-Prussian War received a wound
in his right hand that left it badly crippled; he subsequently
became a high official in the civil service. Frieda had married
Professor Weekley when she was under twenty, and in that
year of 1912 she was thirty-two and her husband was forty-
seven. She says in her memoir of Lawrence that her married
life in that provincial town was not an unhappy one, but that
she was unawakened. Catherine Carswell says in *The Savage
Pilgrimage* that Frieda "lived in a placid dream, which was varie-
gated at times by love-affairs that were equally unreal."

But what Lawrence felt for Frieda was not unreal. Upon
leaving the Weekleys' home after his first meeting with Frieda,
he walked the eight miles across the fields to Eastwood. The
next time he saw Frieda, he annoyed her by telling her that she
was unaware of her husband. She became aware of Lawrence,
she says, when she saw him playing with her children by a
brook, making paper boats for them and floating daisies on the
water. As he bent over, Frieda felt a tenderness for him, and
she knew that she loved him. "After that, things happened
quickly."

She wanted him to spend the night with her when her husband
went away on a trip, but Lawrence refused; he loved her and
wanted her to leave her husband. Frieda was tormented by the
fear of losing her children if she did so. But on the third of
May, she and Lawrence crossed the channel and went to Metz,
where her family lived. Frieda dutifully visited her parents,
but did not tell them about Lawrence, though she presented him
to her two sisters, who liked him. Lawrence and Frieda, who
had few places where they could meet, spent much of their
time walking around the fortifications of Metz. When Lawrence
was arrested on suspicion of being a British officer, Frieda had
to tell her father about him, and through her father's influence
Lawrence was released. The two men met only once, when
Frieda brought her lover home to tea: "They looked at each
other fiercely—my father, the pure aristocrat, Lawrence, the
miner's son. My father, hostile, offered a cigarette to Lawrence.
That night I dreamt that they had a fight, and that Lawrence
defeated my father." And in Lawrence's unconscious, Frieda

was doubtless blotting out the image of his mother, as no other woman had ever done.

Lawrence left Metz for Trier, and after several days there he went on to the Rhineland. On the way, he had to change trains at Hennef, and he wrote a letter to Frieda as he sat "like a sad swain beside a nice, twittering little river, waiting for the twilight to drop, and my last train to come. . . . Now for the first time during today, my detachment leaves me, and I know I only love you. The rest is nothing at all. And the promise of life with you is all richness. Now I know." This letter closely resembles the poem "Bei Hennef" which Lawrence also wrote on the spot; there is the same "little river twittering in the twilight," and "All the troubles and anxieties and pain" are "Gone under the twilight."

> And at last I know my love for you is here,
> I can see it all, it is whole like the twilight,
> It is large, so large, I could not see it before
> Because of the little lights and flickers and interruptions,
> Troubles, anxieties and pains.

"Bei Hennef" first appeared in *Love Poems*, but in the *Collected* edition was put into the *Look! We Have Come Through!* sequence. The last line of the last stanza takes a new turn of thought not suggested by anything in the letter:

> You are the call and I am the answer,
> You are the wish, and I the fulfilment,
> You are the night, and I the day.
>> What else—it is perfect enough,
>> It is perfectly complete,
>> You and I,
>> What more—?
> Strange, how we suffer in spite of this!

Staying with relatives at Waldbröl in the Rhineland, Lawrence was wretched without Frieda, to whom he wrote almost daily. His letters, urging her to be patient, reflected at the same time his own impatience. He and Frieda must have a period of waiting, of vigil: yet they must hasten her divorce. Lawrence even wrote Professor Weekley, who in the intimacy of the situation had become "Ernest"; and Edward Garnett was sent frequent bulletins. Lawrence wrote to Mrs. William Hopkin about the matter, and subsequently informed Jessie Chambers and Helen Corke, as well as a former colleague at Croydon, A. W. McLeod. It was in one of the letters to McLeod that Lawrence first gave an indication that he was no longer interested in a university lectureship: "If I have to beg my bread I'll never teach again." A few months later he told McLeod, "I still dream I must teach— and that's the worst dream I ever have. How I loathed and raged with hate against it, and never knew."

While at Waldbröl, Lawrence casually mentioned to Frieda that his cousin Hannah, recently married to an uninteresting man, was becoming "quite fond" of her young visitor, though it was all "perfectly honorable"; but he wrote somewhat differently to Edward Garnett, saying that Hannah was sorry she was married: "She's getting in love with me. Why is it women *will* fall in love with me?" Frieda began writing from Metz about another man; Lawrence told her she reminded him of the Maupassant story about the hungry peasant and the wet nurse with breasts painfully overfull of milk, who met in a railway compartment and "relieved each other and went their several ways." Where, Lawrence wondered, would Frieda's admirer "get his next feed?"

He had assured Frieda that he was not flirting and would not do so unless he got tipsy. He told Garnett he had no eye for the girls, and wanted only to have Frieda meet him in Munich. He wrote to her that she must not worry if she had become pregnant by him: there should be no interference, for he wanted to have children by her, wanted to marry her. "I think, when one loves, one's very sex passion becomes calm, a steady sort of force, instead of a storm. Passion, that nearly drives one mad, is far away from real love. I am realizing things that I never thought to realize."

It was the beginning of the second phase of Lawrence's writing career—even though parts of the first phase lingered on. New stirrings are evident in the *Look!* poems he began writing when he met Frieda; they will be discussed in connection with the next phase, to which most of them belong. The ending of the first period is marked by the final writing of *Sons and Lovers*. Lawrence had taken up again the manuscript of *Paul Morel* and was working on it "while eating his heart out" at Waldbröl. He went on rewriting the book after he and Frieda had met again; he sent the manuscript to London and, after receiving it back with Garnett's comments and suggestions, completed the book before the year was out. He could do so now because the part of his life with which *Sons and Lovers* is concerned was over at last.

While Lawrence was in Waldbröl, Frieda had considered returning to her husband and children, but instead of going to England went to Munich and stayed with her married sister, Dr. Else Jaffe. Lawrence met Frieda at Munich on the 24th of May, and after a night there they went for a week to Beuerberg in the Bavarian Tyrol, where they wandered through masses of Alpine flowers. They were frequently in conflict but they were happy, too: the struggle and the ecstasy of the experience are recorded in *Look! We Have Come Through!* and in Lawrence's letters to Edward Garnett: "The children are miserable, missing her so much. She lies on the floor in misery—and then is fearfully angry with me because I won't say 'Stay for my sake.'" And: "I *do* love her. If she left me, I do not think I should be alive six months hence." And: "The lovely brooks we have paddled in, the lovely things we have done!"

Professor Alfred Weber of Heidelberg lent Lawrence and Frieda his flat at Icking, about fourteen miles south of Munich, where they stayed until their departure for Italy on the fifth of August. The flat was above a shop, and it had a balcony with a view of grainfields and the cold green Isar River. The conflict between the lovers lessened, Lawrence wrote busily, and visitors provided distractions: Edward Garnett's young son David, on a holiday from college, was a pleasant guest; Frieda's mother, en route to Switzerland, descended upon the lovers for an hour and demanded to know why Lawrence expected a baroness to clean his boots and empty his slops, "the wife of a clever professor, living with him like a barmaid, and he not even able to keep her in shoes"—but Lawrence mollified his future mother-in-law, with whom he was to have a cordial relationship as long as he lived. Lawrence was pleased with reviews of *The Trespasser* which were sent from England, and he was amused at the *Nottinghamshire Guardian's* heading of its review, "A Reprehensible Jaunt." Lawrence told Garnett that love made him feel "barbaric," and that Frieda wanted "to clear out of Europe, and get to somewhere uncivilized." It is interesting to note that this idea, later so important to Lawrence, was originally Frieda's.

When Lawrence and Frieda left Icking, they walked south over the Alps, by way of Mayrhofen, Sterzing, Bozen, and Trient, arriving at Riva in the first week of September. Riva, at the top of Lago di Garda, was then in Austrian territory; they had taken the train there after Frieda broke down at Trient because the cheap hotel with its "doubtful sheets" and dirty toilets upset her, and Lawrence had found her weeping on a bench in the Piazza Dante. Frieda was weary of walking around with a rucksack, dressed like a tramp; she was happy again when she caught up with her trunk at Riva, and she and Lawrence could live at a respectable *pensione*. Then their lives were further brightened when fifty pounds arrived from Duckworth. They left Riva in the middle of September and moved halfway down the lake to Gargnano, in Italian territory, on the western shore. There they took the first floor of the Villa Igéa, the first of their several Italian villas, where they stayed until their return to Germany and England in April 1913. The last draft of *Sons and Lovers* was written at Gargnano, amid the vineyards and olive woods and lemon groves by the purple lake of Catullus. But there is no touch of the South in that emphatically northern novel.

On August 4, Lawrence had told Garnett it would take him three months "to write *Paul Morel* over again." He occasionally referred to the book in subsequent letters to various correspondents and on November 14 notified Garnett that he had mailed the completed manuscript to him the day before, for publication by Duckworth (Heinemann had rejected the novel). The précis of the book given in the November 14 letter to Garnett provides an important starting point for a discussion of *Sons and Lovers*, for it is a summary from the author's point of view, presenting the main outline of the story:

A woman of character and refinement goes into the lower class, and has no satisfaction in her own life. She has had a passion for her husband, so the children are born of passion, and have heaps of vitality. But as her sons grow up, she selects them as lovers—first the eldest, then the second. These sons are *urged* into life by their reciprocal love of their mother—urged on and on. But when they come to manhood, they can't love, because their mother is the strongest power in their lives, and holds them. . . . As soon as the young men come into contact with women there is a split. William gives his sex to a fribble, and his mother holds his soul. But the split kills him, because he doesn't know where he is. The next son gets a woman who fights for his soul—fights his mother. The son loves the mother—all the sons hate and are jealous of the father. The battle goes on between the mother and the girl, with the son as object. The mother gradually proves the stronger, because of the tie of blood. The son decides to leave his soul in his mother's hands, and, like his elder brother, go for passion. Then the split begins to tell again. But, almost unconsciously, the mother realizes what is the matter and begins to die. The son casts off his mistress, attends to his mother dying. He is left in the end naked of everything, with the drift towards death.

The principal thematic point that emerges from this précis is what Freud was first to call the Oedipus complex. Lawrence had not gone deeply into the official aspects of this—he said at the time that he had never read Freud though he knew about him—but his intuition and knowledge led him independently to many of the conclusions at which psychoanalysts were then arriving in the Viennese clinics.

Lawrence came to see the Oedipus complex not just as his own story but as the dilemma of his generation, a widespread condition that had reached fever-peak in the last years of the long Victorian matriarchy. Lawrence wrote in an unpublished foreword that was meant only for Garnett's eyes, "The old son-lover was Oedipus. The name of the new one is legion." He told Garnett in a letter that this was the tragedy of thousands of young Englishmen, perhaps even of Garnett's son.

Some of the autobiographical features of *Sons and Lovers* have already been mentioned; Lawrence said toward the end of his life that the first half of the book was all autobiography. Jessie

Chambers reports that the early version of the manuscript which he sent her seemed strained; the situations were unreal and the writing "tired." She told Lawrence she thought that "what had really happened was much more poignant and interesting than the situations he had invented," and she suggested that he rewrite the whole story, keeping closer to the pattern of actuality.

Apparently the early *Paul Morel* manuscript was, like *The White Peacock*, a wishful fictionizing of unpleasant truth. Lawrence Clark Powell has reported that, in what is probably the earliest surviving holograph of *Paul Morel*, "the father accidentally kills Paul's brother, is jailed and dies upon his release." Once again, as in his first novel, Lawrence was conveniently getting the father out of the way.

Jessie Chambers helped Lawrence write parts of the second draft of *Paul Morel*, in late 1911 and early 1912, before he went to Germany. Frieda Lawrence makes a somewhat similar claim for herself in relation to the final version which Lawrence wrote between July and November 1912 in Germany, Austria, and Italy; she says she "lived and suffered that book, and wrote bits of it" to help present the mother's point of view in certain situations. Jessie Chambers' contributions were chiefly remembrances of events she had taken part in, though she also made numerous emendations to Lawrence's text; several extant manuscripts containing evidences of her assistance are now located at the Humanities Research Center at the University of Texas. Appendix B of the present book is an examination of these manuscripts.

Sons and Lovers in its final form is both a testimony to Jessie Chambers and an effort on Lawrence's part to get her out of his system. She says that she felt "bewildered and dismayed" at the final version of the story: she thought Lawrence had not handled the central problem with integrity, and the sympathetic portrait of the mother irritated her. Lawrence's "bondage was glorified and made absolute," and Miriam was not, Jessie felt, treated justly. Lawrence had "completely left out the years of devotion to the development of his genius. . . . What else but the devotion to a common end had held us together against his mother's repeated assaults." And Jessie felt that he had not faithfully represented "the nature and quality of our desperate search for a right relationship." She apparently did not realize that, although Lawrence was drawing some of his facts from life, he was after all writing a novel.

And Lawrence was consciously writing a novel in the tradition: *Sons and Lovers* is the most normally constructed of his better novels. When he completed the last version of the manuscript, he wrote Garnett, "I tell you it has got form—*form;* haven't I made it patiently, out of sweat as well as blood." *Sons and Lovers* contained much that was new, and it was the first significant work of one of the twentieth century's most important authors. And it was something else: the last novel of the nineteenth century.

The autobiographical novel is essentially a twentieth-century product, although there had been autobiographical novels in the past, and in books such as *David Copperfield* a good deal of personal experience was incorporated into various parts of the imaginary narrative. In the early twentieth century, autobiographical novels were often a direct projection of experience: in *A Portrait of the Artist as a Young Man*, for example, the episodes are skillfully selected and poetically expressed. *Sons and Lovers*, almost the exact contemporary of Joyce's first novel, is less carefully constructed—despite Lawrence's assurances to Garnett—but its very crudeness and the intensive passion of its theme give it at least an equal strength.

Parts of *Sons and Lovers* have an impressive objectivity that does not clash with the prevalent subjectivity. The opening section, for instance, the chapter called "The Early Married Life of the Morels," provides an effectively realistic base for the rest of the novel. Although the author's sympathies are with the mother rather than the father, the bias is not extreme: Lawrence had enough understanding of humanity and, although not overtly, of social conditions, not to let his sympathies pervert the story. Lawrence's feelings of guilt, years later, about his fictional treatment of his father have been mentioned: they were perhaps more intense than they needed to be, for the father is not made out too great a monster in *Sons and Lovers;* actually, the portrait is a humanized one, for even through his antagonism in youth, Lawrence felt some sympathy with his father, and this sympathy is evident in the characterization of Morel.

Sometimes in the evenings, the Morel of the story would

cobble the boots or mend his pit-bottle or the kettle, and those were happy times for the children, who were recruited to help. "He was a good workman, dextrous, and one who, when he was in a good humor, always sang. He had whole periods, months, almost years, of friction and nasty temper. Then sometimes he was jolly again," and he and the children worked happily together at household tasks. He would tell them about the horse, Taffy, in the pit—"Morel had a warm way of telling a story. He made one feel Taffy's cunning."—or about the mice that ran up his arm in the mine, or got into his pocket. Morel was also presented in his comic aspects, as when he saw the photograph of his eldest son's fiancée, a picture that had shocked Mrs. Morel because the girl's shoulders were naked:

Morel found the photograph standing on the chiffonier in the parlor. He came out with it between his thick thumb and finger.
"Who dost reckon this is?" he asked his wife.
"It's the girl our William is going with," replied Mrs. Morel.
"H'm! 'Er's a bright spark, from th' look on 'er, an' one as wunna do him owermuch good neighter. Who is she?"
"Her name is Louisa Lily Denys Western."
"An' come again to-morrer!" exclaimed the miner. "An' is 'er an actress?"

Later, when Lily has come to Bestwood for a visit, Mrs. Morel tries to force a book on her and William says contemptuously that Lily has never read a book. Morel breaks in: " 'Er's like me. . . . 'Er canna see what there is i' books, ter sit borin' your nose in 'em for, nor more can I." In scenes and speeches like these, Morel is viewed with humor—but the humor is not cruel. And toward the end of the book, when his wife is sinking into her fatal illness, Morel is shown as forlorn, "helpless, and as if nobody owned him. . . . He put up his eyebrows for misery, and clenched his fists on his knees, feeling so awkward in the presence of a big trouble." Such passages, contrasting with those in which Morel is revealed as a brute and a drunkard, help round out the portrait of the man, a rich and living portrait.
There is much tenderness in *Sons and Lovers*, expressed without sentimentalism or self-pity. Sentimentalism is lacking because

even in his defeats Paul Morel tries to come to terms with life and does not expect too much of the situation in which he finds himself; self-pity is missing because Paul never laments over his fate and never asks why he, of all mortals, must suffer so much. The tenderness, which is essentially a recognition of the value of a human personality for its own sake, provides continual relief for the reader from the passionate intensity of the main plot: the lives of the characters are presented with a fullness that includes many of the little incidental emotional experiences that enrich human existence. The episode, for example, in which Paul and his mother go to Nottingham together is a fine presentation of what these two feel for one another and for life in general, for in this sequence they are seen in relief against a strange setting. This passage in the chapter "Paul Launches Into Life" was not put into the book merely to deepen atmosphere or even to increase the range of characterization: it is an organic part of the story, for it deals with Paul's beginning to work at Jordan's. Since Paul stays there for a number of years, in contrast with Lawrence's own brief employment in a similar place, and since many of his important experiences come out of his work at Jordan's, such as his meeting with Clara and Baxter Dawes, the sections concerned with his time at the artificial-limb factory are important to the development of the story.

Lawrence's handling of the trip to Nottingham by Paul and his mother, on that day when he "launches into life," is one example among many of the skillful way in which he blends characters and episodes into the main plot in this novel. He does not merely state that Paul and his mother went to Nottingham, but shows them in their mingled anxiety and gaiety as they undertake this little journey which is at once a business trip and an excursion. Paul, at the ticket office at Bestwood, watched his mother, and "as he saw her hands in their old black kid gloves getting the silver out of the worn purse, his heart contracted with pain of love for her." But a few moments later, on the train, "he suffered because she *would* talk aloud in the presence of the other travellers." In Nottingham, seeing the barges in the canal, they compared the place to Venice, and "they enjoyed the shops immensely," remarking how a needlework blouse they saw would "just suit our Annie." After the harsh interview with Mr. Jordan, who finally engaged Paul, the mother and son wandered through Nottingham again, two poor people in a provincial city whose prices were beyond their range. This kind of scene has been presented in literature before and since, but few authors have succeeded in giving it so much emotional force.

Lawrence never expresses directly the underlying meaning of the sequence: it is more than the description of a boy's going to work for the first time—it is in part the realization of his mother's dreams for him, and in part the failure of them. It is a realization of her dreams because she has at least helped the boy escape from the mines. It is a failure because the alternative is merely another phase of bourgeois industrialism: a growing boy must travel sixteen miles by rail each day and arrive at the city as early as a quarter to eight, for which he will receive eight shillings a week. Yet the mother feels they must celebrate; they will eat at a restaurant. Paul had only once or twice before been to such a place, and then only for buns and tea; Bestwood people regarded anything beyond this, such as a cooked dinner, as an extravagance. Paul felt guilty, and they ordered the cheapest dish, kidney pies and potatoes. The mother insisted that Paul have a currant tart, though he begged her not to order it; but because he liked sweets, she was firm—he must have the currant tart. The waitress took her time in coming for the order; she was flirting with some men customers: "Mrs. Morel was angry. But she was too poor, and her orders were too meagre, so that she had not the courage to insist on her rights just then. They waited and waited." Afterward, Mrs. Morel wanted to buy Paul a paintbrush, "but this indulgence he refused," and then they saw some black grapes which made Mrs. Morel's mouth water, but she knew she would "have to wait a bit" for such luxuries. Later she embarrassed Paul when, in the presence of an elegant young lady in a florist shop, she rejoiced over the display of flowers. Paul had nevertheless "spent a perfect afternoon with his mother. They arrived home in the mellow evening, happy, and glowing, and tired."

This episode has been discussed at length for reasons already explained—it is both an important part of the story and a revelation of character—and for the purpose of showing, as concretely as possible, the human force of *Sons and Lovers*. The boy and his mother are the Victorian poor, whose pleasures are few and simple; in adjustment to their lot, they have preserved some of the natural joy of the poor, and although the occasion of their trip to Nottingham is in part a miserable one, they turn it into a kind of holiday. They are always reminded of their poverty, but they find a gaiety in their own relationship; and the continual reminders of their poverty serve to enhance the values of that relationship. And it is this relationship that comprises the central part of the story; *Sons and Lovers* was the first and has remained the most forceful of stories of what Freud called the Oedipus complex.

Freud had begun promulgating his theories along these lines only a few years before Lawrence finished *Sons and Lovers*. By 1912 many of the British intellectuals were reading Freud; as previously explained, Lawrence is not supposed to have read him until somewhat later; Frederick J. Hoffman in *Freudianism and the Literary Mind* quotes a letter from Frieda Lawrence in 1942, in which she says she cannot recall whether or not Lawrence had read Freud or knew of him before 1912, but she was "a great admirer" of Freud, and she and Lawrence "had long arguments" about him. Professor Hoffman believes that these discussions may have caused Lawrence to increase "the emphasis in the novel upon the mother-son relationship, to the neglect of other matters. . . . But the relationship was there long before Lawrence's final revision": he did not allow psychological or clinical commentary to lower the novel's literary excellence, and "it is doubtful, therefore, that the revision of *Sons and Lovers* was more than superficially affected by Lawrence's introduction to psychoanalysis." Murry says in his *Reminiscences*, "It had been discovered that in *Sons and Lovers* Lawrence had independently arrived at the main conclusions of the psychoanalysts, and the English followers of Freud came to see him."

Murry and others who have tried to see all of Lawrence's achievement entirely within the limitations of the Oedipus complex have failed to consider the vitalizing influence of Frieda and the liberating effect of the very writing of *Sons and Lovers*. Goethe, who used literature as a kind of confessional to free himself from entangling experiences, once wrote that, like a snake, he sloughed his skin and started afresh, and another time he said, "People go on shooting at me when I am already miles out of range." The purgative value of such procedures lies in the intensity of the emotional experience of the writing itself: if the emotion is recollected in tranquility, the product is likely to be merely a celebration and perpetuation of the past; on the other hand, if the experience is relived painfully, its harmful effects may often be discharged from the system, in a kind of self-administered psychoanalysis. Frieda says that when Lawrence wrote of the mother's death, he became ill with grief, and that he told her that if his mother had lived he could not have loved Frieda, for his mother would not have let him go. But Frieda believes he got over this attachment, although she admits that its fierceness and intensity had harmed the growing boy. But: "I think a man is born twice: first his mother bears him, then he has to be reborn from the woman he loves." In Lawrence's case, the death of the past and the rebirth into the present and the future were a simultaneous process culminating in the production of *Sons and Lovers*. As Martin Jarret-Kerr points out in *D. H. Lawrence and Human Existence*, Lawrence did not have a continuing obsession with the "Oedipus complex," which made no important appearance in his work after *Sons and Lovers*.

The relationship between Paul and his mother in that book is an extremely complicated one, and Lawrence shows the mother's firmness and harshness as well as her gentleness. Jessie Chambers' resentment at Lawrence's belief in the rightness of his mother has been mentioned: Jessie was irritated because "in *Sons and Lovers* Lawrence handed his mother the laurels of victory." When he was working on the book, Lawrence had continued writing to Jessie from the Continent and kept sending her parts of the manuscript and later the proofs, mentioning Frieda and even suggesting that Jessie come abroad to visit them. The situation became too much for Jessie, who returned Lawrence's why-not-visit-us? letter without comment and never heard from him again.

Frieda Lawrence, in a letter to the author on May 27, 1950, sums up her memories of Lawrence's comments on his relationship with Jessie Chambers: "L. talked to me by the hour about

Jessie Chambers. He owed her a lot, considering L.'s home, but the human relation between them did not work, she was a bluestocking and he had more warmth for her than she for him—she sort of wanted to run him too much in that humble bullying way—she would have wanted him to be a nice, tame english little poet!'"

Jessie's statement to the effect that *Sons and Lovers* could not get beyond the deadlock between the mother and the girl is given apparent corroboration by the early play, *A Collier's Friday Night*, which presents the same situation—and the same deadlock. *Sons and Lovers* in its final version, however, has a range beyond the deadlock: Paul's love affair with Clara Dawes. And the deadlock itself is broken by the mother's death, though Paul has already been neutralized as far as Miriam is concerned.

Jessie Chambers says that Clara is a composite of three women, and that she was created as a compensation for the author's "mood of failure and defeat." Such personally motivated criticism is largely futile: Clara's blonde Junoesque beauty brings an element into the story that is needed, for this ripe woman is an effective foil for both the ageing mother and the dreaming farm girl. Because the relationship with Clara is primarily and almost exclusively physical, there is plenty of dramatic contrast; and the fact that both the mother and Miriam want to possess Paul spiritually subtilizes and enriches the entire situation. To know the background of a story, the geography and the psychological circumstances that went into it, is one matter—information of this kind increases the reader's range of understanding— but to take aesthetic imperatives from such background material is quite another. Once again it must be stated that, whatever the background facts of *Sons and Lovers* are—and they are interesting facts, often relevant to the *understanding* of the story— Lawrence was writing a novel.

In taking his material from life, as a novelist must do, Lawrence probably modeled Clara after three women, as Jessie Chambers says. Certainly Clara has some of the physical characteristics and some of the forthright personality of the woman who had so recently entered his life and was with him when he completed the book—Frieda. Clara was also possibly suggested by Lawrence's one-time fiancée, Louie Burrows, but the woman friend of Lawrence's who most nearly fits the specifications of Clara Dawes is Alice Dax, of whom Lawrence wrote in a letter of 1915, "I like her, and shall always feel her an integral part of my life; but that is in the past, and the future is separate." Close friends have said that "it was understood that she was the Clara Dawes." But, no matter which women Lawrence used compositely for the portrait of Clara, the important thing is the characterization as part of the novel; and, for reasons previously mentioned, Clara brings important elements into the story. The success of the character in fulfilling this function is made possible by the force with which Lawrence presents Clara.

The sections of the book dealing with the mother's illness and death are also forceful; they gain in power because they are not sentimentalized: they are not taken up in wild lamentation but are restrained in their descriptions, giving the death and the ensuing grief an added intensity because of restraint. Many of the incidents of this part of the novel find parallel expression in some of the *Amores* poems, in such lines as "My love looks like a little girl to-night,/But she is old," and "Since I lost you, I am silence-haunted," and in this stanza:

> I was watching the woman that bore me
> Stretched in the brindled darkness
> Of the sick-room, rigid with will
> To die: and the quick leaf tore me
> Back to this rainy swill
> Of leaves and lamps and traffic mingled before me.

The expression in the poetry is more extravagant: the suggestion of controlled extravagance in the prose increases the effect of force in the narrative. The death is described in all its horrible details; when Paul and his sister can no longer bear the mother's suffering, they give her an overdose of morphia pills, putting them into a cup of milk the mother will drink from: "Then they both laughed together like two conspiring children. On top of all their horror flickered this little sanity."

This chapter in which the mother dies is called "The Release": and it is Paul's release not only from his mother but also from Clara, whom he gives back to her husband. Paul had been attracted to Clara almost exclusively at the physical level: she lacked Miriam's spiritual quality. Paul had not yet found the woman who would truly "release" him, the woman who would do for him what Frieda—who attracted Lawrence both physically and spiritually—was doing for Lawrence at the very moment of writing *Sons and Lovers*. And in "The Release," Paul returns Clara to her husband, a man for whom he feels a strange sympathy and compassion. Baxter Dawes, although far less sensitive than Paul, is a kind of "double" of Paul: a man ruined by a woman and caught in the mesh of the social system, he has become a wastrel. But Paul, who is not to go in the direction Dawes has taken, helps regenerate Dawes, although the other man has hated Paul and once even thrashed him badly. Dawes, existing at a lower level than Paul, can yet be saved by Clara, originally the cause of his trouble. Paul, knowing Clara will not ultimately fulfill him any more than Miriam could, reunites the Daweses and walks out of their lives. He is then "left . . . naked of everything, with the drift towards death."

In the last chapter, "Derelict," Paul meets Miriam once again. She wants to renew the old relationship, but will not give him sex without marriage; and he rejects her again. The culmination of Lawrence's prose writing up to this time is the concluding passage of *Sons and Lovers*, in which Paul Morel walks miserably through the night after his final parting from Miriam. It is a prose that surges and sings, and it has in it all the immensity of a great Midland night. And at the end Paul does not go out to the oblivion that beckons him but turns back to life: the last word in the book, "quickly"—in the sentence in which Paul turns away from the darkness and walks "towards the faintly humming, glowing town, quickly"—is not intended to signify *rapidly* but is rather used in Lawrence's favorite way to mean *livingly*. The last word in *Sons and Lovers* is an adverb attesting not only the hero's desire to live but also his deep ability to do so. But this was implicit from the first, for through all the book's trials and sorrows, Paul's consciousness has remained "quick":

He shook hands and left her at the door of her cousin's house. When he turned away he felt the last hold for him had gone. The town, as he sat upon the car, stretched away over the bay of railway, a level fume of lights. Beyond the town the country, little smouldering spots for more towns—the sea—the night—on and on! And he had no place in it! Whatever spot he stood on, there he stood alone. From his breast, from his mouth, sprang the endless space, and it was there behind him, everywhere. The people hurrying along the streets offered no obstruction to the void in which he found himself. They were small shadows whose footsteps and voices could be heard, but in each of them the same night, the same silence. He got off the car. In the country all was dead still. Little stars shone high up; little stars spread far away in the flood-waters, a firmament below. Everywhere the vastness and terror of the immense night which is roused and stirred for a brief while by the day, but which returns, and will remain at last eternal, holding everything in its silence and its living gloom. There was no Time, only Space. Who could say his mother had lived and did not live? She had been in one place, and was in another, that was all. And his soul could not leave her, wherever she was. Now she was gone abroad into the night, and he was with her still. They were together. But yet there was his body, his chest, that leaned against the stile, his hands on the wooden bar. They seemed something. Where was he?—one tiny upright speck of flesh, less than an ear of wheat lost in the field. He could not bear it. On every side the immense dark silence seemed pressing him, so tiny a spark, into extinction, and yet, almost nothing, he could not be extinct. Night, in which everything was lost, went reaching out, beyond stars and sun. Stars and sun, a few bright grains, went spinning round for terror, and holding each other in embrace, there in a darkness that outpassed them all, and left them tiny and daunted. So much, and himself, infinitesimal at the core a nothingness, and yet not nothing.

"Mother!" he whimpered—"mother!"

She was the only thing that held him up, himself, amid all this. And she was gone, intermingled herself. He wanted her to touch him, have him alongside with her.

But no, he would not give in. Turning sharply, he walked towards the city's gold phosphorescence. His fists were shut, his mouth set fast. He would not take that direction, to the darkness, to follow her. He walked towards the faintly humming, glowing town, quickly.

PART TWO

Lawrence in his correspondence during the months preceding the publication of *Sons and Lovers* said that he might have to go back to teaching if the book failed. When it appeared in May 1913, its initial sale was not great, but *Sons and Lovers* definitely established Lawrence as an author to be watched, and for a while he felt more secure.

From this point forward, to the time of his last illness in the spring of 1930, the man belonged so completely to his writings that they must take precedence over all else in considerations of Lawrence. His life and works are more closely related, overtly at least, than those of most writers, because he was more directly autobiographical than most of them. But the works themselves remain the central thing: Lawrence's "life" is found most truly in them. He was so prolific, through all the vicissitudes of travel and poverty and ill health, that he has left hardly a moment of his existence unrecorded. But his most essential record is his thought-adventures, and those will henceforward be our chief concern.

In Lawrence's fourth and fifth novels, *The Rainbow* and *Women in Love*—originally intended to be a single book—he began writing in a new way. The change had been prefigured in his poetry, in the verse composed while he was working on the final version of *Sons and Lovers*: poems later included in the volume entitled *Look! We Have Come Through!*

The *Look!* poems first make frequent use of the image that, as both image and symbol, was to become increasingly important in Lawrence's work: darkness. It is the darkness of the mines: what Lawrence's mother had fought so bitterly to save him from haunted him all his life. Although he ran off to the hot, bright places of the world, the Mediterranean fringe and Mexico, his spirit returned at times to the cold, damp Nottinghamshire mines where his former schoolfellows were laboring in the broken darkness.

The main theme of the *Look!* series, however, is a love-conflict of another kind than Lawrence had known in his experiences with his mother and with Jessie Chambers. The volume, originally entitled *Man and Woman*, is prefaced by an Argument which explains that the man and the woman in the story go to a strange country, "she perforce leaving her children behind. The conflict of love and hate goes on between the man and the woman, and between these two and the world around them, till it reaches some sort of conclusion, they transcend into some condition of blessedness." Lawrence later omitted the last clause from his *Collected Poems*.

Look! We Have Come Through! was first published in December 1917, though many of the poems were written five years before. Eroticism blooms luxuriantly in them. Lawrence was already formulating the central philosophy of his life, which he expressed in a letter of January 1913: "My great religion is a belief in the blood, the flesh, as being wiser than the intellect. We can go wrong in our minds. But what our blood feels and believes and says, is always true."

Most of the *Look!* poems are dramatizations of the struggle between the two lovers, set against the magnificent background of the places Lawrence and Frieda passed through on their southward walking tour in 1912, from Bavaria, through the Tyrol, to northern Italy. "First Morning," which contains this passage, is thematically and scenically typical:

> In the darkness
> > with the pale dawn seething at the window
> > through the black frame
> > I could not be free,

not free myself from the past, those others—
and our love was a confusion,
there was a horror,
you recoiled away from me.

Here we have the mine-like darkness oppressing the consciousness: even the dawn at the window suggests the pale light in a mine, while the "seething" suggests the effect of the sputtering of a mine-lamp. But later in the poem, in the full outdoor light of the high morning of the mountains, the poet finds safety among the risen flowers; the man and the woman can bind together the flowers and the distant mountains, and infuse them with new life and meaning. But in the poem directly following ("And Oh—That The Man I Am May Cease To Be—"), there is a perverse crying out for the darkness: not the shafted, half-lit mine-darkness, but the utter darkness of obliteration. It is only natural that when Lawrence's consciousness yearns for destruction he should see it in terms of his most destructive symbol:

I wish that whatever props up the walls of light
would fall, and darkness would come hurling heavily down,
and it would be thick black dark for ever.
Not sleep, which is grey with dreams,
nor death, which quivers with birth,
but heavy, sealing darkness, silence, all immovable.
. . . .
I wish it would be completely dark everywhere,
inside me, and out, heavily dark
utterly.

It is noteworthy that Lawrence, in willing this destruction upon himself, frequently employs images that suggest disaster in a mine:

the darkness falling, the darkness rising, with muffled sound
obliterating everything.

And this leads to the final "heavy, sealing darkness."

The poem called "In The Dark" has the woman telling the

man that he peoples the sunshine "with shadows." "Mutilation" represents the poet as feeling that if he is cut off from the woman he will be a cripple. If she leaves him—and Lawrence in his letters to Edward Garnett in 1912 told how Frieda was torn between the idea of staying with him and the idea of returning to her children—if she leaves him, his convulsions will break open the sky. But the lovers become reconciled, the poems take on a happy tone. A number of them picture summer roses and have rose-names. And so the poems go on, through all the lovers' counterpoising affections and antagonisms. The darkness motif persists, as when the man is left alone for a few days:

> I wonder where
> Ends this darkness that annihilates me.

The effect of landscape upon persons continually manifests itself. There are a number of passages such as the one written at Glasshütte, where the poet feels his own smallness before the immensity of the mountains:

> I hold myself up, and feel a big wind blowing
> Me like a gadfly into the dusk, without my knowing
> Whither or why or even how I am going.

Altogether, the *Look!* poems portray one of the fullest and richest love experiences of our time, the alternations of conflict and harmony in a man and woman entangled in the problems of our complex world, all of this expressed with compelling intensity and, however crudely at times, with poetic force.

Both the geographical and the social aspects of Italy and Germany enhanced the change that was taking place in Lawrence at this time. It was while he and Frieda were going over the Alps that he wrote his sketch "Christs in the Tirol," a shockingly vivid account of the *Martertafeln* in the Bavarian and Austrian mountains—the great wooden crucifixes at the wayside shrines. The Christs in the north were heavy peasant types; the farther south Lawrence got the less effective he found them—some were merely quaint, some foppish. The most gripping of all was in a chapel in a valley near St. Jakob. The Christ there was a huge, powerful man:

And the look of the face, of which the body has been killed, is beyond all expectation horrible. The eyes look at one, yet have no seeing in them, they seem to see only their own blood. For they are bloodshot till the whites are scarlet, the iris is purpled. These red, bloody eyes with their strained pupils, glancing awfully at all who enter the shrine, looking as if to see through the blood of the late brutal death, are terrible. The naked, strong body has known death, and sits in utter dejection, finished, hulked, a weight of shame. And what remains of life is in the face, whose expression is sinister and gruesome, like that of an unrelenting criminal violated by torture. The criminal look of misery and hate on the fixed, violated face and on the bloodshot eyes is almost impossible. He is conquered, beaten, broken, his body is a mass of torture, an unthinkable shame. Yet his will remains obstinate and ugly, integral with utter hatred.

This quotation is from one of the three extant versions of "Christs in the Tirol," the one which appeared in Lawrence's first travel book, *Twilight in Italy*. This volume, an account of his first acquaintance with the Italian peasants who were in time to become one of his philosophic mainstays, was written in 1912, but did not appear until 1916. Besides its striking natural descriptions and its enjoyable sketches of Americanized Italians returned home and of provincial actors playing *Hamlet* and *Ghosts, Twilight in Italy* contains valuable comments on the general way of life in the southern countries. The sketches of Gargnano—which has hardly changed from the Gargnano Lawrence knew in 1912-13—are particularly sharp and moving. Some of this material was altered by Lawrence before he published it in book form four years later, but the basic substance was not changed greatly. Lawrence also subsequently made a fictional use of the Tyrolian crucifixes, at the end of *Women in Love*, where they provide a forceful symbol.

Militarized pre-war Germany, where Lawrence was once seized by the authorities and accused of being a British officer on a spying assignment, gave him the suggestion for one of his finest short stories, "The Prussian Officer." This was written during a brief second visit to Germany, when he and Frieda were returning to England from Italy. Lawrence called the story "Honour and Arms," and it struck a prophetic note when it appeared in the *English Review* for August 1915; when Garnett, later that year, changed the name to "The Prussian Officer" and used that for the title of Lawrence's first volume of short stories, Lawrence indignantly asked his agent, "What Prussian Officer?"

The officer in the story is an incarnation of something the entire world was becoming aware of at the time the tale was published. The basic situation in "The Prussian Officer" is not unlike that of Ernest Hemingway's story, "A Simple Enquiry," which also concerns the relations of a captain and his orderly, but the outcome is far different. In "A Simple Enquiry," the conflict between the Italian officer and the orderly who attracts him is skillfully subtilized; in his story, Lawrence with equal skill shows a more violent conflict leading to an outburst of homosexual-sadistic frenzy.

Lawrence wrote another story about the German army at this time, "The Thorn in the Flesh," originally called "Vin Ordinaire." It sympathetically tells of the dilemma of a young soldier with a weakness, fear of height, which makes him a misfit in the German military organization. Some time earlier Lawrence had written a poem, sent in a letter to Edward Garnett and later printed in the *Letters*—"The Young Soldier With The Bloody Spurs"—which portrayed the cold cruelty of another German trooper in his relations with a servant girl. Lawrence's attitude to militarism, particularly of the German brand, was firmly set some time before the war began.

Many of Lawrence's first short stories appear in *The Prussian Officer:* those early short pieces "Goose Fair," "Odour of Chrysanthemums," and "A Fragment of Stained Glass," as well as some longer stories such as "The Daughters of the Vicar," which tells of the romance of a young miner and the girl who nursed his mother through her last illness. The miner is shy, and the girl has to do most of the wooing; and since her clergyman father is humiliated because his daughter is to marry a collier, the young couple plan to emigrate to Canada. The story has good atmospheric touches and believable characters, including the vicar's elder son-in-law, also a clergyman, a lifeless intellectual. Throughout, in its examination of class distinctions, the story is expertly satirical. Virtually all the stories in *The Prussian Officer* are at this same level of excellent workmanship: that Lawrence afterward wrote more deeply and richly tends to diminish the values of this earlier work.

Most of the *Prussian Officer* stories had appeared in magazines before the book came out at the end of 1914; in the main they represent Lawrence's earlier phase rather than his post-*Sons and Lovers* period, but their themes point to later developments in his work.

Several of these pieces—"Odour of Chrysanthemums," "The Prussian Officer," "The Thorn in the Flesh," "A Fragment of Stained Glass," "Goose Fair," and "The Daughters of the Vicar"—have already been discussed. The title story is the most significant because it is "darker" than the others, and more passionate. This story and "The Thorn in the Flesh," with their German-army setting, are the most effectively written tales in the collection, exhibiting the growing mastery of rhythm and of color usage that is also noticeable in the prose of *Sons and Lovers*. The other stories resemble *The White Peacock* stylistically: the writing is simple and competent, but it lacks the distinction of Lawrence's later idiom.

Of the six *Prussian Officer* stories not previously discussed, two are concerned with *White Peacock* and *Sons and Lovers* material: "Second Best" and "The Shades of Spring." Both of them deal with a Midlands girl who has been dropped by the young man she loves. In each story he is a cultivated, educated young man, and in each of them the girl takes a somewhat cruder successor. One story is reflected almost entirely from the girl's point of view, the other from that of the youth who has discarded her.

The young man does not even appear as a character in "Second Best"; he is merely mentioned by the girl, Frances, and her sister. Frances, who is twenty-three, suffers "a good deal"; she tells her sister that Jimmy, whom she has loved for five years ("having had in return his half-measures"), has received his Doctor of Chemistry degree and has become engaged to another girl. This recapitulates Jessie Chambers' experience with Lawrence, and it is not difficult to imagine Jimmy as a kind of Cyril Beardsall-Paul Morel young man eluding his Miriam. Frances' "second best," a young man named Tom who is beginning to attract her as the story ends, is likeable enough, one of the vigorous, natural types Lawrence often admired in his fiction. Tom can speak in a cultivated way if he wishes, but like Mellors in the much later *Lady Chatterley's Lover*, or like Lawrence himself when he sniffed social snobbery in the air, Tom occasionally talks "broad"—that is, in Midland dialect.

The sisters in the story scold him for this. But though Tom is not quite a gentleman, Frances will ultimately accept him: his careful progress toward mastery over her is finely dramatized. One of the most interesting features of the story is its animal symbolism, which is effectively but unobtrusively woven into the main pattern. The moles, which are agricultural pests, suggest the relationship of Jimmy and Frances: she has no urge to kill them, and is shocked when her younger sister murders one that bites her while she is playing with it. Later, when Tom tells Frances that it is "necessary" to kill moles because of the damage they do, she seeks one out and kills it and brings it to him, and this is the beginning of their relationship.

"The Shades of Spring" was written at Croydon. In this story, John Syson returns to Willey Water Farm (it is Willey Farm in *Sons and Lovers*) to see the girl he used to be in love with, Hilda Millership. On his way through the woods, Syson is stopped by a young man with a gun: this is Hilda's new lover, Arthur Pilbeam, and quite appropriately he is a gamekeeper. Because Syson is married, Pilbeam reproaches him for continuing to send Hilda letters and books and poems—as Lawrence used to send such things to Jessie Chambers after he had gone away with Frieda Weekley-Richthofen. Syson in the story feels no resentment or jealousy of the gamekeeper—Lawrence's young men seem to admire rather than dislike their rivals, as Paul in *Sons and Lovers* feels strangely drawn to Baxter Dawes, who has thrashed him for having a love-affair with his wife. When Syson meets Hilda again, however—in a scene which re-creates the family life at the *Sons and Lovers* farm—he is a bit disturbed at her independence, her freedom from him. Later, as they walk through the woods, she tells him that here, in the gamekeeper's setting, she gave herself to him on the night Syson was married. The heroine of "The Shades of Spring"—which when it first appeared in a magazine in 1913 was called "A Soiled Rose"— indirectly reproaches Syson for not having seduced her. This forerunner of Connie Chatterley even takes Syson to her lover's hut, hung with skins of rabbits and calves and stoats, where they are soon joined by the sulking gamekeeper. After Syson leaves them, he hears them at the edge of the wood discussing their possible marriage; when a bee stings the keeper's arm, Hilda sucks the wound, then kisses Pilbeam with her blood-smeared mouth, and Syson walks away from this symbolic Lawrencean scene, in which blood is emphatically conquering intellect.

"The Christening" is a quite different kind of story, representing Lawrence's other range: besides these tales of love and passion, in which the emotions of the characters are intensified by the natural setting, Lawrence could also produce stories of character, in which a group of Trollope-like or Dickens-like men and women act out a little comedy of situation. "The Christening" is one of these, dealing with the comic-pathetic baptism of an illegitimate child in a lower-class Midlands household. A somewhat different version of this story comprised one of the episodes in an early draft of *The White Peacock*. The grandfather who dominates the family in the short story is a yeoman patriarch of a particularly interesting kind, earthy, tyrannical, vital. He finds a satisfaction in his own way of life, though he is cut off from his children because he has crushed them.

One of the remaining three *Prussian Officer* tales to be considered, "The White Stocking," is, like "A Fragment of Stained Glass," a later shaping of a story Lawrence submitted to the Nottingham newspaper competition before he was a published author. "The White Stocking" has also a similarity to the other two *Prussian Officer* stories not previously discussed, "A Sick Collier" and "The Shadow in the Rose Garden," in that they are all concerned with young marriage.

"The White Stocking" is a comedy about a flirtatious and attractive little wife whose husband discovers after two years of married life that she is still receiving presents from her former employer. The setting is the city of Nottingham, and the three principal characters are neatly sketched: the petit-bourgeois husband of twenty-eight, the overweening older man, and the well-meaning but careless girl. The husband in this case is unreservedly jealous; he feels no subtle sympathy for the other man. Lawrence shows in this, even more than in most of his early stories, a fine understanding of the tight-drawn problems of marriage; and among these tensions there is also a believable atmosphere of married intimacy.

"A Sick Collier" is another comedy, with somewhat more serious suggestions. The scene is Lawrence's native town, and the principal characters are a young collier and his wife. After they are married a year, he is injured in a pit accident, brought home in an ambulance, and confined to bed. The pain from the accident—a torn bladder—continually drives Willy Horsepool out of his mind, and in his frenzies he tries to kill his wife: "The peen—I ha'e such a lot o' peen—I want to kill 'er!" The story is little more than a statement of situation; a girl neighbor stops Willy in one of his murderous frenzies, and the wife hopes that news of his actions will not get about lest his injury-compensation pay be stopped. Lawrence has given the slightly absurd little dilemma an acid underlining by showing the unconscious tendencies of an apparently happy husband.

"The Shadow in the Rose Garden" is in all respects a more serious tale. The original (unpublished) version, called "The Vicar's Garden," probably written when Lawrence was in college, tells of a honeymooning couple who admire a clergyman's garden and learn that he keeps his insane son there, a former soldier. The young couple are shocked, and "The honeymoon will not, I fear, be spent by that bonny northern bay." The later version of "The Shadow in the Rose Garden," as published in *The Prussian Officer*, uses the same idea but in a subtler, deeper, and more dramatic way. The bride has lived in this seaside town before, but begs her husband not to mention this to the people he meets, since she does not wish to be recognized. On a walk by herself, she visits the vicar's rose garden and there sees a ghost from the past: the vicar's son, who she had been told was killed in the Boer War. He is mad and does not know her, though when she asks him whether or not he does, he tells his keeper that she is an old friend. The woman returns to her husband in such noticeable distress that he demands to know what has happened and learns the whole story, or at least her version of it. He asks whether she and the former officer had gone "the whole hogger," and upon learning that they had, is hurt and angry. But there is a suggestion that the trouble between this husband and wife may in time be mended: "The thing must work itself out. They were both shocked so much, they were impersonal, and no longer hated each other." Lawrence could occasionally write an effective story without a fully resolved ending—as later in "The Fox"—and this is one of the times the method worked satisfactorily. The story is brought to a pitch, the characters recognize certain things in one another, and the author indicates that the solution lies in the difficult future. It is a Russian method, mainly Chekhovian, and Lawrence did not always use it so effectively as he did in "The Shadow in the Rose Garden." His friend Katherine Mansfield, not only one of the most expert of short-story writers but also an acute critic of the genre, said in a letter that this was one of Lawrence's "weakest" stories, but went on to state that it stood out above the work of other authors in a contemporary collection: "It is so utterly different from all the rest that one reads it with joy. When he mentions gooseberries these are real, red, ripe gooseberries that the gardener is rolling on a tray. When he bites into an apple it is a sharp, sweet, fresh apple from the tree. Why has one this longing that people shall be rooted in life?"

These early stories of Lawrence have been focused upon so intently because their features indicate values and potentialities which will be developed in Lawrence's later work: these will be of importance in the total estimate of his achievement. And now that the stories in *The Prussian Officer* have been considered, it will be necessary to look at some similar material of that period, stories written at about the same time as those in that book but, with a few exceptions, unpublished until after Lawrence's death. Most of these are found in the volumes *Love Among the Haystacks* and *A Modern Lover*.

For the most part these stories are not of the same quality as the majority of those in *The Prussian Officer*, though two or

three of them seem as good as several in that collection, and one
of them—the story entitled "Love Among the Haystacks"—ranks
with any of them below "The Prussian Officer" itself.

"Love Among the Haystacks" is a lively story of young love,
with some excellent Midland-landscape backgrounds. Stylistically it is on a par with *Sons and Lovers* and with "The Prussian Officer," which was composed some months after the
completion of that novel. Lawrence's descriptive gift is in evidence throughout the "Haystacks" tale, which among other
excellent passages contains this one:

Far away was the faint blue heap of Nottingham. Between, the
country lay under a haze of heat, with here and there a flag of
colliery smoke waving. But near at hand, at the foot of the hill,
across the deep-hedged high road, was only the silence of the
old church and the castle farm, among their trees.

This passage has faults, particularly the two inversions,
". . . was the faint blue heap" and ". . . was only the silence,"
an obsolescent kind of construction; it is nineteenth-century
writing rather than twentieth. The inversion in the last sentence
is particularly awkward because of the three sets of modifying
phrases preceding the verb, but once the verb is passed the
sentence becomes extremely effective; the farm and church and
trees are conveyed not only by image but also by adroit blending of syllables. The first sentence, even with its "English-in-
reverse" flaw, is extremely effective; how could it be put better
than "Far away was the faint blue heap of Nottingham"? The
middle sentence, with the "haze of heat" over the countryside
and with its brilliant metaphor bringing in the nearby coal mines
in a single deft stroke, neatly joins foreground and background
together.

The people in the story are not magnificent or large-scale
human types, but they are wonderfully vital and true. The two
brothers Maurice and Geoffrey are sketched in at the beginning,
and they are immediately individualized. Geoffrey, twenty-three,
is slower than his brother, who at twenty-one is entering into
his first love experience, with the Polish governess at the nearby
vicarage. Geoffrey is jealous and unhappy, but he meets a girl

of his own age, a tramp coming along the roads with her worth-less, rodent-like husband. This girl, Lydia, spends the night with Geoffrey in the hut adjoining the hayfield, and a magnetic tenderness unites these two lost human beings; Lydia decides to leave her husband and marry Geoffrey. Meanwhile, in the night of rain, Maurice and his Paula are high in the haystack, under its cloth covering. They have a small quarrel, originating in a mistake, which is settled at the end of the story. The two women are, like the brothers, sharply individualized: the little wanderer had begun to take on a hard and haggard look, but under the touch of Geoffrey's love she begins to bloom into attractive femininity. This is one of the first Lawrence stories in which the magic influence of simple touch is of great importance in establishing a relationship between two human beings, a relationship that will have a regenerative force, as in the later "touch" stories of the *England, My England* collection. And if Lydia, the fierce little vagrant who begins to soften under tenderness, is a brightly living character, the same may be emphatically said about the governess Paula, with her alternations between gaiety and melancholy.

Three other pieces written at that time are also included in the *Love Among the Haystacks* volume: "A Chapel Among the Mountains," "A Hay Hut Among the Mountains," and "Once." The first two are slight travel sketches of Lawrence's walking tour with Frieda through the Tyrolean Alps; "Once" is a rather naturalistic story of little merit, based chiefly on the reminiscence, by a Frieda-like German woman, of a brief love affair with a young German officer.

The other posthumous collection of Lawrence's early tales, *A Modern Lover*, brought out in 1934, was decidedly inferior to *The Prussian Officer*, and it is understandable that editors did not accept all six of the short stories in the volume. Two of the weakest of them were published, however, in two issues of the *Saturday Westminster Gazette*, in September 1913, when Lawrence was becoming widely and favorably known as the author of *Sons and Lovers*. These stories appear in *A Modern Lover* as "Her Turn" and "Strike Pay." "Her Turn" is little more than an anecdote, though the characters, even within the imposed confines, are alive as Lawrence's people usually are:

when Mrs. Radford's husband is on limited strike pay, he refuses
to give her a share for the weekly household money although he
has used some of his union stipend to drink at a tavern; he
changes his tune when Mrs. Radford takes what is left of her
household savings and buys linoleum, a new mattress, some
dishes, and other long-needed items. "Strike Pay" is also anecdotal: Ephraim Wharmby, a young collier, goes revelling with
his union allowance and comes home to an unhappy wife and
a sarcastic mother-in-law.

"The Old Adam" is a sketch of the Jones family whom Lawrence lodged with during his Croydon schoolmastership. Lawrence draws Mrs. Jones sympathetically, and gives a brief,
amusing picture of the little girl—who is also the subject of
his earlier poem "Baby Running Barefoot"—but he presents the
ex-football player Mr. Jones in a harsher light. Lawrence himself is Edward Severn, another Cyril Beardsall-like young man,
who at twenty-seven is "quite chaste"; "when in repose, he had
the diffident, ironic bearing so remarkable in the educated youth
of today, the very reverse of that traditional aggressiveness of
youth"—but when he gets into a fight with the Mr. Thomas of
the story, he nearly strangles him. After that, the formerly
friendly Mrs. Thomas is cool to Severn, who had not known that
he could be so "uncivilized," but Mr. Thomas looks upon him
with a kind of friendly respect. There is a servant girl in the
background, who is leaving because she is too "insolent" for the
Thomases, and there is a current of intrafamily antagonism that
is a constant in Lawrence's fiction. But the story is essentially
thin, interesting today only as an autobiographical picture of the
young Lawrence and as an example of his apprentice writing.

The same may be said of "The Witch à la Mode," in which
the same rather ineffectual young man appears, this time with
a name less like that of the hero of a Victorian novel: the name
Bernard Coutts has a distinct Midland flavor, and indeed that
surname is to be found in other stories by Lawrence, including
Lady Chatterley's Lover. The setting is in the suburbs of South
London, and the girl in the story, Winifred Varley, is another
version of Helena of The Trespasser. But the story, despite its
somewhat exciting climax when Coutts, symbolically and accidentally, nearly sets the girl's house on fire, is—like many of

these others—merely interesting as a manifestation of the early Lawrence. "New Eve and Old Adam" is likewise a tale with little intrinsic value to later readers: the Lawrencean young man with the Frieda-like wife becoming a little weary of him in a London flat, figures in an anecdote of the consequences of a mistake in identity. The story's principal interest for later readers lies in its depiction of the rising and falling antagonisms and reconciliations of the married couple. While these do not have much outward similarity to the series of marriages described in *The Rainbow*, they point in the direction of the author's development.

The remaining shorter piece in this collection is the title story, "A Modern Lover." This is in some ways similar to "The Shades of Spring" in *The Prussian Officer:* the Cyril Beardsall young man is this time called Cyril Mersham, and Miriam is Muriel. On his return to the Midlands he finds her involved with a young mine-electrician, but the ending is different from that of "The Shades of Spring." Cyril triumphs this time; the girl clings to him and does not wish to let him go.

Another of the *Prussian Officer* stories ("Odour of Chrysanthemums") bears a resemblance, previously mentioned, to Lawrence's most effective play, *The Widowing of Mrs. Holroyd*. The story apparently came first; the play adds erotic interest in the person of a young electrician named Blackmore, in love with the collier's wife. One incident is given almost identical treatment in both play and story: the washing of the dead collier by his mother and his wife.

Lawrence said in one of his letters that Mrs. Holroyd was his aunt, and that the original version of the play was a product of the first phase of his writing career. The play as published, however, was extensively rewritten on the proofsheets sent by an American publisher, Mitchell Kennerley, during Lawrence's second visit to Italy in 1913-14. Lawrence had written three other plays before *Mrs. Holroyd: The Married Man* and *The Merry-Go-Round*, both set in Lawrence's native Midland, and *The Fight For Barbara*, a story of Lawrence's first sojourn in Italy.

Married Man is a light comedy about the flirtations of a young doctor who tries to conceal the fact of his marriage from the girls he flirts with; like all Lawrence's works it has a certain amount of animation, and the people are fresh and lively, but the play is crudely put together.

The Merry-Go-Round also has the Lawrencean verve, but structurally it is crowded and disorganized. The characters live in a mining community and there are some good bits of dialect, as when a miner's old wife is telling of the passion a local girl has for her son: " 'E'd only ter stick 's 'ead out 'o the door, an'er'd run like a pig as 'ears the bucket"; but the situations often strain too hard after comic effects, as when the Polish nobleman who is the local vicar goes with his wife to beat lovers out of the lane at night—comic enough this far—and starts a free-for-all in the darkness, in which most of the characters stiffly and incredibly take part. The Polish vicar, it is amusing to note, was an actual person in Eastwood whom Lawrence disliked: the Reverend Rodolph von Hube.

The Fight For Barbara is about a young man who runs off to Italy with a married woman; her aristocratic parents and even the abandoned husband descend upon the couple. Except for the last-mentioned feature, the play reproduces the Lawrence-Frieda situation after their elopement and uses for its setting the house they lived in at Lago di Garda during their first residence in Italy. *The Fight For Barbara* is dramatically more effective than the two plays mentioned above, but it does not go far toward establishing Lawrence as an authentic dramatist.

✦ ✦ ✦ ✦

Lawrence's fourth novel, *The Rainbow*, grew out of the fictional material he began working at when he finished *Sons and Lovers*. A good part of *The Sisters*, as it was then called, was written at Fiascherino on the Gulf of Spezia in 1913-14. Later, the first part of this material—so far as chronological development of plot is concerned—was rechristened *The Wedding Ring*. Still later this first part became *The Rainbow*, which had a note at the conclusion of its final typed manuscript, "End of Volume I." The recasting of the rest of the original version of *The Sisters* became, in 1916, *Women in Love*.

After Lawrence completed *Sons and Lovers* at Gargnano late in 1912, he and Frieda planned to return to England for a short visit in relation to her forthcoming divorce from Professor Weekley. When they left Italy in April they went back for a while to the region south of Munich, where they stayed in the little house belonging to Frieda's brother-in-law, Professor Jaffe, in a pinewood at Irschenhausen. Lawrence was working on *The Sisters* and on *The Insurrection of Miss Houghton*, the novel he was to complete after the war and call *The Lost Girl*.

It was at this time—the spring of 1913—that the Lawrence-Jessie Chambers relationship was finally broken off; as previously mentioned, she returned without comment Lawrence's letter with its strange suggestion that she join him and Frieda at Irschenhausen. Jessie's later memoir of Lawrence ends at this point, but a 1933 letter of hers to Helen Corke refers to her "seeing" him again at the time he died. This letter, published in 1950 in the British literary magazine, *Arena*, indicates once again Jessie's essential antagonism to Lawrence; she admires him when he deals artistically "with the immediate and the concrete," but as a thinker he is "superficial, unconvincing, and quite soon boring" to her. "I returned his last letter in 1913, and since then no word ever passed between us, and I never heard news of him; his name was never mentioned to me."

When Lawrence and Frieda arrived in England in June, they stayed for a while at the Garnetts' country home in Kent, later going to London and then to Kingsgate, on the Kentish coast, before leaving England in August. In London they met John Middleton Murry and Katherine Mansfield, editors of *Rhythm*, a "little magazine" to which Lawrence had contributed. He had previously spoken of *Rhythm* as "a daft paper, but the folk seem rather nice." In July he and Frieda went to see for themselves when they called on the editors at their combination flat and office in Chancery Lane. "Lawrence was slim and boyish," Murry recalls; "he wore a large straw hat that suited him well. Mrs. Lawrence, a big Panama over her flaxen hair. Straw hats, and sunshine, and gaiety." Such was the beginning of the intense friendship between Lawrence and Murry that was not destined to remain a matter of straw hats, and sunshine, and gaiety.

Middleton Murry, who had not long since broken away from

Oxford and come to London to earn a sparse living as a critic, was four years younger than Lawrence in 1913 and had not yet published a book. He was at this time trying to form himself out of doubts and anguishes that were of a different kind from Lawrence's. He was an urban—really a suburban—product, lower middle class, with a systematized Classical education. On a trip to Paris he had fallen in love with a prostitute, but had abruptly deserted her. His friendship with the sculptor Henri Gaudier-Brzeska had come to a violent end when Gaudier overheard him and Katherine Mansfield making fun of Gaudier's girl, Sophie. Like Lawrence and Frieda, Murry and Katherine were not yet married: Murry has confessed that when Katherine, one evening by her fireside, first proposed that they become lovers, he lay on the floor waving his legs in the air and saying, "I feel it would spoil everything." But he later gave in. Their love affair was always—despite the fact that there were no abandoned children to stand as a reproach between them—shot through with even more difficulties and uncertainties than the relationship of Lawrence and Frieda.

At the time she met Lawrence, Katherine Mansfield had published little, and she was almost completely unrecognized. She and Lawrence felt for one another a kind of sympathy mixed with antagonism. She was rarely enthusiastic over his writings, as her reviews, letters, and journal-entries show. Lawrence in turn felt that she was only a minor talent, and after her death he chided Murry for lack of perspective in referring to her as great. Frieda, however, had liked Katherine whole-heartedly from the first, and felt that the nervous, big-eyed girl was "a perfect friend" and "like a younger sister." Frieda was delighted, at the time of their first meeting, when they were all going to Soho for lunch, to see Murry and Katherine making faces at one another in the bus, like children. "I think theirs was the only spontaneous and jolly friendship that we had."

Frieda had met her children on the street, on their way to school, and they had danced around her happily and asked when she was coming back home. She suffered because she could not take them with her, and she says that when she "tried to meet them another morning they had evidently been told that they must not speak to me and only little white faces looked at me as if I were an evil ghost." Lawrence was enraged and power-less, but Katherine Mansfield helped Frieda by going to visit the children and taking them letters from their mother.

When Lawrence and Frieda left for Kingsgate, Murry and Katherine promised to come down and see them. After they had failed to appear, Murry admitted that it was because they lacked the money for railway fare, and Lawrence scolded the younger man for not borrowing from him. Later Murry and Katherine did come down and the two couples had a gay time; Lawrence cooked steak and tomatoes for their dinner, of which Murry wrote many years later, "Somehow those tomatoes gleam very red in my memory." Not long afterward, when Lawrence and Frieda had returned to Italy and Murry again did not visit them after promising to do so, Lawrence again scolded him, this time for refusing to draw upon Katherine Mansfield's allowance from her family.

At Kingsgate, Lawrence and Frieda had discovered that Edward Marsh was nearby. He had called on them and brought them to meet Herbert and Cynthia Asquith, who became good friends of Lawrence and Frieda and remained so for a number of years. The beautiful Cynthia Asquith, soon to become Lady Cynthia, reminded Frieda of Botticelli's Venus, and Lawrence greatly admired her too; indeed, although he never overtly revealed it, he was partly in love with her. He had a faculty similar to that of his German contemporary, Rilke, for arousing the sympathy of high-born women. Lawrence, it will be recalled, had married a baroness.

Frieda made little progress that summer in relation to her divorce. At last she and Lawrence again set out for Italy, once more stopping at Irschenhausen, where on August 11 Lawrence wrote in a letter that Frieda was "getting better of her trouble about the children, for the time being, at least."

In the middle of September Frieda went to visit her parents at Baden-Baden while Lawrence walked or sailed on steamers across Switzerland. By the end of the month he and Frieda had found the house where they would spend the winter; it was at Fiascherino, near the town of Lerici on the Gulf of Spezia. Their *villino* was "a four-roomed pink cottage among vine gardens, just over the water and under the olive woods. . . . You run out of the gate into the sea, which washes among the rocks at the mouth of the bay."

By May 1914 Lawrence had completed what was to be the next-to-last draft of *The Rainbow*, at this time still called *The Wedding Ring*. Edward Garnett continually found fault with the book as he received sections of it. The correspondence between him and Lawrence at the time is one between an older man trying to keep his protégé in line with tradition, and a younger man aware that he was going headlong in a new direction. At the end of December he had told Garnett that the book was *"very* different from *Sons and Lovers:* written in another language almost." A month later, while admitting that some of Garnett's criticisms were pertinent, Lawrence explained, "It is my transition stage—but I must write to live, and it must produce its flowers, and if they be frail and shadowy, they will be all right if they are true to their hour. It is not so easy for one to be married. In marriage one must become something else. And I am changing, one way or another." But he destroyed his manuscript, and in the middle of February told another friend in England that he was beginning the novel once more, "for about the seventh time. . . . It was full of beautiful things, but it missed—I knew that it just missed being itself. So here I am, I must sit down and write it out again." In April he wrote to Garnett that he was sure of the new version, and shortly afterward he told Murry, in relation to the novel, that he hoped he would have a few friends to believe in him "a bit." And then in June he wrote to Garnett:

I don't think the psychology is wrong: it is only that I have a different attitude to my characters, and that necessitates a different attitude in you, which you are not prepared to give. As for its being my *cleverness* which would pull the thing through—that sounds odd to me, for I don't think I am so very clever, in that way. I think the book is a bit futuristic—quite unconsciously so. But when I read Marinetti—"the profound intuitions of life added one to the other, word by word, according to their illogical conception, will give us the general lines of an intuitive physiology of matter"—I see something of what I am after. I translate him clumsily, and his Italian is obfuscated— and I don't care about physiology of matter—but somehow—that

which is psychic—non-human, in humanity, is more interesting
to me than the old-fashioned human element—which causes one
to conceive a character in a certain moral scheme and make him
consistent . . . You musn't look in my novel for the old stable
ego of the character. There is another ego, according to whose
action the individual is unrecognizable, and passes through, as it
were, allotropic states which it needs a deeper sense than any
we've been used to exercise, to discover are states of the same
single radically-unchanged element. . . . You must not say my
novel is shaky—it is not perfect, because I am not expert in
what I want to do. But it is the real thing, say what you like.
And I shall get my reception, if not now, then before long.

Lawrence wrote this just before he and Frieda left Italy. They
could now return to England to marry, for in London on May
28, in the Probate, Divorce, and Admiralty Division of the High
Court of Justice, with Mr. Justice Bargrave Deane presiding, the
nisi decree was granted in the divorce case of "Weekley v.
Weekley and Lawrence."

Lawrence walked north through Switzerland while Frieda
again went to visit her parents in Baden-Baden. It was the last
time Frieda was to see her father; on the eve of the European
war, the sick old baron kept muttering, "I don't understand the
world any more."

Lawrence and Frieda were in London by the end of June,
staying at the Kensington home of their friend the Irish barrister
Gordon Campbell (later Lord Glenavy). With Campbell and
Murry as witnesses, Lawrence and Frieda were married on July
13 in the Register Office of the District of Kensington.

The Lawrences planned to visit western Ireland and later
return to Italy, but a few weeks after their marriage the war
came. Confined to England, they took a cottage at Chesham in
Buckinghamshire, near the windmill where the novelist Gilbert
Cannan and his wife Mary lived; the Murrys were in a cottage
only two miles across the fields. Catherine Jackson, the Scottish
journalist who was soon to marry the Scottish barrister Donald
Carswell, was one of the Lawrence's new friends who came to
visit them at Chesham. The translator S. S. Koteliansky was
another; he had been one of several men on a Westmorland
walking tour with Lawrence at the time the war began.

One of Koteliansky's Hebrew songs contained the word *Rananim*, and Lawrence took that word to name the Utopia he had begun to dream of: he told all his friends that they must leave the wars and other corruptions of civilization and find an island they could call Rananim. Katherine Mansfield once punctured Lawrence's enthusiasm by providing a mass of information about actual islands; he became bitterly silent at this flippancy. For another ten years he tried to find a Rananim and to found an ideal colony; he gave up only after the disillusionment of New Mexico, long afterward.

Lawrence's seriousness on the subject of Rananim in the early days of World War I is evident in a letter to W. E. Hopkin in January 1915:

I want to gather together about twenty souls and sail away from this world of war and squalor and found a little colony where there shall be no money but a sort of communism as far as necessities of life go, and some real decency. It is to be a colony built up on the real decency which is in each member of the community. A community which is established upon the assumption of goodness in the members, instead of the assumption of badness.

What do you think of it? We keep brooding on the idea—I and some friends.

Lawrence's horror of the war, of humanity lacerating itself, is perhaps most forcibly expressed in a letter he wrote to Lady Cynthia Asquith early in 1915. He tells her that when the war broke out, he had been "in Westmorland, rather happy, with water-lilies twisted round my hat," but that "since I came back, things have not existed for me. I have spoken to no one, I have touched no one, I have seen no one. All the while, I swear, my soul lay in the tomb—not dead, but with a flat stone over it, a corpse, become corpse-cold. And nobody existed, because I did not exist myself. Yet I was not dead—only passed over—trespassed—and all the time I knew I should have to rise again."

It was during an illness in the autumn of 1914, a few months before he left Buckinghamshire, that Lawrence grew the beard which for the remaining fifteen years of his life was his red badge of identity. He wrote to Catherine Carswell, "I think I look hideous, but it is so warm and complete, and such a clothing to one's nakedness, that I like and shall keep it." Murry, used to the young man with the ginger moustache, noted in his journal that the beard "lends him an age which makes it hard to connect with the D. H. L. who appeared at Chancery Lane a year ago last summer." But Lawrence was now not the same young D. H. L. who had appeared at Chancery Lane, and the prophet-like beard was an outward sign of the inner change.

While at Chesham, Lawrence worked on a study of Thomas Hardy and began rewriting *The Rainbow*. In January 1915, Viola Meynell invited him and Frieda to live in Sussex: "It is the Meynell's place. You know Alice Meynell, the Catholic poetess, rescuer of Francis Thompson. The father took a big old farmhouse at Greatham, then proceeded to give each of his children a cottage. Now Viola lends us hers."

Lawrence completed *The Rainbow* at Greatham in the spring, and Viola Meynell typed it. At Greatham and on trips to London, Lawrence saw many old and new literary friends. There was even a visit to Bertrand Russell at Cambridge; he and Lawrence, both opposed to war, planned to give a series of joint lectures in London, but the project fell through when they quarrelled over philosophic issues. E. M. Forster came to Greatham for a visit, to be appropriately scolded for his ways, and the Lawrences visited Garsington, the Oxfordshire country home of the famous hostess, Lady Ottoline Morrell. Frieda says in her memoir that in those days she wondered whether she should not "leave Lawrence to [Lady Ottoline's] influence; what might they not do together for England? I am powerless, and a Hun, and a nobody."

The war continued to make Lawrence unhappy, and he could upon occasion become furious at individuals. He preferred to go bankrupt at this time rather than pay Frieda's divorce costs. "I wouldn't pay if I were a millionaire," he told Russell at the end of April, referring to the solicitors as "bugs, beasts, leeches."

But in spite of his famous bitterness, Lawrence was capable of great gaiety and loveableness. This is an important point for those who read about him to remember, for most of his biographers have played up his outbursts of rage—indeed, most of the *incidents* reported of Lawrence are of this nature. Such incidents have a concreteness of a kind not found in abstract discussions of the "better side" of Lawrence, and consequently they give an unbalanced picture of the man. Since many examples of Lawrence's irascibility must necessarily appear in the pages of the present book, a few of the statements as to the other side of his nature will be quoted at this point.

Catherine Carswell, always prone to see the best in Lawrence, wrote an account of him in *Time and Tide* of March 14, 1930 that foretold the friendly tone of her subsequent biography, *The Savage Pilgrimage*. Like that book, the *Time and Tide* article was actually a letter of complaint against the Lawrencean obituaries. Mrs. Carswell, who had known him for sixteen years "as friend, hostess and guest in varying circumstances, often of the most trying kind," felt that the obituaries which made Lawrence out as morose and frustrated were in themselves disgraceful. He was no more morose than an open flower, no more tortured or hysterical than a humming bird: "Gay, skillful, clever at everything, furious when he felt like it, but never grieved or upset, intensely amusing . . . He was at once the most harmonious and the most vital person I ever saw." Mrs. Carswell pointed to his achievements in the face of poverty, hostility, and ill health: "He painted and made things and sang and rode," writing an amazing number of books "of which even the worst pages dance with a life that could be mistaken for no other man's." He lacked vices, had most of the human virtues, and was the husband of one wife: "Scrupulously honest, this estimable citizen yet managed to keep free from the shackles of civilization and the cant of literary cliques."

Richard Aldington, whose *Portrait of a Genius, But . . .* is a friendly picture of Lawrence that does not blink at mentioning his faults, assembled several other friendly witnesses when he wrote the *Spectator* (issue of April 28, 1950) to protest against Hesketh Pearson's review of that book. Aldington said, in part:

It was an American who said of Lawrence: "He is the gentlest, kindest person in all human relations that anyone could be on this earth." It was a Dane who said: "He is so reasonable and so overwhelmingly good that there is no end to it." Luckily it was an Englishman, but he happens to be the most intelligent of his generation, who recognized in Lawrence a man "superior in kind, not degree" to all his contemporaries.

According to the accounts of observers, Lawrence seemed to be particularly irascible at two periods of his life: during World War I, and during the years he spent in the New World. But it is important to know that he was not always smashing crockery and bickering with people: too many of those who knew him have testified to the gaiety and generosity that he so often manifested.

✦ ✦ ✦

The Lawrences left Greatham at the beginning of August 1915 and settled at Number 1 Byron Villas, in the Hampstead section of London. They were living there when *The Rainbow* was published on September 30, 1915 and when it was suppressed in the first week of November, after Robert Lynd, James Douglas, and Clement Shorter had attacked it in the newspapers as indecent. The book was condemned in a police court, and the *Daily Express* reported: "Obscene Novel to be Destroyed—Worse Than Zola." Lawrence on November 6 wrote his agent J. B. Pinker, "I heard yesterday about the magistrates and *The Rainbow*. I am not very much moved: am beyond that by now. I only curse them all, body and soul, root, branch, and leaf, to eternal damnation." Nine years later he wrote, "Methuen published that book, and he almost wept before the magistrate, when he was summoned for bringing out a piece of indecent literature. He said he did not know the dirty thing he had been handling, he had not read the work, his reader had misadvised him—and *Peccavi! Peccavi!* wept the now be-knighted gentleman."

A few of Lawrence's fellow-authors stood by him—among them John Drinkwater, Arnold Bennett, and May Sinclair, the last two in print, though rather belatedly. Catherine Carswell, who had reviewed books for the *Glasgow Herald* for ten years, was debarred from further writing for that paper because she had praised *The Rainbow* in its columns. Her husband Donald Carswell wanted to defend the book in court, and Philip Morrell, Lady Ottoline's husband, asked a question in Parliament about the suppression. But no effective action was ever undertaken, even though the Authors' Society had become interested in the matter.

Lawrence had letters from Sir Oliver Lodge and others and told Pinker that he hoped "we might make a good row," but aside from his letters to personal friends he seems to have done nothing himself. He was of course seriously hampered by a lack of funds; he was so poor at this time that the Morrells, Edward Marsh, and other friends (the Morrells even persuaded George Bernard Shaw to make a small contribution) got up a small fund to help the Lawrences go to America. But although they were granted passports through the help of Lady Cynthia Asquith, and although they spoke of definite ships and sailing dates all through the last part of 1915, they did not leave the country at that time, and when at last they tried to do so, in February 1917, the Government would not indorse the passports.

A study of Lawrence's correspondence and of his activities in the period following the suppression of *The Rainbow* suggests that he was bewildered at this time—more bewildered, actually, than angry. But he always defended his book sharply. Immediately after the suppression, he wrote to Edward Marsh: "You rather jeered at *The Rainbow*, but notwithstanding, it is a big book, and one of the important novels in the language. I tell you, who know." And in December he wrote to his agent: "Tell Arnold Bennett that all rules of construction hold good only for novels which are copies of other novels. A book which is not a copy of other books has its own construction, and what he calls faults, he being an old imitator, I call characteristics." Lawrence—who nine years later was to write at his New Mexican ranch that "there is no more indecency or impropriety in *The Rainbow* than there is in this autumn morning"—knew that novel had the quality he used to speak of later as "the quick of a new thing." His previously quoted letters to Edward Garnett, written while he was working on the last draft of the book, indicate what he felt about it.

The Rainbow begins as a novel of the soil. The opening passages provide a general account of the Brangwen family, of their Marsh Farm, and of the surrounding country. The Brangwens "were fresh, blond, slow-speaking people" who lived on rich land but were never rich in money "because there were always children, and the patrimony was divided every time." They were a hard-working race not because of economic necessity but because of their vitality:

They felt the rush of the sap in spring, they knew the wave which cannot halt, but every year throws forward the seed to begetting, and, falling back, leaves the young-born on the earth. They knew the intercourse between heaven and earth, sunshine drawn into the breast and bowels, the rain sucked up in the daytime, nakedness that comes under the wind in autumn, showing the birds' nests no longer worth hiding. Their life and inter-relations were such; feeling the pulse and body of the soil, that opened to their furrow for the grain, and became smooth and supple after their ploughing, and clung to their feet with a weight that pulled like desire, lying hard and unresponsive when the crops were to be shorn away. The young corn waved and was silken, and the lustre slid along the limbs of the men who saw it. They took the udder of the cows, the cows yielded milk and pulse against the hands of the men, the pulse of the blood of the teats of the cows beat into the pulse of the hands of the men. They mounted their horses, and held life between the grip of their knees, they harnessed their horses at the wagon, and, with hand on the bridle rings, drew the heaving of the horses after their will.

The principal figure that emerges out of the generations in the first part of the book is Tom Brangwen, clumsiest of a set of brothers, who fell heir to the farm when the cleverer ones moved to the cities and became bourgeois. The clod Tom is unawakened until he sees Lydia, the Polish woman, widow of a revolutionary patriot, who has come to the village with her little girl. The child is blonde, as the Brangwens are, and her head is like a dandelion, but the mother is dark, preserving a darkness within herself: "She was like one walking in the Underworld, where the shades throng intelligibly but have no connection with one."

This is the first time Lawrencean darkness has, in one of his novels, been centered in a person: this Polish alliance will bring into the family of British farmers a darkness that will channel out to all the future Brangwens. But although Lydia (also the name of Lawrence's own mother) is to have two sons, it is not through her but her daughter Anna (née Lensky) and in turn through Anna's daughter Ursula, that the family and the story will be carried on. Anna, who always has a strong bond with her foster-father Tom, grows up to fall in love with Tom's nephew Will, son of one of the brothers who has left the farm. Will is a Ruskinized young man who loves church architecture. And it is in his love scenes with Anna (who is the more aggressive partner) that we get the first important sign of the changed Lawrence.

After *Sons and Lovers* the way was open for Lawrence to become one of the most popular of English novelists, perhaps a kind of successor to Meredith, with the wide public that likes well-written novels which are not too disturbing. Lawrence had a supreme gift for evoking his native landscape and he had the Dickens-like knack of touching a character to life with a few deft strokes: the humorous way the father is sometimes presented in *Sons and Lovers* is an excellent example of this, and many of the characters in the short stories previously discussed give additional evidence. If Lawrence had exploited his talents along these lines, fame, comfort, and riches would probably have come to him. But this was not Lawrence's way. He felt the challenge to go in another direction, to explore the phases of human consciousness which the novel as a medium had not previously exploited.

Now all this was in the *Zeitgeist:* Freud had recently pried open the Pandora's box of the unconscious, and while Lawrence asserted that he largely rejected Freud, he could not escape the ambient influence of the Viennese doctor. Other novelists had been working in consciousness-technique experiments, those writers who were Henry James's spiritual descendants—Proust, Joyce and Dorothy Richardson. But Lawrence was working in another direction as he was writing *The Rainbow* in Italy and in Sussex, and his experiments in consciousness were of an altogether different kind from those of the other writers, who were for the most part investigating the mental aspects of consciousness. Lawrence was exploring almost entirely the *emotional* properties of consciousness. Consider the passage in *The Rainbow* which describes Will and Anna harvesting the wheat sheaves in the moonlight; how different it is from the previously quoted paragraph about the earlier Brangwens and their earth-feelings:

Into the rhythm of his work there came a pulse and a steadied purpose. He stooped, he lifted the weight, he heaved it toward her, setting it as in her, under the moonlit space. And he went back for more. Ever with increasing closeness he lifted the sheaves and swung striding to the centre with them, ever he drove her more nearly to the meeting, ever he did his share, and drew towards her, overtaking her. There was only the moving to and fro in the moonlight, engrossed, the swinging in the silence, that was marked only by the splash of sheaves, and silence, and a splash of sheaves. And ever the splash of his sheaves broke swifter, beating up to hers, and ever the splash of her sheaves recurred monotonously, unchangingly, and ever the splash of his sheaves beat nearer.

Here the physical action takes on a rhythm that becomes part of the consciousness of the participants, as well as of the "infeeling" or empathic reader. But how different again a later scene of a somewhat similar kind is—this occurs a generation after, and one of those taking part is Ursula Brangwen, the grown daughter of Will and Anna. After one of Ursula's uncles is married at Marsh Farm, there is dancing out-of-doors in the moon-bright farmyard. Ursula's lover is yet another Polish young man, Anton Skrebensky, and once again it is the woman who is the aggressive partner, Ursula more fiercely so than her mother:

They went towards the stackyard. There he saw, with something like terror, the great new stacks of corn glistening and gleaming transfigured, silvery and present under the night-blue sky, throwing dark, substantial shadows, but themselves majestic and dimly present. She, like glimmering gossamer, seemed to burn among them, as they rose like cold fires to the silvery-bluish air. All was intangible, a burning of cold, glimmering, whitish-steely fires. He was afraid of the great moon-conflagration of the cornstacks rising above him. His heart grew smaller, it began to fuse like a bead. He knew he would die.

It is not immediate physical death that Skrebensky "knows" he will undergo in the presence of this ecstasy: what he feels as a menace is the destruction of his personality, of his identity, and how right he is in feeling this dread will be shown by his later experiences with Ursula.

At the time of this episode Ursula is only seventeen; her lover soon leaves England to fight against the Boers, and it is some six years before he returns. Ursula has an unsatisfactory time, first at training school, then as a teacher in uncongenial surroundings, and finally as a student at Nottingham University College, which she feels to be a deadening place. She has no further sexual relations with men, but for a while at the training school she has a lesbian attachment to one of her teachers. This does not prove to be fulfilling. Skrebensky comes back while she is at the university; he is a lieutenant on leave, scheduled to go out to India in a few months. Ursula, upon seeing him again, feels a compelling physical passion for him. They go away together several times and there are rhapsodic love-scenes. But Ursula will not marry him: once when she tells him this as they drive through London in a cab, he collapses into hysteria and cannot stop weeping. After one more attempt at passion she leaves him; he has not fulfilled her.

The chief point to be remembered here is that in its later stages *The Rainbow* breaks away from the main line of the traditional novel and assimilates many of the properties of poetry. That is to say, many of the statements in the book are made emotionally, musically, rather than in terms of straight narrative or dramatized logic. This is similar to the method of the French *symbolistes*, which will be discussed later.

Two erotic passages in particular brought about the suppression of *The Rainbow;* one of them occurred in the account of a love scene between Ursula and Winifred Inger, and the other in that of a love scene between Ursula and Anton Skrebensky. The lesbian passage was modified in later editions. Readers have become used to lesbian stories, but even now *The Rainbow* stands out from other books containing such material, because in that novel love between women is not merely suggested but passionately described.

The next-to-last chapter, "The Bitterness of Ecstasy," is a series of prose poems representing Ursula's exaltations and dejections: many of the crucial factors determining her behavior are not conveyed by ordinary novelistic notation but by the presentation of a mood-state, a reaction to physical surroundings, a magnificently described depression or ecstasy which has a value other than itself—it is an important psychological motivation. This is even more pronounced in the final chapter, which bears the same name as that of the book; here Ursula is left alone after casting off Skrebensky, and the way her life will take is presaged by symbols coming out of nature: these embody a special meaning for her.

Ursula's relationship with Skrebensky fails because of his inadequacy in the ultra-sexual necessity Ursula is seeking. It should be noted that the fault is partly hers: she is not quite sure what it is she wants, and it is not until after the Skrebensky experience that she will know. She has been nettled by his constant nagging about marriage, though from time to time she weakens and even considers going out to India as his wife. But she is always seeking something more than he can give, something more than the ordinary concept of love, which has "so much personal gratification"—or so she explains it to a woman friend who "could feel that Ursula was already hankering after something else, something that this man did not give her."

At the last it is in the "beyondness of sex" that Skrebensky fails—where Birkin in *Women in Love* will not fail with Ursula later. Skrebensky becomes identified in Ursula's mind with the civilized, empire-spreading, mechanized way of life that seems so null to her. And while she says none of these things, lets none of them enter her consciousness during the final torturing love-frenzy on yet another moon-charged night, the clues have been given, the values she has been seeking without exact knowledge of what they are have become dominant in her unconscious, and the reasons for Skrebensky's pitiful collapse become implicit. This, the last of the intense love scenes of the book, is set on the Lincolnshire coast. The next morning, when the lovers part in a muffled half-dead way, Ursula cannot put into words the explanation Skrebensky wants, and she does not place all the blame upon him.

Later Ursula discovers she is with child and writes to Skrebensky in India; she feels she must submit, and she writes with humbleness. But Skrebensky, escaping from Ursula's tormenting ecstasy, has married his colonel's daughter. Ursula, not knowing this, has meanwhile felt again a revulsion at the idea of entering Skrebensky's world, and one rain-streaked day in a woodland she has a vision of being pursued by gigantic horses. There is no implication until the conclusion of the scene that Ursula might be in a fever: she has simply gone for a walk in the afternoon and those terrible, destructive beasts out of Freudian mythology loom in her path. The writing in the early part of the chapter has been realistic in Lawrence's poetic way, and Ursula's walk through the rainy countryside has been presented normally enough. Then abruptly these huge beasts appear in the woodland, which at once becomes a nightmare world. Ursula's horror and her frantic efforts to escape while the horses circle around her and cut off retreat in every direction she takes—these are invested with Lawrence's powers of description, psychological dramatization, and compulsion of atmosphere. The horses come up out of the page so huge and fierce, they are so *aware*—Ursula saves herself only by climbing an oak and dropping on the other side of a thick hedge that holds back the horses.

Was it a vision after all? These people live in such a tense, anxiety-charged atmosphere that it is not always easy to distinguish the hallucinated from the actual. But whatever did happen, Ursula becomes unconscious after her escape. She has two weeks of illness and delirium, and through it all she feels bound to Skrebensky by nothing but the expected child. She sees her situation through one of Lawrence's most consistent metaphors, the kernel freeing itself:

And again, in her feverish brain, came the vivid reality of acorns in February lying on the floor of a wood with their shells burst and discarded and the kernel issued naked to put itself forth. She was the naked, clear kernel thrusting forth the clear, powerful shoot, and the world was a bygone winter, discarded, her mother and father and Anton, and college and all her friends, all cast off like a year that has gone by, whilst the kernel was free and naked and striving to take new root, to create a new knowledge of Eternity in the flux of Time. And the kernel was the only reality; the rest was cast off into oblivion.

Later, Ursula is glad when she learns that she will have no child; and when Skrebensky's cablegram arrives ("I am married"), she knows that the man she must have will come out of the Infinite, "out of Eternity to which she herself belonged." So as she recovers she expects a new creation. The houses in the little mining communities are a deathly horror to her. But one day she sees a rainbow, and understands its promise: "She saw in the rainbow the earth's new architecture, the old, brittle corruption of houses and factories swept away, the world built up in a living fabric of Truth, fitting to the over-arching heaven."

This is the end of the book, the rainbow's message to Ursula that tells her she will escape the mean little world she identified with Skrebensky: and the moment of her vision is the moment of her release.

The passages it has been necessary to quote from *The Rainbow* illustrate not only how Lawrence's ideas and outlook but also how his style of writing had changed. The book is palpably the work of a visionary, of a man at the edge of mysticism. The Old Testament pulse-beat in the style is in keeping with the Book-of-Genesis episodes in the story. The patriarchal world of the earlier Brangwens is destroyed by flood when the elder Tom Brangwen drowns: like Noah he has been drunk and has exposed himself before his family (his tipsy speech at Anna's wedding), but unlike Noah he is not saved. After the flood, and his death, there is a new beginning: the rest of the story is Ursula's. And it is she who has, though long after the flood, the vision of the rainbow.

In order to exalt this family of British yeomen, bring them within the range of his own heightened sensitivity, Lawrence introduced a foreign strain: the later phases of the Brangwen dynasty are centered in three women of Polish strain. Lydia is half-Polish, half-German, and her daughter Anna had a Polish father; Anna's daughter Ursula is only half-English, and her erotic transports are shared by the Polish Skrebensky. Lawrence had used Polish characters before—the ardent governess in the story "Love Among the Haystacks" and the fussy vicar in the play *The Merry-Go-Round*—but never so importantly and so functionally as in *The Rainbow*. These passionate Slavs with their "dark" souls are the proper denizens of his new-created

world, celebrants of the condition that gives its name to one of
the chapters of the book: the bitterness of ecstasy.

Lawrence's essay "The Crown" was apparently written in
the summer of 1915, after he had left Greatham and was living
in the Hampstead section of London. This essay does not seem
to be the "philosophy" Lawrence continually referred to in his
letters to Lady Ottoline Morrell and Bertrand Russell in the
spring and early summer of 1915; Lawrence's projected "philosophy" book, *The Signal*—parts of which he sent in manuscript
to these correspondents—was apparently never finished. Some of
the ideas contained in it, however, may have been repeated in
"The Crown."

In 1924 Lawrence said that this essay "was written in 1915,
when the war was already twelve months old, and had gone
pretty deep." If his memory is accurate, this would place the
composition of "The Crown" in August 1915. It was at the
beginning of that month that the Lawrences had moved to
Hampstead. Murry in two of his books says that Lawrence
wrote "The Crown" for the *Signature*, a little magazine to which
he and Murry and Katherine Mansfield were the sole contributors. After two issues in October and one in November, the
publication went out of business. Lawrence did not take the
venture so seriously as Murry did; at the time, Lawrence's letters
about it to his friends were not violently enthusiastic, and nine
years later he wrote of the *Signature* as "a little escapade"—a
statement which Murry has challenged. Lawrence at least took
his own essay seriously, and in 1924 he included it, with some
changes, in the volume *Reflections on the Death of a Porcupine*.

"The Crown" tells a good deal of what was in Lawrence's
mind at the time of *The Rainbow*, and it is the first importantly
definite statement he made about one of the things darkness
symbolized for him—in this instance the flesh, the senses, in their
everlasting war with the spirit. Dark and light were the lion and
the unicorn fighting for the crown, and the crown was a symbol
of the consummated true self; Lawrence also used the iris, or
rainbow, to emblemize this.

The true self will be created, realized, only after the individual
has fulfilled the possibilities of both the warring extremes in his

nature, the suffering that comes from the dark side, the joy that comes from the light:

And when a man has reached his ultimate of enjoyment and his ultimate of suffering, *both*, then he knows the two eternities, then he is made absolute, like the iris, created out of the two. Then he is immortal. It is not a question of time. It is a question of being. It is not a question of submission, submitting to the divine grace; it is a question of submitting to the divine grace, in suffering and self-obliteration, and it is a question of conquering by divine grace, as the tiger leaps on the trembling deer, in utter satisfaction of the Self, in complete fulfillment of desire. The fulfillment is dual. And having known the dual fulfillment, then within the fulfilled soul is established the divine relation, the Holy Spirit dwells there, the soul has achieved immortality, it has attained to absolute being.

✦ ✦ ✦ ✦

Like *The Rainbow, Women in Love* developed—as previously explained—out of the fictional material Lawrence began working on in 1913, originally called *The Sisters. Women in Love* was not published until 1920, when Thomas Seltzer in New York brought out a limited edition. This was followed by trade editions in 1921 (London) and 1922 (New York); Seltzer defeated a move to have the latter suppressed by the authorities. In England, the composer Philip Heseltine ("Peter Warlock") collected damages from Martin Secker because the character Halliday in the book supposedly resembled him; Lawrence under protest changed the color of Halliday's hair in later editions.

Lawrence referred to *Women in Love* as "something of a sequel to *The Rainbow*"; it has several of the same characters, and Ursula is the central figure in each book, yet they do not seem in all ways to be the same people: much had happened to Lawrence between the publication of *The Rainbow* and the finishing of the last draft of *Women in Love*. He was a man who had undergone anguishing changes. The war, the suppression of *The Rainbow* in November 1915, and his quarrels with various friends had made Lawrence more cynical, bitter, and lonely, and more contemptuous of public opinion. When he went over *Women in Love* for the last time, in Cornwall in

1916, he added in fictionized form many of the recent events of his life, as well as portraits of several people he had but lately come to know.

The Lawrences had moved to Cornwall in the last week of 1915, after five months at Hampstead. Early in March 1916 they took a cottage at Zennor, near St. Ives, five pounds a year: "The place is rather splendid. It is just under the moors, on the edge of the few rough stony fields that go to the sea. It is quite alone, as a little colony." Lawrence hoped that Murry and Katherine Mansfield would take an adjoining cottage that had a tower room: "I call it already Katherine's house, Katherine's tower." Lawrence wrote Murry that he wanted "no more quarrels and quibbles. Let it be agreed for ever. I am a *Blutbruder:* a *Blutbrüderschaft* between us all. Tell K. *not* to be so queasy."

Lawrence also wrote to Bertrand Russell suggesting that he too visit Cornwall: "So let us have a good time to ourselves while the old world tumbles over itself. It is no good bothering. Nothing is born by taking thought. That which is born comes of itself. All we can do is to refrain from frustrating the new world which is being born in us." The statement is from the last extant Lawrence letter to Russell. Lawrence, after intermittently scolding Russell for almost a year, began this letter in a tone of appeasement: "Are you still cross with me for being a schoolmaster and for not respecting the rights of man? Don't be, it isn't worth it." But Russell, at forty-three a noted philosopher and distinguished mathematician, was weary of being coached by this poet just turned thirty who flaunted the claims of instinct and intuition in the face of an apostle of intellect and reason.

Russell did not go to Cornwall at this time, but Murry and Katherine Mansfield did so, although they were reluctant to leave Bandol, on the French Riviera, where they were having a happy time. They arrived at Zennor on a grey day of April in 1916. From the first they disliked the place and its gulls that cried forlornly overhead.

Lawrence and Murry almost at once began quarrelling. Murry has in several books since that time meditated publicly as to what exactly might have been the cause of their trouble. He found Lawrence, he says, in a condition of spiritual blackness, trying to sink into "mindlessness" and demanding some kind of

House on Victoria Street, corner of Scargill, in Eastwood, Nottinghamshire, where D. H. Lawrence was born, 1885.

Above: The Breach, company-owned miners' quarters north of Eastwood; "The Bottoms" of *Sons and Lovers*; *below:* Brinsley Colliery at Brinsley, north of Eastwood, where Lawrence's father worked from childhood to old age.

Left: "End House," No. 49, The Breach, home of the Lawrence family, 1887-1893; *right:* two colliers from Brinsley pit, 1932.

Felley Mill, northeast of Eastwood; "Strelley Mill" of *The White Peacock*.

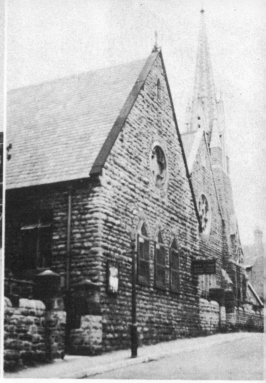

Left: Hilltop Wakes being set up, Eastwood; the carnival of *Sons and Lovers* before tavern which was favorite (as "The Moon and Stars") drinking place of the father in that novel; *right:* Congregational Chapel which Lawrence family attended, Albert Street, Eastwood; Lawrence first taught school, 1902-1903, in building in foreground.

The true "Lawrence Country," north of Eastwood. The Haggs, "Miriam's" farm in *Sons and Lovers,* is upper left center; Felley Mill, "Strelley Mill" of *The White Peacock,* lower right; Underwood steeple on horizon.

The Haggs, home of Jessie Chamber's family, "Miriam Lievers'" family in *Sons and Lovers*.

Top: mowing fields at Greasley, Nottinghamshire, scene of *Love Among the Haystacks*; also described in *Sons and Lovers*; *bottom left:* farm near Cossall, close to Nottingham Canal and Derbyshire border; "Marsh Farm" where "Brangwens" lived in *The Rainbow*; *bottom right:* church in Cossall, Nottinghamshire, the "Cossethay" of *The Rainbow,* where the "Brangwens" attended services.

blood-brotherhood ceremonial, one that was apparently more athletic than sexual (Murry refers to the wrestling scene in *Women in Love*). Murry says that he and Katherine heard Lawrence crying out to Frieda one night, "Jack is trying to kill me," and that Lawrence called Murry "an obscene bug sucking his life away." Murry and Katherine removed to Mylor, on the south coast, and for a long time the relationship of the two couples was cool.

Like Lawrence, Murry was occasionally called up by the conscription authorities; Lawrence was unable to obtain educational work for national service, but Murry—who in the *Signature* had written of the war that "this monstrous thing does not exist"—went into the War Office on a kind of public-relations assignment from which he ultimately emerged with an Order of the British Empire.

As Murry has pointed out, Lawrence wrote a penetrating account of his own experiences at the time, in the "Nightmare" chapter of *Kangaroo:* this chapter is discussed in the subsequent analysis of that novel written in 1922. "The Nightmare" is a picture of Cornwall during the war; the character representing Lawrence tries to forget, amid an atmosphere heavy with the spirit of ancient Druidic blood-sacrifices, that the civilized world is tearing itself apart. "The Nightmare" also describes Lawrence's experiences with conscription boards and the police.

Lawrence's bitterness during the war years was increased by his poverty; he was still in disgrace because of *The Rainbow*, publishers were but slightly interested in his work, and he persistently refused to write the kind of trash that would have made him a popular author. He continued to plan Utopias in other lands—in Florida, in South America—but lack of a passport prevented any of these projects from getting beyond the talking stage.

Lawrence's relations with the Cornish people were unhappy. Even the farmer with whom he had a close friendship, a mystically inclined man of the soil named William Henry Hocking, was somewhat influenced by the general feeling against Lawrence. Most of the Cornish people distrusted the bearded intellectual who had a German wife; these outsiders were suspected of signalling submarines and of otherwise giving aid to the enemy. The Lawrences did not allay suspicion when in their cottage at night they exuberantly sang Hebridean songs which the eavesdropping local Celts thought were German. Finally, on October 12, 1917, the police searched the cottage and delivered orders expelling the Lawrences from Cornwall.

Furious and humiliated, they went to London; Hilda Doolittle, the American poet H. D., whose husband Richard Aldington was a British officer on the Western Front, lent them her flat at 44 Mecklenburgh Square. They lived there until late December —occasionally pestered by agents of the Criminal Investigation Department—when they moved to Hermitage, near Newbury, Berkshire. There they rented Chapel Farm Cottage from Dollie Radford, member of a minor literary family. When the Radfords needed the house some months later, Lawrence and Frieda moved to the Midlands. Lawrence's sister Ada rented a cottage for him for a year—Mountain Cottage at Middleton-by-Wirksworth, Derbyshire—and he and Frieda took it over at the beginning of May. "It is in the darkish Midlands, on the rim of a steep deep valley, looking over darkish, folded hills—exactly the navel of England, and feels exactly that."

After a year at Mountain Cottage, the Lawrences returned to Hermitage, where they remained until autumn. Lawrence was so poor at this time that he could not afford to buy fuel for the cottage; he had to burn wood chips he picked up after trees had been cut down for use in the war industries.

The long-awaited passports finally came through in that autumn of 1919. In October Frieda went to Baden-Baden to visit her mother. Lawrence wanted to avoid seeing Germany so soon after the war; he went to Florence, via Paris, in early November, and Frieda joined him on December 3.

When the ship Lawrence sailed on was leaving England, he looked back and saw the land "like a long, ash-grey coffin slowly submerging"—this was the image he gave to the departure of Alvina in The Lost Girl, which he wrote during the next year; and in Kangaroo two years after that, his autobiographical character, Somers, saw the receding island as "a grey, dreary-grey coffin sinking in the sea behind, with her dead grey cliffs and the white, worn-out cloth of snow above."

This account of biographical events pertaining to Lawrence in wartime and in the year after the Armistice has taken the discussion beyond the composition of *Women in Love*. That novel was completed by December 1916, nearly a year before the Lawrences were driven out of Cornwall, but they had been under suspicion for some time before the book was finished. Lawrence's quarrel with Russell lay in the background, as well as the unhappy visit of Murry and Katherine Mansfield, the suppression of *The Rainbow*, and Lawrence's despair over the war.

The shifting and seething mass of these background elements must certainly have affected *Women in Love*—they certainly did not decrease its intensity. The vision that had enabled Lawrence to create the superb landscapes of *Sons and Lovers* and "The Prussian Officer" and "Love Among the Haystacks" now had attained a kind of Van Gogh febrility that made them waver and vibrate like the wind-touched or haze-filmed or sun-shaken landscapes of actual life, that beat upon the retina of the beholder. Lawrence had undoubtedly been stimulated by the natural settings in Hardy's books; in a study of Hardy written in the autumn of 1914, though not published until after his death, Lawrence spoke of the power of Hardy's "great background, vital and vivid, which matters more than the people who move upon it. Against the background of dark, passionate Egdon, of the leafy, sappy passion and sentiment of the woodlands, of the unfathomed stars, is drawn the lesser scheme of lives."

Lawrence's landscapes are more careless, more jagged, with here and there a hasty impressionist dab or a reckless scratchline, but they live. Lawrence was aware that he had a "style," though he rarely discussed the technical side of literary matters. One of the few statements he ever made on this subject was in a special preface he wrote in September 1919 for *Women in Love*, which after three years of neglect was about to appear in America: "Fault is often found with the continual, slightly modified repetition. The only answer is that it is natural to the author; and that every natural crisis in emotion or passion or understanding comes from this pulsing, frictional to-and-fro which works up to culmination."

This explains much about Lawrence's prose: the blending of syllables, the "slightly modified repetition," and the resultant musical capture of the emotions.

One other technical aspect of Lawrence's writing needs to be discussed briefly before *Women in Love* is dealt with in some detail: Lawrence's use of the technique of *symbolisme* in both *The Rainbow* and *Women in Love*.

First it must be stated that this adaptation must have been coincidental rather than deliberate, for Lawrence seems to have had little acquaintance with the school of Mallarmé and its doctrines, though in his youth he knew in the original the poetry of Baudelaire, from whom those doctrines were in part taken, as well as the poetry of Verlaine, whom the *symbolistes* eventually adopted; and in *The Trespasser* Lawrence revealed a familiarity with the methods of that other *symboliste* idol, Richard Wagner. In one of his early letters (1914) Lawrence made a reference to "Maeterlinck and the Symbolistes, who are intellectual."

Lawrence of course always used symbols, but these were in the general literary tradition: the symbolism of the title in *The White Peacock*, in which the bird is identified with certain types of women, or the symbolism of Lawrence's later short novel, "St. Mawr," in which the fierce and vital horse is identified with the savage maleness that civilization wants to crush. These are examples of a kind of symbolism poets have always used. The French *symbolisme* of the late nineteenth and of the early twentieth century was somewhat different.

It has already been explained that Lawrence's early work has nothing in common with this movement—indeed Lawrence does not in any period belong even remotely to any movement, and he has little resemblance to any other author—yet a similarity of method between his work and some of that of the *symbolistes* may be discerned in *The Rainbow* and *Women in Love*. It is found chiefly in these two books and in parts of *Look! We have Come Through!*: it makes them unique among all his works, and gives them a quality which even the finest of his later books do not possess.

Symbolisme is a post-Romanticist revolt against materialism and naturalism in which the vision of the poet discerns, through "universal analogy," the most deeply hidden secrets of nature. The symbols the poet uses in this process are his own mystical or metaphysical response to life; the symbols are private rather than public—they are not usually comprehensible at once or without a special study of the poet, and some of them remain inscrutable. They are never simple, as when a flag represents a country or white stands for purity, and they are not even like the more complicated but understandable symbols of writers such as Dante. The symbols of the poets belonging to this movement suggest or intimate rather than reveal. They often have the elusive quality of music, and they often have that blending of the senses, technically known as synaesthesia, which Baudelaire's famous sonnet suggests. The method is an intuitional one, an intuitional way of *knowing:* the poet seeks to express his inner experience in new and exact metaphors and symbols, and when one of these is a dominant element in a work of art, that work of art is truly *symboliste.*

Now Lawrence in *The Rainbow,* in some of the early *Look! We Have Come Through!* poems, and in *Women in Love* often writes in this way. He does not always do so, however, in his later work, where he continues to employ symbols in the usual literary manner, but in this second period of his writing he does so in the three books mentioned. The excerpts already quoted indicate this—the mine-darkness passages from the *Look!* poems, the stackyards scene and Ursula's encounter with the horses in *The Rainbow,* as well as most of the later meetings of Ursula and Skrebensky, in which, as previously pointed out, the changes in Ursula are indicated by suggestion rather than by explicit statement. There are further examples in *Women in Love,* notably the episode in which Birkin is stoning the image of the moon in the pond, and Ursula is secretly watching him from the adjoining woodland:

He stood staring at the water. Then he stooped and picked up a stone, which he threw sharply at the pond. Ursula was aware of the bright moon leaping and swaying, all distorted, in her eyes. It seemed to shoot out arms of fire like a cuttle-fish, like a luminous polyp, palpitating strongly before her.

And his shadow on the border of the pond, was watching

for a few moments, then he stooped and groped on the ground.
Then again there was a burst of sound, and a burst of brilliant
light, the moon had exploded on the water, and was flying
asunder in flakes of white and dangerous fire. Rapidly, like
white birds, the fires all broken across the pond, fleeing in
clamorous confusion, battling with the flock of dark waves that
were forcing their way in. The furthest waves of light, fleeing
out, seemed to be clamoring against the shore for escape, the
waves of darkness came in heavily, running under towards the
centre. But at the centre, the heart of all, was still a vivid,
incandescent quivering of a white moon not quite destroyed,
a white body of fire writhing and striving and not even now
broken open, not yet violated. It seemed to be drawing itself
together with strange, violent pangs, in blind effort. It was
getting stronger, it was re-asserting itself, the inviolable moon.
And the rays were hastening in in thin lines of light, to return
to the strengthened moon, that shook upon the water in triumphant reassumption.

Birkin stood and watched, motionless, till the pond was
almost calm, the moon was almost serene. Then, satisfied of so
much, he looked for more stones. She felt his invisible tenacity.
And in a moment again, the broken lights scattered in explosion
over her face, dazzling her; and then, almost immediately, came
the second shot. The moon leapt up white and burst through
the air. Darts of bright light shot asunder, darkness swept over
the centre. There was no moon, only a battlefield of broken
lights and shadows, running close together. Shadows, dark and
heavy, struck again and again across the place where the heart
of the moon had been, obliterating it altogether. The white
fragments pulsed up and down, and could not find where to
go, apart and brilliant on the water like the petals of a rose that
a wind has blown far and wide.

Yet again, they were flickering their way to the centre, finding the path blindly, enviously. And again, all was still, as
Birkin and Ursula watched. The waters were loud on the shore.
He saw the moon regathering itself insidiously, saw the heart of
the rose intertwining vigorously and blindly, calling back the
scattered fragments, winning home the fragments, in a pulse and
in effort of return.

And he was not satisfied. Like a madness, he must go on. He
got large stones, and threw them, one after the other, at the
white-burning centre of the moon, till there was nothing but

a rocking of hollow noise, and a pond surged up, no moon any more, only a few broken flakes tangled and glittering broadcast in the darkness, without aim or meaning, a darkened confusion, like a black and white kaleidoscope tossed at random. The hollow night was rocking and crashing with noise, and from the sluice came sharp, regular flashes of sound. Flakes of light appeared here and there, glittering tormented among the shadows, far off, in strange places; among the dripping shadow of the willow on the island. Birkin stood and listened and was satisfied.

Ursula was dazed, her mind was all gone. She felt she had fallen to the ground and was spilled out, like water on the earth. Motionless and spent she remained in the gloom. Though even now she was aware, unseeing, that in the darkness was a little tumult of ebbing flakes of light, a cluster dancing secretly in a round, twining and coming steadily together. They were gathering a heart again, they were coming once more into being. Gradually the fragments caught together re-united, heaving, rocking, dancing, falling back as in panic, but working their way home again persistently, making semblance of fleeing away when they had advanced, but always flickering nearer, a little closer to the mark, the cluster growing mysteriously larger and brighter, as gleam after gleam fell in with the whole, until a ragged rose, a distorted, frayed moon was shaking upon the water again, re-asserted, renewed, trying to recover from its convulsion, to get over the disfigurement and the agitation, to be whole and composed, at peace.

Birkin lingered vaguely by the water. Ursula was afraid that he would stone the moon again. She slipped from her seat and went down to him, saying:

"You won't throw stones at it any more, will you?"

"How long have you been there?"

"All the time. You won't throw any more stones, will you?"

"I wanted to see if I could make it be quite gone off the pond," he said.

"Yes, it was horrible, really. Why should you hate the moon? It hasn't done you any harm, has it?"

"Was it hate?" he said.

Passages of this kind provide the most characteristic developments of the latter half of *The Rainbow* and of most of *Women in Love*. John Middleton Murry, whose interpretations of the literary and technical phases of various authors are often as

correct as his readings of the philosophical and psychological
are erroneous, suggests that in this episode "Birkin is destroying Aphrodite, the divinity under whose cold light Ursula annihilated the core of intrinsic male in Lawrence's last incarnation
as Skrebensky." The first part of this provides a reasonable interpretation; in the second part, the identification of Lawrence
with Skrebensky, and the further speculative Murryisms in the
continuation of this passage from *Son of Woman* are certainly
wrong. Skrebensky was palpably the anti-Lawrence figure in
The Rainbow; Birkin, who may in part be reasonably identified with certain aspects of Lawrence, is able to satisfy Ursula
as Skrebensky had been unable to do. Birkin, as we shall see
later, gratifies not only Ursula's sexual nature but also her desire
to get beyond the materialistic and beyond the husk, the rind, of
modern life.

Again and again in *The Rainbow* and *Women in Love*, theme
matches language. For all their exciting travelogue passages, and
occasional supreme dramatizations of conflict between people,
The Lost Girl and *Aaron's Rod* and *Kangaroo* and *The Boy in
the Bush* never quite achieve the integrated effectiveness of *The
Rainbow* and *Women in Love*. The style of those later novels
becomes at times more skillful, flexible, and vari-colored, and
improves in narrative consistency. But the total effect is lacking because the stories are not in themselves so powerful as
those two novels Lawrence wrote after the catharsis of *Sons
and Lovers*, and under the influence of the reality of his marriage, the bitterness of the war, and his ultimate realization that
the chasm between himself and the friends he had counted on
was also a chasm between himself and all the people of England.
Twice again he was to challenge the achievements of his second
period: in *The Plumed Serpent*, where the language is richer
than the thesis is convincing, and in *Lady Chatterley's Lover*,
where the colors of the style are beginning to fade and the
rhythms to slacken. In that book, even a vital theme—somewhat
hampered by obvious and ineffective symbolism—cannot lift the
story to the level of *The Rainbow* and *Women in Love*.

The setting of the latter novel is mostly Nottinghamshire,
occasionally London, and at last the Tyrol. Beldover, the town
to which the Brangwens had moved toward the end of *The*

Rainbow, is modeled after Quorn, in Leicestershire, where Louie Burrows lived; some of her personality is doubtless reflected in the portraits of the Brangwen girls. The principal woman character besides Ursula Brangwen is her sister Gudrun, who had been a quite unimportant figure in the previous novel. The parents appear but slightly; they are the older generation, reactionary now. The two men who count most are Gerald Crich, the heir to vast mining properties, and Rupert Birkin, an inspector of schools.

The action takes place several years after that of *The Rainbow;* as previously explained, Ursula—the most important link between the two books—is a somewhat different person than in the earlier story. Lawrence put several of his recent friends into the novel; Lady Ottoline Morrell is caricatured as the dominating Hermione Roddice, and Russell makes a brief but unmistakable appearance as Sir Joshua Malleson, "a learned, dry baronet of fifty, who was always making witticisms and laughing at them heartily, in a harsh horse-laugh." The stiff-bodied "elderly sociologist," whose "mental fibre was so tough as to be insentient," comes in for various jibes. Some of his statements are points taken from Russell's philosophy, which are of course effectively refuted by the Lawrencean figure, Rupert Birkin. (Note: In some texts, Malleson is Matheson.)

Murry and Katherine Mansfield were assigned the most important rôles, though with more outward disguise than the others had been given. Murry indeed failed to recognize himself, and in his autobiography he says he was astonished when Frieda Lawrence one day informed him that he was Gerald Crich. "Anyhow, that was a rough way of putting it; I was not Gerald Crich, but it probably is true that Lawrence found the germ of Gerald in me, as he found the germ of Gudrun in Katherine." Because these characters were "our counterparts in the pre-mental realm of which we had no cognizance and in which Lawrence's imagination liked to dwell," Murry thinks it scarcely a matter for wonder that he and Katherine did not recognize themselves.

The dark-complexioned Middleton Murry is really quite different from the efficient young coal baron, Gerald Crich, with his blond Viking "glisten," his adventures in the Boer War, his industrial experiences, and his explorations along the Amazon. Yet, Murry points out, some of the discussions between Rupert Birkin and Gerald Crich were "taken from conversations between Lawrence and me," and "a few of the incidents of Gudrun's life were taken without any sea-change from Katherine's." He refers particularly to Gudrun's snatching away of Birkin's letter which Halliday is reading to a jeering group at the Pompadour. This incident actually took place at the Café Royal, where a group of former friends of Lawrence were mocking at a copy of his *Amores*. Katherine Mansfield walked over to their table, asked to see the volume, and stalked out of the café with it into the London night.

Actually, the outward aspects of Gerald were borrowed from the heir of the Barber and Walker coal mines, Thomas Philip Barber. A noted figure in the County, he became a Major in the First World War, retiring from active service after three fingers of his left hand were blown off. He retained ownership of the mines until the Atlee government took them over after the Second World War. Like Gerald Crich, Major Barber (now Sir Thomas Barber) had installed modern machinery in the collieries; like him, he had accidentally killed his brother in childhood; and like Gerald he had fought in the Boer War. The drowning of Gerald's sister in *Women in Love* is also taken from life. Thomas Philip Barber was about ten years older than Lawrence, who often saw him, though he did not meet him socially; Barber's appearance, even to the detail of the steely blue eyes, is accurately carried over into the book. The combination of this verisimilitude and Murry's "dark" relationship with Lawrence-Birkin gives Gerald a particular depth and richness.

The *roman à clef* aspect of *Women in Love*, so apparent in the foregoing paragraphs, does not hamper it as an imaginative story. The book is in part a society novel, and Lawrence drew upon the actual materials of society, but the social satire is merely an incidental feature. Lawrencean passion runs through the center of *Women in Love*.

Birkin is the book's hero. He discovers "the way of freedom," which is "the paradisal entry into pure, single being, the individual soul taking precedence over love and desire for union, stronger than any pangs of emotion, a lovely state of free, proud singleness." This state accepts "the obligation of the permanent connection with others, and with the other, submits to the yoke and leash of love, but never forfeits its own proud individual singleness, even while it loves and yields."

When Birkin comes to this conclusion, after much suffering, he is ready for his first proposal of marriage to Ursula. Birkin has escaped from the clutches of Hermione, who is wealthy and domineering, the supreme embodiment of Lawrence's loathing of the overintellectualized modern woman who seeks to dominate others by her will. Birkin shakes himself free of her after she tries to smash his skull with a ball of lapis lazuli.

Gerald has an affair with a corrupt little model Birkin introduces him to in the Bohemian set in Soho, but he soon turns to Gudrun. There is also a relationship of a mystical-physical kind between the two men, intensified in the wrestling sequence which leaves them dazed and feeling as if they have performed some kind of *Blutbrüderschaft* sacrament.

The relations between Birkin and Ursula in *Women in Love* are a continuation of some of the themes of *The Rainbow*, though the Ursula of this story is an Ursula who seems either to be without the benefit of the experience she underwent in the previous novel, or left in a weakened condition because of it. This time it is Birkin who is questing for the deeper, darker, ultra-sexual relationship. He has been through what he calls "the flux of corruption," he has known the "white" world of the spirit that is now running to dissolution—the world of Hermione and of the Soho-Bloomsbury Bohemians. He is seeking the farthest limits of the other direction now, to get beyond the sensual experience itself. Ursula releases the power of "otherness" in him:

After a lapse of stillness, after the rivers of strange dark fluid richness had passed over her, flooding, carrying away her mind and flooding down her spine and down her knees, past her feet, a strange flood, sweeping away everything and leaving her an essential new being, she was left quite free, she was free in complete ease, her complete self. So she rose stilly and blithe, smiling at him. He stood before her, glimmering, so awfully real, that her heart almost stopped beating. He stood there in his strange, whole body, that had its marvellous fountains, like the bodies of the sons of God who were in the beginning. There were strange fountains of his body, more mysterious and potent than any she had imagined or known, more satisfying, ah, finally, mystically-physically satisfying. She had thought there was no deeper source than the phallic source. And now, behold, from the smitten rock of the man's body, from the strange marvellous flanks and thighs, deeper, further in mystery than the phallic source, came the floods of ineffable darkness and ineffable richness.

Once again we have material presented poetically rather than logically: it is to be understood more through the emotions—which are themselves the subject-matter—than through the intellect; again Lawrence makes use of *symbolisme*. But there are phases of Birkin's love which he can explain with a certain amount of clarity, as when he tells Ursula, at the beginning of their attachment, of a "final me which is stark and impersonal and beyond responsibility. So there is a final you. And it is there I would want to meet you—not in the emotional, loving plane—but there beyond, where there is no speech and no terms of agreement. . . . What I want is a conjunction with you—not meeting and mingling;—you are quite right:—but an equilibrium, a pure balance of two single beings:—as the stars balance each other." A bit later she accuses him of saying he wants a satellite, but he denies that he has said this: "I did not say, nor imply, a satellite. I meant two single equal stars balanced in conjunction—."

This stems from the essay "The Crown"; Lawrence had groped after it narratively in *The Rainbow*, and it leads into the future essays, *Psychoanalysis and the Unconscious* and *Fantasia of the Unconscious*. The idea is also stated in "Manifesto," the longest and one of the last of the *Look!* poems, whose cycle Lawrence was completing. His theory of "polarity" was coming into being. But this must be studied later, in its proper place, in the discussion of the two books on the unconscious, written in Lawrence's next period.

The relationship of Birkin and Ursula, who marry, is successful because they realize a "balanced conjunction." But Gerald and Gudrun do not: Gudrun tries to make Gerald her instrument. She eventually drives him to his death, which is described in the next-to-last chapter, "Snowed Up." The two couples have gone to the Austrian Tyrol, and the last scenes are acted out against a dazzling background of mountains and snow, which Lawrence's prose brings up livingly from the page.

The story here seems to have something of a mythological framework: when the little sculptor who comes between Gerald and Gudrun is introduced, his name Loerke catches the imagination at once—this gnomish creature with full, mouse-like eyes seems to have much in common with Loki, the Evil One of Scandinavian mythology. We remember that Gudrun is the name of Siegfried's wife in the Eddic version of the Siegfried story, and that the name Gerald is the old Teutonic word for spear-bearer, warrior. Just what Lawrence may have had in mind is not altogether clear; he was certainly not following the Volsung-Nibelung myth so closely as, during these same years, James Joyce was patiently working out his Homeric parallel in *Ulysses*. But in a sense the mythological usages of both men have a similarity: Joyce shows how Leopold Bloom, by reasserting his will, annihilates his wife's lovers *in the mind of his wife;* this is the modern way, in contrast with Odysseus' massacre of his rivals in the banquet hall, and it tells much about the change in humanity which has taken place in the time that has passed between the days of the winedark sea of Homer and those of the snotgreen sea of Joyce.

Lawrence does not have his Siegfried killed by a boar spear; he dies a "psychological" death when his will-to-live is broken. In the old story it is Loki who brings up from the Underworld the gnomes' ring which will cause the death of Sigurd (Siegfried). We cannot follow too far whatever Lawrence may have had in mind, but it is possible that he was using rather loosely the symbolism G. B. Shaw found implicit in Wagner's musical version of the myth, the symbolism of modern capital and industry. Certainly there is much about capital and industry in *Women in Love,* and it binds together the two characters—Gerald, the entrepreneur, and Loerke, the artist who makes his work subserve industrial needs. But whatever effects Lawrence did or did not strive after, the mythological parallel faintly apparent in the story helps to produce an unusual suggestion of *Heldstod,* hero's death, that has an almost symphonic force.

Gerald's death occurs at the end of the book. He overtakes Gudrun and Loerke in the snow, at twilight, and knocks the little sculptor off his feet. Then Gudrun brings down her clenched hand on the face and breast of Gerald in a terrible blow, repeating one she had given him earlier in the story, and "A great astonishment burst upon him, as if the air had broken. Wide, wide, his soul opened in wonder, feeling the pain." In a laughing ecstasy he starts to strangle her, but finally his disgust and contempt are so great that he abruptly leaves her and the dazed Loerke. Gerald goes up the high, snow-crusted mountain in the *Gotterdämmerung* moonlight, and his death when it comes is a death from within outward; he is broken inwardly before the physical accident happens. Lawrence had learned, since the days of *The Trespasser*, how to kill off a leading character.

As Gerald, "not really conscious," drives himself onward along the snow-ridges, he dimly sees "a half-buried crucifix, a little Christ under a little sloping hood, at the top of a pole." He sheers away, in terror now; he is going to be murdered: "Lord Jesus, was it then bound to be—Lord Jesus! He could feel the blow descending, he knew he was murdered. . . . But he wandered unconsciously, till he slipped and fell down, and as he fell something broke in his soul, and immediately he went to sleep."

It is not of course the orthodox Christ that has "murdered" Gerald, but Christ as the symbol of values opposed to Gerald's materialism. Lawrence has prepared the reader for Gerald's death, in a passage earlier in the book. It is in the chapter "Moony," after Birkin has hurled his stones into the bright pond; it is the next day that he thinks over the different ways of life and finally decides to ask Ursula to marry him in "the way of freedom." While brooding on the "awful African process" of ancient, "dark" sensuality, Birkin thinks of the different "way" of the white races who, "having the arctic north behind them, the vast abstraction of ice and snow, would fulfill a mystery of ice-destructive knowledge, snow-abstract annihilation." Birkin thinks of Gerald as "one of these strange white wonderful demons from the north, fulfilled in the destructive frost-mystery. And was he fated to pass away in this knowledge, this one process of frost-knowledge, death by perfect cold? Was he a messenger, an omen of the universal dissolution into whiteness and snow?"

After Gerald's death, Birkin helps Gudrun with the authorities. Gerald's frozen body horrifies him, and he remembers Hamlet's lines about "Imperial [sic] Caesar, dead and turned to clay. . . ." He says to Ursula, "He should have loved me. I offered him." Ursula says that for Birkin to want a fulfilling friendship with a man, as well as her love, is "an obstinacy, a theory, a perversity," and that the idea is "false, impossible." Birkin answers, "I don't believe that."

Some of Lawrence's critics have cried out that this is homosexual. Such a charge is not particularly shocking, in the age of Proust and Mann and of a host of lesser writers who have dealt with such themes, but it has a special significance in Lawrence's case because he was a prophetic writer. He was more than a recorder; he was creating a world of values.

And certainly Lawrence was intensely interested in the idea of male comradeship, from the exaltation of it in some of the George-and-Cyril scenes in *The White Peacock* through the leadership novels of his third period. The concept was given its fullest treatment in *Women in Love.*

The year after Lawrence's death, Murry's *Son of Woman* seemed to many readers an accusation of homosexuality, as well as of impotence, against Lawrence himself. But five years after *Son of Woman*, Murry in his autobiographical *Between Two Worlds* said of Lawrence and another dead friend, the sculptor Gaudier-Brzeska, that he wished to "make it perfectly clear that I am not at all attributing to them what is generally understood by the word homosexuality." Lawrence's cruelest biographer, Hugh Kingsmill, discounts any charge of sexual perversion against Lawrence, though Richard Aldington in his latest book on Lawrence says "he had a streak of homosexuality in him." Catherine Carswell says in *The Savage Pilgrimage* that Lawrence told her he felt sexual perversion was "the sin against the Holy Ghost, the hopeless sin." In a letter of February 1915 he told Russell he felt that the man who committed sodomy was a man chained to a rock.

The question remains—What, with all due obeisance to imaginative literature, did the Gerald-Birkin relationship mean? It is a question which will perhaps never be answered satisfactorily. It is possible that the *Blutbrüderschaft* of Lawrence's ideal was not homosexual in the limited, obvious sense. Mrs. Carswell said Lawrence "cherished the deep longing to see revived a communion between man and man which should not lack its physical symbols. He even held that our modern denial of this communion in all but idea was largely the cause of our modern perversions. To recover true potency, and before there could be health and happiness between man and woman, he believed that there must be a renewal of the sacredness between man and man."

The question remains. And perhaps the best place to seek the answer is in Lawrence's own writings, particularly in *Women in Love*. The wrestling scene in the chapter "Gladiatorial," in which Birkin, who had studied jiujitsu, astonishes the apparently stronger Gerald, is a scene both athletic and mystic, but it does not seem sexual. It is possible that Lawrence, who believed so ardently in the "electric" sense of touch was, in writing such scenes, merely indulging in a form of compensation: he was perhaps giving his own frailness an identification with strength. This is suggested only as a possibility—based, however, on the observation that none of these scenes suggests any form of *sexual* gratification.

Compensatory action of the kind suggested here is of course an indication of weakness; it does not normally bespeak full maturity and complete emotional adjustment. But conditions of this kind are fairly common in the disordered world of the twentieth century: Lawrence in this was again being a modern of the moderns.

The condition was, however, one he was to grow out of, for after the three leadership novels, *Aaron's Rod, Kangaroo,* and *The Plumed Serpent*, he turned at last to the completer personal fulfillments suggested by *Lady Chatterley's Lover* and *The Escaped Cock*. (An interesting sidelight on the interrelationship of the *Women in Love* people is found in some unpublished parts of the book, including a prologue and an epilogue section. These chapters, whose manuscripts are now at the University of Texas, are described in *The Intelligent Heart*. The prologue was discussed by George H. Ford in the Spring 1963 issue of the *Texas Quarterly*, which printed that prologue.)

But what of the readers who are antagonized by such themes as the Rupert Birkin-Gerald Crich relationship? These readers can, for one thing, find much in *Women in Love* that is enjoyable in the usual way of novels. Beyond the circle of intense, delicate-nerved characters in the foreground, there is a whole normal world of villagers, innkeepers, miners. The comic scene with the young couple Birkin and Ursula meet and buy a chair for in the marketplace is another testimony to Lawrence's ability to present living people and incidents in the traditional way. The social satire of the "Pompadour" (Café Royal) crowd is nimbly done, and there are vivid chapters such as "Water-Party," with its dramatic episode of a drowning amid the gaiety of a night party on Willey Water. And *Women in Love* has other rewards for the reader who expects a true novel: the book's correlatives with the novel-form go deeper than mere chapter-divisions or the manner in which the dialogue is handled. For life pours richly through it. Such scenes as Birkin's stoning of the moon's reflection in the water are of the kind that become an important part of one's reading experience. To those who are capable of appreciating such effects, the poetry the book is fleshed in is also a significant experience. Certainly the friendship-glorification passages represent a weakness—of immaturity or of physical frailty seeking compensation—but the reader may overlook or "forgive" these sections as he may do with parts of Lawrence's mysticism which are nonsensical, such as the professed belief in the great "lost wisdom" of sunken continents. There is also much common sense in Lawrence, and surely some of his aberrations, even of prophecy, may be "forgiven" for the sake of the magnificant writing. Above all, there is the saneness-amid-chaos of Birkin's efforts to establish a "balanced conjunction" with Ursula: the central theme of this novel.

Those who find it difficult to respond philosophically to all or several of the points Lawrence was trying to make philosophically might think of the book in relation to T. S. Eliot's statement in reference to Dante, to the effect that "it must be possible to have full literary or poetic appreciation without sharing the beliefs of the poet."

PART THREE

A NEW LAWRENCE EMERGED IN THE WANDER-
years after the war, the prolific writer of the 1920-1925 period
in which his most important productions were the three novels
concerned with leadership themes. Like many another man who
had seen the Victorian dream shattered, Lawrence wanted a
social order of guaranteed security. In the spirit of the times
this was a search for brotherhood, and it also became a quest
for a father: stepping out of the ruins of the old matriarchal
molds, Lawrence as he groped toward symbols of assurance
was personalizing the issues that on the one hand were driving
masses of people toward socialism and communism and, on the
other, toward facism. During this 1920-1925 period Lawrence
projected himself into the most important contemporary experiences when he wrote the leadership novels; prophet-like, he was
far ahead of the majority of mankind in understanding what the
trends of those years were, and in charting them. Finally he
dropped the leadership themes, and abandoned his own attempts
to be a leader, even of a little colony of faithful life-seekers.
That phase of his activity and of his writing career was ended.
But while it lasted he produced some of his most brilliant work,
and though it seems always to have a core of darkness, its surface
flares with rich tropical colors as Lawrence travels back and
forth across the warm belts of the earth.

He left England after the war, and returned only a few times, for brief visits. He became a wanderer, deracinated, always looking futilely for a place where he could establish a new way of life, and always searching for people who would share it with him. The first of the three novels which dramatized his quest was *Aaron's Rod* (published 1922), a semi-autobiographical story with English and Italian backgrounds; this was followed by *Kangaroo* (1923), a prophetic Australian novel with a political theme, and by *The Plumed Serpent* (1926), a Mexican story with both political and religious idealizations. These novels are complemented by several others and by some long stories, by Lawrence's books on the unconscious, by his travel sketches, and by the poems collected in *Birds, Beasts and Flowers* (1923).

Since Lawrence travelled so much during this period of his writing, a brief sketch of his movements from 1919 to 1925 might be helpful to the reader at this point. Some of these movements will be referred to in detail later; the present account is inserted as a helpful résumé.

In November 1919 Lawrence went to Italy while Frieda visited her mother at Baden-Baden. Frieda soon rejoined him in Florence, and after a brief trip to the mountains of south-central Italy, they went to the island of Capri before the new year. In March 1920 they took a villa at Taormina, in Sicily, which remained their home for two years while they travelled around the Mediterranean and in Germany.

The Lawrences went to Ceylon in March 1922, where they stayed for about six weeks with their friends the Brewsters. They travelled to Australia in May, finally settling in a bungalow at Thirroul, on the coast below Sydney. In August they sailed for America by way of Tahiti. After landing at San Francisco early in September they went to Taos, New Mexico, where they maintained a base for the next three years. They went to Old Mexico in the spring of 1923, accompanied by the American poet Witter Bynner. After a short stay in Mexico City, Lawrence and Frieda lived for nearly two months in the province of Jalisco. In July they returned to the United States and took a ship from New Orleans to New York. They lived for a while in New Jersey, and in August Frieda went to Europe alone. Lawrence turned westward again, this time going to Los Angeles, and later journeying down the west coast of Mexico.

In November he sailed for England from Vera Cruz, to rejoin Frieda, with whom he had quarrelled; there was even the possibility of a separation. But peace was made in London.

At the end of January 1924, Lawrence and Frieda went from London to Baden-Baden. In March they returned to New York, accompanied by the painter Dorothy Brett. They all went to New Mexico, the Lawrences to the ranch which had been given them in the Sangre de Cristo mountains. In October they returned to Mexico, going to Oaxaca. Lawrence was severely ill there and in February 1925 moved to Mexico City. The doctor found him to be tuberculous. By April Lawrence had returned to his ranch, where he rested and took sunbaths. In September he and Frieda sailed for England; he was leaving America for what proved to be the last time.

As explained, this brief sketch may provide the reader with a reference chart for the pages to follow, since in them Lawrence's work will generally be discussed in terms of publication dates, though occasionally, for reasons that will be self-evident in the text, his writings will necessarily be described in relation to time of composition. It is, for example, necessary at this point to swing back and look over some of the material Lawrence was writing toward the end of the war.

One of his projects after his expulsion from Cornwall was a history book which he completed early in 1919 while living above the huge Derbyshire ravine, the Via Gellia, near Middleton-by-Wirksworth. *Movements in European History* is a vivid textbook in which past events are envisioned not in terms of outstanding personalities, but as parts of "great, surging movements which rose in the hearts of men in Europe, sweeping human beings together into one great concerted action, or sweeping them far apart for ever on the tides of opposition." The book, which begins with the last days of Rome and ends with the unification of Germany, was published by Oxford Press in 1921; originally the authorship was ascribed to "Lawrence H. Davison," but in the later (1925) edition D. H. Lawrence was given full credit for the work. Lawrence was not a true historian, a scholar investigating and interpreting source material; he was not even a trained historiographer, experienced in selecting and proportioning data; but his narrative skill, his reading of Gibbon and other historians and of Frazer and other anthropologists, and his ability to present facts imaginatively and dramatically to school children, contribute toward making the book an exciting popularization. It has occasioned some bitter criticism because its last paragraph speaks of Europe's need for a great leader:

But we must never forget that mankind lives by a twofold motive: the motive of peace and increase, and the motive of contest and martial triumph. As soon as the appetite for martial adventure and triumph in conflict is satisfied, the appetite for peace and increase manifests itself, and *vice versa*. It seems a law of life. Therefore a great united Europe of productive working-people, all materially equal, will never be able to continue and remain firm unless it unites also round one great chosen figure, some hero who can lead a great war, as well as administer a wide peace. It all depends on the will of the people. But the will of the people must concentrate in one figure, who is also supreme over the will of the people. He must be chosen, but at the same time responsible to God alone. There is a problem of which a stormy future will have to evolve the solution.

Throughout *Movements in European History*, Lawrence manifests an interest in the hero, in leadership. From the admiration of Augustus in the first chapter (he "had some of the beauty and noble gentleness of Christ") to the descriptions of Bismarck in the last (as "remarkably great" and "a powerful figure"), the emphasis is on history's strong men. Lawrence particularly vivifies Attila:

He was a squat, broad-backed man with a large head and a flat face. But his little eyes sparkled with tremendous passions, his body had great nervous energy. A haughty little creature, he had a prancing way of walking, and he rolled his eyes fiercely, filling the onlookers with terror, enjoying the terror he inspired.

A comparison with Gibbon's description of Attila will show that Lawrence borrowed from the great historian:

His features, according to the observation of a Gothic historian, bore the stamp of his natural origin; and the portrait of Attila exhibits the genuine deformity of a modern Calmuk; a large head, a swarthy complexion, small, deep-seated eyes, a flat nose, a few hairs in the place of a beard, broad shoulders, and a short square body, of nervous strength, though of a disproportioned form. The haughty step and demeanor of the king of the Huns expressed the consciousness of his superiority above the rest of mankind; and he had a custom of fiercely rolling his eyes, as if he wished to enjoy the terror which he inspired.

This sample suggests the extent of Lawrence's raid on Gibbon. It is interesting to see how Lawrence reworked the original, making it simpler and more dramatic for the sake of his schoolchildren readers. The essential difference between the passages is that between fine prose of the late eighteenth century and good prose of the early twentieth. This particular passage left a seed in Lawrence's consciousness that sprouted some ten years later, in the *Pansies* volume, in the poem:

> I would call Attila, on his little horse
> A man of peace. . .

because "he helped to smash a lot of old Roman lies."

> And after all, lying and base hypocrisy and treachery
> are much more hellishly peaceless than a little straightforward
>   bloodshed
> which may occasionally be a preliminary to the peace that
>   passes understanding.

Another prose piece Lawrence wrote after completing *Women in Love*—the series of essays called "The Reality of Peace"—also contains the germ of a later poem. In the second of the essays he writes:

If there is a serpent of secret and shameful desire in my soul, let me not beat it out of my consciousness with sticks. Let me bring it to the fire to see what it is. For a serpent is a thing created. It has its own *raison d'être*. In its own being it has beauty and reality. Even my horror is a tribute to its reality. And I must admit the genuineness of my horror, accept it, and not exclude it from my understanding. . . . Come then, brindled abhorrent one, you have your own being and your own righteousness, yes, and your own desirable beauty. . . . But keep to your own ways and your own being. Come in just proportion, there in the grass beneath the bushes where the birds are. . . . But since it is spring with me, the snake must wreathe his way secretly along the paths that belong to him, and when I see him asleep in the sunshine I shall admire him in his place.

This passage belongs to the spring of 1917. In Sicily several years after, Lawrence wrote one of the most remarkable of all his poems, "Snake," which appears in the *Birds, Beasts and Flowers* collection. In this poem, Lawrence tells of a hot afternoon when "with Etna smoking," he went in his pajamas down to the water-trough and there saw a snake:

He reached down from a fissure in the earth-wall in the gloom
And trailed his yellow-brown slackness soft-bellied down, over the edge of the stone trough
And rested his throat upon the stone bottom,
And where the water had dripped from the tap, in a small clearness,
He sipped with his straight mouth,
Softly drank with his straight gums, into his slack long body,
Silently.

The poet confesses he likes the snake, yet his human education tells him the snake must be killed. Another voice within him tells him he is a coward for not killing the snake. The man and the serpent look at one another. Then as the snake starts back "into that horrid black hole," the man is overcome by a revulsion, and he throws a log at the reptile, which quickly disappears:

And immediately I regretted it.
I thought how paltry, how vulgar, what a mean act!
I despised myself, and the voices of my accursed human education.

And I thought of the albatross,
And I wished he would come back, my snake.
For he seemed to me again like a king,
Like a king in exile, uncrowned in the underworld,
Now due to be crowned again.

And so I missed my chance with one of the lords
Of life.
And I have something to expiate:
A pettiness.

It is possible that when Lawrence wrote this poem he did not consciously remember the prophetic and symbolic prose passage he had written some three years before. The prose is prophetic because it outlines figuratively an episode that was to occur later, and it is symbolic because in its very figurativeness it tells us what the episode would mean to Lawrence. The poem "Snake" is readily enough understandable in human terms—the uninitiated reader can easily grasp Lawrence's feeling for the majesty of this representative of the animal world—but there is also a meaning beyond the apparent, a deeper Lawrencean meaning, and the prose excerpt from "The Reality of Peace" gives a clue to that meaning.

The snake is the horror of "the other way of life," the way of dissolution—and "The Reality of Peace" is a study of this way of dissolution and of the ways to bring it into balance with the creative way. Unfortunately, the last three of the seven sections of this essay series are apparently lost; the first four have been preserved (and published in the posthumous *Phoenix* volume) because they appeared in four issues of the *English Review* in the summer of 1917. These parts that have been saved are important for a complete understanding of Lawrence, for they contain later developments of some of the points in "The Crown," and they lead the way toward the two subsequent books on the unconscious.

These "Reality" essays mark the break between Lawrence's second and third periods. If part of the material is a restatement of the opposed dualism of dark and light as presented in "The Crown," the later development is also a subtilization of the ideas, an enrichment of their possibilities. Lawrence, incidentally, differs from most Romantic writers in that he has this almost Platonic type of dualism; he comes closest to being away from this in the passages where his characters have a Romantic feeling of oneness with landscape.

In writing a series of essays in the middle of a war and calling

them "The Reality of Peace," Lawrence was not speaking of
the possible end of hostilities between the warring powers:
although he was certainly affected by the war, he was not writing directly of its issues but of a timeless peace, the peace of the
soul. And he found that this peace was essentially the drifting
of the soul toward the unknown. The will cannot itself take us
in this direction; it can merely act as rudder or helmsman once
the "flow" has begun—the flow to which will and understanding must submit. This condition is not a yielding to death, even
with the Red Indian's courage or with Sappho's in her leap into
the sea or with Empedocles' leap into the volcano. These are
"easy," for death will come anyhow: "But a living man must
leap away from himself into the much more awful fires of creation." And in the struggle between death and creation, man
must realize that he is not only a creature "of light and virtue"
but that he is also "alive in corruption and death." The opposition of these forces produces the condition of dualism that is
the subject of "The Reality of Peace." Again we find dualism in
Lawrence, and a struggle for the reconciliation of opposites, a
struggle for balance. In the books on the unconscious he later
used the word polarity to express this.

Where in "The Crown" Lawrence had used darkness in a
rather literary way, and as a fairly simple denotation of the
flesh and the senses, in "The Reality of Peace" he faces the
"dark" side of life with a deeper realization of evil, of the meaning of dissolution. The snake symbol already quoted is but one
of many: "that side" of life is "a slow stream of corruption"
in our own bowels, it is a marsh, it is a hell of putrescence. But
it must not be denied; it must be brought into a balanced relationship with its opposite.

Although the essay series as we have it is incomplete, the
missing three sections could hardly have added more to what
Lawrence was trying to say. Toward the end of the fourth
essay, two paragraphs in particular resolve the various proposi-
tions:

When the darkness of which I am an involved seed, and the
light which is involved in me as a seed, when these two draw
from the infinite sources towards me, when they meet and

embrace in a perfect kiss and a perfect contest of me, when they
foam and mount in their ever-intensifying communion in me
until they achieve a resultant absolution of oneness, a rose of
being blossoming on the bush of my mortality, then I have
peace.

It is not of love that we are fulfilled, but of love in such
intimate equipoise with hate that the transcendence takes
place. . . . There is a new heaven and new earth, the heaven
and earth of the perfect rose.

Lawrence said, in relation to the books on the unconscious,
that with him ideas were experienced first in imaginative creation—in his novels—and written of philosophically later. This
process operated in "The Reality of Peace," for many of the
passages about dissolution and corruption are a development of
the experience of Rupert Birkin in *Women in Love*.

The discussion of that book mentioned that Birkin had
decided to marry Ursula after realizing that "the way of freedom" was "the paradisal entry into pure, single being"—he had
come to these conclusions after brooding over one of Halliday's
African statuettes of "a woman, with hair dressed high, like
a melon-shaped dome. . . . She had thousands of years of purely
sensual, purely unspiritual knowledge behind her." Thousands
of years ago these Africans must have undergone the experience
that was imminent in him: "The goodness, the holiness, the
desire for creation and productive happiness must have lapsed,
leaving the single impulse for knowledge in one sort, mindless
progressive knowledge through the senses, knowledge arrested
and ending in the senses, mystic knowledge in disintegration
and dissolution, knowledge such as the beetles have, which live
purely within the world of corruption and cold dissolution."
But the "awful African process" would be fulfilled differently
by the white races, in a kind of "snow-abstract annihilation"
of the kind to be represented by the death of Gerald in that
novel. Birkin turned away from such possibilities, and to "the
paradisal way" of union with Ursula. But the other way, that
of the dark old dissolution that Birkin speculated about, is
explored far more thoroughly in "The Reality of Peace."

This essay, then, is on the one hand an important connection
between *The Rainbow* and "The Crown" and *Women in Love*

and, on the other hand, the two books dealing with the unconscious. After *Women in Love* Lawrence was reworking some
of the ideas he had previously developed, and he was setting in
motion the processes which would evolve his concept of leadership, along with its associated theme of polarity. As we have
seen, leadership is the principal concern of Lawrence's third
period, which began to assume a definite identity after he went
to Italy in 1919.

But before we can get Lawrence out of England at that time,
we must look at a few more of his writings that come between
the completion of *Women in Love* and the beginning of the
new bloom in the Mediterranean region.

There is, for example, the play *Touch and Go* which Lawrence wrote while living at Hermitage, Berkshire, in 1919. This
drama of a colliers' strike in the Midlands was published in 1920,
in the Plays of a People's Theatre series edited by Douglas
Goldring. *Touch and Go* is at times more assured, more force-
fully dramatic than any of Lawrence's other plays except *The
Widowing of Mrs. Holroyd*, yet its two themes—the mine exec-
utive's love affairs and his relation to his workers—are neither
integrated nor effectively counterpoised. Lawrence might have
done better if he had confined himself to the theme of the strike,
or if he had invented a new set of characters to represent the
mine owners and their friends instead of using several of the
people from *Women in Love* with some of the problems from
the novel, irrelevant here, still clinging to them. Lawrence does
present several new characters, among them his Eastwood socialist friend William E. Hopkin (to whom he sent a copy of the
play inscribed, "Here you are, Willie!"), who becomes Willie
Houghton; but most of the principal people are from the novel.
Gerald Barlow is Gerald Crich again, though he lacks Crich's
mastery over the colliers; Oliver Turton is a pale shadow of
Birkin, and Anabel Wrath is Gudrun Brangwen, the art teacher
(as in the novel) of Gerald's little sister, who is again named
Winifred. The house is Lilley Close instead of Lamb Close. In
the play, Gerald and Anabel have already been through their
Women in Love experience; she tells Turton, "It was terrible,
Oliver. . . . You don't realize how awful passion can be, when
it never resolves, when it never becomes anything else. It is

hate, really. . . . I left him for reason's sake, for sanity's sake. We should have killed one another." This is a gloss on the last section of *Women in Love*, but it does little for *Touch and Go* except provide part of the reason for Gerald's attitude toward the colliers; Turton tells Anabel she has "dehumanized" Gerald. But the Norwegian lover she left Gerald for has died, and she has come back to Gerald; and though she is a witness to some of the events leading up to his final struggle with the men, she is not dramatically necessary to the play. She is, for example, rather ineffectually present in the last scene, when Gerald is mauled by the strikers. The play itself, like some of Lawrence's short stories, lacks a definite ending: it closes with Gerald shaking himself free of the men and saying that, like them, he wants a new way of life, but that he will not be bullied. He does not indicate what he means by a new way of life.

Lawrence, who also wanted a new way of life, had taken a step toward realizing it when he left England in the autumn of 1919. The two books on the unconscious, written after he had settled in the Mediterranean region, mark the actual beginning of the third phase of his writing career. *Psychoanalysis and the Unconscious* was first published in America; in May 1921 his new publisher, Thomas Seltzer, brought it out in New York; London publication by Martin Secker followed in July 1923. *Fantasia of the Unconscious* was issued by Seltzer in October 1922, with Secker's edition following by eleven months.

But before these books can be discussed, another work of Lawrence's which is related to them must be mentioned: his series of essays, "Education of the People," first published posthumously in *Phoenix*. These essays were apparently begun late in 1918, when Lawrence was living in the Derbyshire cottage and writing *Movements in European History*, also an educational book. As we have seen, Lawrence was poor at this time; he did not wish to return to teaching, but in September 1918 he asked Lady Cynthia Asquith whether she could help him get a job in the Ministry of Education; he had been trained in education and wanted a position where he would not be ashamed: "Not where I shall be kicked about like an old can: I've had enough of that." He was weary of being "pawed" by the "military *canaille*," who in his last medical examination had marked him down for sedentary work: "I don't care much what I do—so long as it is nothing degrading. I would like to do education."

The first version of "Education of the People" was perhaps in part an attempt by Lawrence to establish himself as something of an authority on the subject. Toward the end of 1918 he told Katherine Mansfield that he had been asked to write for the educational supplement of the *Times*, by "Freeman"— George Sydney Freeman—and in Jauary 1919 he wrote Catherine Carswell that Freeman had returned the essays with the suggestion that they be made into a book. The publisher Stanley Unwin saw the manuscript and suggested that Lawrence expand the material to about twice its length. Apparently, however, Lawrence did not begin revision until 1920, when an entry in a surviving diary indicates that he "began Education of the People" on June 15. Lawrence evidently rewrote the essays Freeman had seen—apparently four—and at this time added the remaining eight that comprise the total text as it appears in *Phoenix*.

"Education of the People" is, then, an even more definite connection than "The Reality of Peace" was, between Lawrence's second and third periods. In the first part of the "Education" essays, Lawrence suggests a scheme that has much in common with Plato's ideas of state education in the *Republic*. Like Plato, Lawrence believes that those unfit for further education be dropped at appropriate stages along the way. He admits that this will produce different classes of society, and as Lawrence envisions them they do not seem greatly different from Plato's class divisions of workers, warriors, and elders:

The basis is the great class of workers. From this class will rise also the masters of industry, and, probably, the leading soldiers. Second comes the clerkly caste, which will include elementary teachers and minor professionals, and which will produce local government bodies. Thirdly we have the class of the higher professions, legal, medical, scholastic: and this class will produce the chief legislators. Finally, there is the small class of the supreme judges: not merely legal judges, but judges of the destiny of the nation.

If this seems almost pure Platonism, adapted of course to modern society, we must remember that Lawrence disliked Plato; in his essay "The Novel," which appeared in *Reflections on the Death of a Porcupine*, in 1925, Lawrence wrote that someone should have kicked Plato "in the wind, and set the whole school in an uproar"; which would have put Plato "into a much truer relation to the universe." Lawrence felt that "if, in the midst of the *Timaeus*, Plato had only paused to say: 'And now, my dear Cleon—(or whoever it was)—I have a belly-ache, and must retreat to the privy: this too is part of the Eternal Idea of man,' then we need never have fallen so low as Freud."

In the later parts of "Education of the People," Lawrence is definitely in his third period, using the idiom and ideas of the books on the unconscious. He speaks of "affective centres," of polarity, of the necessity of training a man to arise "in his own dark pride and singleness, his own sensual magnificence in single being." Again the struggle for reconciliation of the opposite sides of man's nature is described. Since human consciousness is dual, Lawrence asks, "why try to make a mushy oneness of it?" The two modes of activity, "the mental consciousness and the affective or physical consciousness," can never be "one save in their incomprehensible duality." Since their rapport "is always a polarity of contradistinction," they should be left separate: "what connexion is necessary will be effected spontaneously." Education should begin, Lawrence says, as a nonmental function, and that aspect of it should be kept up through all training.

The educational note of the essays is carried over into the two books on the unconscious, though why the earlier series of essays went unpublished is not known at this time. The two later books seem to be a rewriting and expansion of the "Education" series. Those two volumes, however, seem closer than the "Education" essays to Lawrence's imaginative writing experience. As he says in the Foreword to *Fantasia of the Unconscious:*

This pseudo-philosophy of mine—"pollyanalytics," as one of my respected critics might say—is deduced from the novels and poems, not the reverse. The novels and poems come unwatched out of one's pen. And then the absolute need which one has for some sort of satisfactory mental attitude towards oneself and things in general makes one try to abstract some definite conclusions from one's experiences as a writer and a man. The novels and poems are pure passionate experience. These "pollyanalytics" are inferences made afterward, from the experience.

Lawrence in these "psychoanalysis" books rejects Freud in the main but uses Freud's term *the unconscious* because the word *soul* has fallen into such disrepute. In the first of these two volumes Lawrence says: "On the first field of human consciousness—the first plane of the unconscious—we locate four great spontaneous centres, two below the diaphragm, two above. These four centres control the four great organs. Functional and psychic at once, this is their first polar duality." But there is a further polarity: "The horizontal division of the diaphragm divides man forever into his individual duality, the duality of the upper and lower man, the two great bodies of upper and lower consciousness and function." There is eight-fold polarity when a satisfactory total relationship exists between two individuals.

Later, the *Fantasia* defines the four centers as the solar and cardiac plexuses, the lumbar and thoracic ganglions. The solar plexus is to Lawrence "the greatest and most important centre of our dynamic consciousness"; it is "the greatest nerve-centre situated behind the stomach. From this centre we are first dynamically conscious." Lawrence builds upon this speculation a whole philosophy of education and sexual and societal relationship, of dreams, and of man's relation to the plants and to the universe itself. The book is meant to be a guide for the instruction of humanity, a manual for the rearing of children. It also attempts to give general clues to successful living, and suggests how a man may find polarization in a woman and how he must associate with other men in a purposeful activity which, Lawrence repeatedly states, is non-sexual.

Fantasia is a complicated book, whose contents can only be thinly outlined here. Again, as in such essays as "The Reality of Peace," the total effect depends so much upon music and repetition that neither excerpts nor summaries can do full justice to the theme.

ght: Jessie Chambers (the late Mrs. *hn* R. Wood), the "Miriam" of *ns and Lovers,* in middle life; *cen- ·:* house next to Cossall Church *here* "Will and Anna Brangwen" *ed* after their marriage, in *The ainbow; bottom:* No. 143 Lynn *oft* Road, Eastwood, where Law- *ace's* mother, "Mrs. Morel" of *ns and Lovers,* died in 1910; house *right* is home "Aaron Sisson" ran *ay* from in *Aaron's Rod.*

Frieda von Richthofen as a young woman in Germany.

Left: Villa Igéa at Gargnano, Lago di Garda, Italy, where Lawrence and Frieda lived, 1912-1913; *right:* home of Professor Alfred Weber, Icking, near Munich, Germany, where Lawrence and Frieda lived, summer 1912.

Home of Professor Edgar Jaffe and Dr. Else Jaffe-Rich-
hofen, where Lawrence and Frieda lived during parts of
1912 and 1913; Irschenhausen, near Icking.

Lawrence's first grave at Vence, Alpes Maritimes,
France, where he died in 1930.

Frieda Lawrence at Kiowa Ranch, near Taos, New Mexico, after her return there, 1933.

Lawrence was an expert botanist and at one time had been a successful teacher of science, but here he asserts that he is an amateur rather than a scientist, and in his Foreword he launches an almost Carlylean attack on science. He pays one of his first tributes to earlier civilizations, and gives a hint of what he is striving to resurrect: "I honestly think that the great pagan world of which Egypt and Greece were the last living terms, the great pagan era which preceded our own era, once had a vast and perhaps perfect science of its own, a science in terms of life. In our own era this science crumbled into magic and charlatanry. But even wisdom crumbles." Lawrence said he believed that the science of this great epoch of the past, when "men wandered back and forth from Atlantis to the Polynesian continent as easily as men now sail from Europe to America," was esoteric but universal, expounded by a large priesthood just as mathematics and physics are taught in the same terms all over the world today. But "the melting of the glaciers and the world flood" broke up this ancient order:

The refugees from the drowned continents fled to the higher places of America, Europe, Asia, and the Pacific Isles. And some degenerated naturally into cave men, neolithic and paleolithic creatures, and some retained the marvelous innate beauty of life-perfection, as the South Sea Islanders, and some wandered savage in Africa, and some, like Druids or Etruscans or Chaldeans or Amer-indians or Chinese, refused to forget, but taught the old wisdom, only in its half-forgotten, symbolic forms. More or less forgotten, as knowledge: remembered as ritual, gestures, and myth-story.

Lawrence believed that he was "only trying to stammer out the first terms of a forgotten knowledge. But," he explained, "I have no desire to revive the dead kings, or dead sages. It is not for me to arrange fossils, and decipher hieroglyphic phrases. I couldn't do it if I wanted to. But then I can do something else. The soul must take the hint from the relics our scientists have so marvelously gathered out of the forgotten past, and from the hint develop a new living utterance. The spark is from dead wisdom, but the fire is life."

Lawrence admits that he has taken suggestions from "all kinds of scholarly books, from the Yoga and Plato and St. John the Evangel and the early Greek philosophers like Herakleitos down to Frazer and his *Golden Bough,* and even Freud and Frobenius." He says that he remembers only hints, and proceeds by intuition. And the reader is told that he is free to put aside this "whole wordy mass of revolting nonsense, without a qualm."

Professor William York Tindall, in *D. H. Lawrence and Susan His Cow,* does some scholarly sleuthing to trace Lawrence's sources as exactly as possible, revealing Lawrence's debt to the *Upanishads* through Mme. Blavatsky and theosophy in general, and—more particularly—to a Blavatsky disciple named James M. Pryse. A one-time resident of Dublin, Pryse for a time lived in the same household as William Butler Yeats and A.E., and instructed A.E. in magic and initiation rites.

T. S. Eliot, I. A. Richards and Louis MacNeice have compared Lawrence to Yeats; Eliot and Richards view these poets as men who, feeling lost because society has in our time no basic religious and moral standards, have had to seek out a past that had such standards. Both men, too, looked to nature for inspiration; as MacNeice points out, Lawrence's approach was more immediate and physical than that of the Irish poet, whose nature-images beside Lawrence's are merely heraldic. Each of these writers was seeking a body of beliefs, a scheme to base his poetry upon, and this scheme did not have to be literally "true." It is not strange that these men, finding Christian doctrine inadequate for them in their time, should both have been influenced by Eastern philosophies.

Perhaps Lawrence did not deeply believe in the "lost magic" nonsense he writes of in the *Fantasia;* Yeats admitted that he was not sure how firmly he believed in his own "magical wheel" in *A Vision.* One thing is certain about Lawrence's books on the unconscious: he did not fight for them at the time they were issued, and his later references to them in his published correspondence, including the letters to his mystical friends the Brewsters, are perfunctory. In these two volumes, particularly in the *Fantasia,* Lawrence made a number of doctrinal statements that became part of his continuing philosophy, yet a good many of the thoughts expressed in the book he never repeated.

The anatomical speculations are so patently the work of an amateur that their principal value to us now is symbolic: they are merely signs or emblems of many things Lawrence was trying to express. They are unsuccessful not only because they are amateurish but also because they are too rigid to fit into Lawrence's essentially Heraclitean philosophy. Middleton Murry believed that *"Fantasia of the Unconscious* is his greatest book; and, absolutely, it is a great book. . . . I cannot doubt that it will be a fountain of life for many years to come, and to generations yet unborn." It is particularly significant that he does not put at the top of Lawrence's achievement one of his creative masterpieces, but rather a book whose value is merely secondary. The *Fantasia*, like its predecessor, helps to explain some of the things that were in Lawrence's mind, and that is its principal use today.

It has been necessary to examine Lawrence's general thought-scheme in order that the stories and poems under discussion can be more readily interpreted. The prophet in Lawrence was rising so strongly that from this point forward most of his work—even the simplest poems and tales—is directed by his beliefs; hereafter there is very little of the "pure lyric." Some of the last of it is found in the little volumes of poetry that appeared in 1918 and 1919, *New Poems* and *Bay*.

A few of the "new" poems had come out in magazines as long before as 1910, and were merely extra verses that had not been printed in the two previous volumes. Others, like "Seven Seals" and "Two Wives," were undoubtedly the product of later experience. They reveal a later mood, but no great technical change. Many of these poems reflect Lawrence's first London years—pictures of the Embankment, Parliament Hill, Piccadilly. But none of them is so effective as the blackout mood depicted in one of the *Bay* poems, "Town in 1917." To quote two stanzas:

> London
> Original, wolf-wrapped
> In pelts of wolves, all her luminous
> Garments gone.

London, with hair
Like a forest darkness, like a marsh
Of rushes, ere the Romans
Broke in her lair.

Most of *Bay* is war poems—soldiers in troop trains, imagined battle experiences, and similar themes: Lawrence was vicariously living through things that his health did not permit nor his inclination approve of. But the air, even in stony, druidical Cornwall, or in other country places where he lived, in Berkshire, Sussex, and Derbyshire, was full of war.

Lawrence's arrival in Florence in November 1919, and some connected subsequent events in Sicily and Malta, account for that strange document which he felt was his best sustained piece of prose, his Introduction to *Memoirs of the Foreign Legion*, by M. M. This Introduction tells of Lawrence's experiences with a little down-at-heel theatrical manager, Maurice Magnus (a grandson, on the bar-sinister side, of the German Kaiser Frederick III), whose book appeared posthumously after Lawrence made strenuous efforts on its behalf. The whole affair has been another cause of bitterness against Lawrence: Norman Douglas, who appears in the Introduction with no more disguise than his initials, wrote a pamphlet against Lawrence in 1924, accusing him of falsification and of obtaining unlawful profits from the Magnus book. Now it is true that Lawrence often put people he knew into books and did so in a cruel way, but Norman Douglas should be the last man on earth to reproach another author for doing this. Douglas was infuriated at the portrait of himself as Argyle, in *Aaron's Rod*, which he found to be, like the portrait of Maurice Magnus, inaccurate; but Richard Aldington says Argyle is a vivid and "realistic" portrait of Douglas. As to the charge that Lawrence profited illegally from the publication of the Magnus *Memoirs*, his best defense is a letter written to him by Douglas several years before his anti-Lawrence pamphlet. Lawrence had this letter published in the *New Statesman* after Douglas's attack had been reprinted in a book of essays in 1926; the letter said in part (the italics are Douglas's): "By all means do what you like with the MS. As to M. himself, I may do some kind of memoir of him later on—independent of foreign legions. Put me into your introduction, if you like. . . . *Pocket all the cash yourself.*"

A further bit of information about Douglas's anti-Lawrence pamphlet is provided in Richard Aldington's autobiography, *Life For Life's Sake* (1941). Aldington, a good friend and admirer of both Lawrence and Douglas, takes Lawrence's side in the dispute, and says, "It is no credit to Norman that he accepted a gift of a hundred pounds to write the pamphlet, from a rich woman who had a grudge against Lawrence." Douglas denied this in his *Late Harvest* (1946), but Aldington in *Pinorman* (1954) said the denial was ineffective and repeated the charge.

Magnus's *Memoirs* are inferior literature, valuable principally for their sociological picture of barracks life in North Africa; but Lawrence's long Introduction is a superb narrative. It opens on a rainy night in Florence, expands descriptively and thematically in the passages about the great old monastery at Monte Cassino, and reaches a sordid climax on dusty, bone-dry Malta. Aside from their intrinsic value, the sections about Monte Cassino are particularly important in that they preserve the lost beauty of this bomb-smashed place in a way that even the surviving photographs cannot do.

The settings of the narrative, essentially four southern backgrounds, provide a proper framework for the central figure, the writhing and fugitive little Magnus. We see him first in Florence, of which we are given only a back-alley perspective— Magnus knew the short cuts in virtually every European city— with occasional interiors of a musty *pensione;* he is next shown living rather impressively at Monte Cassino, but leaving hastily when the police approach; then he is glimpsed as an unwelcome visitor at the Lawrence's villa at Taormina in Sicily, begging for money; and he is finally seen at Malta, inflated with hope and enterprise, with the inevitable police closing in and suicide the last exit. The portrait of the futile little man—"he stuck his front out tubbily, like a bird, and his legs seemed to perch behind him, as a bird's do"—is unforgettable; and if the characterization throughout is cruel, it is also sympathetic.

But no matter how Lawrence might waver, in regard to Magnus, between sympathy and distaste, his pen never falters in the sketch. Even Douglas, calling Lawrence unfair or mocking at his bourgeois standards in relation to money and respectability, has to express admiration for the writing; he particularly praises the description of Magnus in the early morning:

He was like a little pontiff in a blue kimono-shaped dressing-gown with a broad border of reddish purple: the blue was a soft mid-blue, the material a dull silk. So he minced about, in demi-toilette. His room was very clean and neat, and slightly perfumed with essences. On his dressing-table stood many cutglass bottles and silver-topped bottles with essences and pomades and powders, and heaven knows what. A very elegant little prayer book lay by his bed—a life of St. Benedict. For M—— was a Roman Catholic convert. All he had was expensive and finicking: thick leather silver-studded suit-cases standing near the wall, trouser-stretcher all nice, hair-brushes and clothes-brush with old ivory backs. I wondered over him and his niceties and little pomposities. He was a new bird to me.

Although not published until 1924, the Introduction to *Memoirs of the Foreign Legion* was written in Sicily early in 1922. A year before, the Lawrences had visited Sardinia on a ten-day trip memorialized in another of Lawrence's outstanding prose achievements, *Sea and Sardinia*, first published in 1921, in New York, with striking illustrations by Jan Juta. This is a direct record of experience, from the cold, pre-dawn awakening and bustling of Lawrence and his wife in their house in Sicily on the morning of their departure, through the concrete details of their journey to the island of Sardinia and of the trip back to Italy. The pitch of description is sustained from page to page: Etna "low, white, witch-like under heaven, slowly rolling her orange smoke and giving sometimes a breath of rose-red flame"; Cagliari from the sea, "a naked town rising steep, steep, golden-looking . . . like a town in a monkish, illuminated missal"; oxen in the Sardinian hills who "lift their noses to heaven, with a strange, beseeching, snake-like movement, and taking tiny little steps with their frail feet"; the bright-costumed peasants, the smoky little country inns—the book, written through Lawrence's gay or fussy moods but always under the control of a penetrating vision, deserves a whole reading, like a good poem. And, like a good poem it may be continually read and reread without wearing thin. Here is part of the description of the departure from the house in Taormina:

Under the lid of the half-cloudy night sky, far away at the rim of the Ionian sea, the first light, like metal fusing. So swallow the cup of tea and the bit of toast. Hastily wash up, so that we can find the house decent when we come back. Shut the door-windows of the upper terrace and go down. Lock the door: the upper half of the house made fast.

The sky and sea are parting like an oyster shell, with a low-red gape. Looking across from the veranda at it, one shivers. Not that it is cold. The morning is not at all cold. But the ominousness of it: that long red slit between a dark sky and a dark Ionian sea, terrible old bivalve which has held life between its lips so long. And here, at this house, we are ledged so awfully above the dawn, naked to it. . . .

Very dark under the great carob tree as we go down the steps. Dark still the garden. Scent of mimosa, and then of jasmine. The lovely mimosa tree invisible. Dark the stony path. The goat whinnies out of her shed. The broken Roman tomb which lolls right over the garden track does not fall on me as I slip under its massive tilt. Ah, dark garden, dark garden, with your olives and your wine, your medlars and mulberries and many almond trees, your steep terraces ledged high up above the sea, I am leaving you, slinking out. Out between the rose-mary hedges, out of the tall gate, on to the cruel steep stony road. So under the dark, big eucalyptus trees, over the stream, and up towards the village. There, I have got so far.

It is full dawn—dawn—not morning, the sun will not have risen. The village is nearly all dark in the red light, and asleep still. No one at the fountain by the Capucin gate: too dark still. One man leading a horse round the corner of the Palazzo Corvia. One or two dark men along the Corso. And so over the brow, down the steep cobble-stone street between the houses, and out to the naked hill front. This is the dawn-coast of Sicily.

Nay, the dawn-coast of Europe. Steep, like a vast cliff, dawn-forward. A red dawn, with mingled curdling dark clouds, and some gold. . . .

The best way to indicate the power of Lawrence's writing is to provide a generous sample of it; the passages just quoted are typical of Lawrence's post-*Women in Love* style. This is writing of the improvisational type: a master at the keyboard playing brilliantly if a little carelessly, but more wonderfully than a calculative performer.

✓ ✓ ✓ ✓

Lawrence's first novel after *Women in Love* was *The Lost Girl*, apparently a later version of an uncompleted book he referred to in a 1913 letter from Germany as *The Insurrection of Miss Houghton*, which he said he was putting aside for a while after page 200. He mentioned it in a letter to the publisher Secker from Capri in January 1920; it had lain in Bavaria since 1914, was two-thirds finished, and would probably be called *A Mixed Marriage*. *The Lost Girl* was finished in Sicily in May 1920; it was published in that same year and awarded the James Tait Black Prize given by Edinburgh University.

This story of a Midlands girl who, to escape boredom, first becomes a nurse and afterward marries an Italian strolling player, had little in it that would shock its readers; Lawrence felt it was "quite amusing: and quite moral." The first part of the story, which deals with James Houghton's finery shop in a Midlands mining town, is somewhat in the Arnold Bennett manner, but the Italian experience toward the end is pure— though not too profound—Lawrence. It is interesting to observe how the Italian-mountain landscape affected the British heroine Alvina, for this is a reflection of the way it touched Lawrence; he had found life there too primitive and cold, and escaped to Capri. He was beginning, in *The Lost Girl* and *Sea and Sardinia*, to give expression to the potentialities he felt in the Italian peasants; at the end of his life he was to think of the peasants almost worshipfully, but at this time he had not yet begun to approach that extreme. The physical discomfort of their surroundings stood in the way of *rapport* with these peasants:

these discomforts are plangently complained of in *The Lost Girl* and *Sea and Sardinia,* though in the novel Alvina stays with her Italian husband Ciccio (Cicio in the English edition). This is the first enunciation of a recurrent Lawrencean theme, the Anglo-Saxon woman becoming a "dark" man's mate. The plays about Red Indians put on by Ciccio's provincial theatrical troupe seem somewhat of a lampoon of Lawrence's future "dark-race" theories. The prissy theatrical manager, Mr. May, is another (an earlier) portrait of Maurice Magnus. The cinema venture at Lumley is a fictional account of a similar one at Langley Mill, adjoining Eastwood; its owner, James Houghton, was actually George Cullen, a well-known Eastwood merchant whom Lawrence drew upon for the character. His daughter Florence was the "lost girl," though Lawrence's sister Ada says the Alvina of the book was chiefly imaginary.

Two days after he finished *The Lost Girl,* Lawrence began a new novel, *Mr. Noon.* He seems never to have gone beyond the first part, which he completed and sent to his agents some months later, in February 1921. Lawrence wanted *Mr. Noon* serialized; perhaps the agents' failure to sell it to a magazine on that basis discouraged him from going on with the story. Only the first part was found after Lawrence's death; it was published with the six short stories, previously discussed, from Lawrence's earliest period that were collected in the 1934 volume, *A Modern Lover.*

Mr. Noon was, as far as it went, an amusing comedy of the Midlands. Lawrence returned to the mood of the first part of *The Lost Girl,* even taking the same town for his setting—Woodhouse, which was of course his native Eastwood. And the heroine of *The Lost Girl,* Alvina Houghton, appears as a background character. Gilbert Noon, the flirtatious science instructor, is based not so much upon Lawrence himself as upon the Don Juanish friend Lawrence had written Edward Garnett about in March 1912, who made quite a career out of flirting. This friend, "our George Henry," had indeed a Noonish flavor. Lawrence ends the first part of his novel with Gilbert Noon forced out of his teaching position, in somewhat the same way that Lawrence's friend had been; there is a possibility of Noon's going to Germany for his doctorate, and there he doubtless would have fluttered the pigtailed Fräuleins in some provincial university town. But as we have it, the story never gets out of the British Midlands. The atmosphere is again that of Lawrence's pre-war plays, *Married Man* and *Merry-Go-Round*, with flirtatious young men (Noon and the doctor in *The Married Man* have much in common), spooning couples, and irate elders attacking in the darkness. But here the comedy grows out of character rather than contrivance; the situations are more credible, psychologically, than those in the plays. Because Lawrence was not limited by the dramatic form in *Mr. Noon*, he wrote more freely, and the result is that this fragment of some one hundred-and-thirty pages is one of his best pieces of comedic writing.

✯ ✯ ✯ ✯

Lawrence again used a Midland setting for the first sections of his next novel, *Aaron's Rod*, which like *The Lost Girl* swings to Italy for its final scenes. This first of the three leadership novels was completed while the Lawrences were at Baden-Baden in the spring of 1921. *Aaron's Rod* was apparently begun in England in 1918, then abandoned, and finally taken up again after Lawrence had gone to the Mediterranean.

The story, which opens soon after the war, crosses social borders as early as the third chapter, when a rather degenerate group of young upper-class intellectuals meet Aaron Sisson, a miner's checkweighman who is running away from his wife and children on Christmas Eve. Some sketches of Aaron's family life are provided: it is very much like that of Siegmund in *The Trespasser*, though Aaron has no young pupil to elope with. But, like Siegmund, Aaron is a musician, a flautist. And it is at Covent Garden Opera that the group of young intellectuals around Jim Bricknell, whom they really loathe, see once more the stranger they had met on Christmas Eve: Aaron, again like Siegmund, is in the Covent Garden orchestra. The Bricknell set immediately adopts Aaron, and he is introduced to Rawdon Lilly, a self-portrait of Lawrence, who is to become a dominant figure in Aaron's destiny. (Aaron is partly based on a one-time Eastwood neighbor of the Lawrences, Thomas Cooper, a checkweighman who was a flute player.)

Before Lilly and Aaron become intimate friends, Lilly goes through a relationship with Jim Bricknell which Jim forces upon him. Uninvited, Jim visits Lilly and his Norwegian wife Tanny in their Hampshire cottage; he says Lilly is the one man in England who can "save" him, he wheezes about the wonder of Christ, and he ravenously devours bread to fill the hollowness he feels inside. Before Lilly can get rid of him (Tanny irritatingly encourages Jim) there is a comic scene in which Lilly's goading drives Jim to punch him in the stomach, and Lilly has to sit silently trying to hide the fact that his wind has been knocked out. "It isn't that I don't like the man," Jim explains after the blow. "But I knew if he went on I should have to do it." Jim is the degeneration of the young-heir-to-mining-interests type; he lives in what is essentially the same house Gerald Crich lived in, and he is what the Gerald or Leslie Tempest type has become in the post-war world. (It is interesting to note that Jim is modelled after Captain James Robert White, known as Jack White, who took part in various Irish revolts against the English.)

When Tanny goes to Norway to visit her parents—as Frieda preceded Lawrence to the Continent after the war—Lilly takes a room above Covent Garden market. One day he sees Aaron collapse on the street below, a victim of influenza. He seems also the victim of a soul-sickness he has caught from one of the women in the Bricknell set.

Lilly rubs him with oil—"as mothers do their babies whose bowels won't work," he explains to the sullen Aaron. The touch brings Aaron back to life, and after his recovery he attaches himself to Lilly. But one day Lilly arouses Aaron's anger by coolly announcing that he has just booked passage for Malta. The two men have been strongly in accord, especially in their condemnation of the existing state of marriage, which permits women to use their men as instruments, to "get them under" with children and keep them under. But Lilly has a dimly felt mistrust of Aaron. There is a good deal of the Lawrence-Murry relationship here: the similarity goes deeper than Lawrence's nursing of Murry during a spell of grippe in Sussex in 1915.

The fundamental antagonism between Lilly and Aaron comes out in a quarrel which Aaron in his irritation begins after the men have been visited by an officer who was nerve-wrecked in the war. Lilly comments that he himself had known the war was false, from the point of view of both sides. When Aaron defends the use of poison gas, Lilly tells him he will have to leave in the morning, and Aaron says "Everybody's got to agree with you—that's your price." After a period of silence Lilly tells him, "I'm *not* going to have friends on the face of things. No, and I *don't* have friends who don't fundamentally agree with me. A friend means one who is at one with me in matters of life and death. And if you're at one with all the rest, then you're their friend, not mine."

Lilly feels, as Lawrence did about Murry, that Aaron is not at one with him in matters of life and death. Lilly, like Lawrence, expects a great deal. As a creator, he needs Aaron's response, and he seeks a living relationship, not complete mastery over another human being. Like Zarathustra, who cries out at the end of the Prologue to *Thus Spake Zarathustra*, that he wants not dead but living companions, Lilly knows that a creator cannot be a necrophile. The other person, the other spirit, must be considered. How generously Lawrence was willing at this time to consider the other spirit is problematical; in any event, in fiction he could wish events into a kind of inevitability: and after Lilly has left for the Mediterranean, Aaron feels that the other man has made a "call" upon his soul. He goes back to the Midlands for a secret, Enoch-Arden view of his family, which he has provided for financially, and then he follows Lilly down to Italy.

The descriptions of the English country and of London are in Lawrence's best vein, and the accounts of the Italian scenery are on a par with *Sea and Sardinia;* Aaron's progress southward is a heightened travelogue, one of Lawrence's finest. Though Aaron is at one level a not-too-articulate proletarian, he is also partly Lawrence; many of Lawrence's actual experiences, such as being robbed on the street in Florence, have been given to him. The visits Lawrence as a minor literary celebrity made en route to Florence, and his reactions to his hosts, are also given to Aaron.

Aaron distinctly represents still another important aspect of Lawrence, the Nottinghamshire-miner-heritage side. But Lawrence was not altogether successful in creating double characters. There is one awkward spot when he is forced to explain to the reader that Aaron did not have all his fine thoughts in so many word-concepts, as given in the text. All Lawrence's subsequent fiction except his last important creative work, *The Escaped Cock*, has such awkward moments, digressions, collapses of theme and structure: *The Rainbow* and *Women in Love* had an integration, perhaps because of their essential *symboliste* quality, not found in the later novels.

Aaron's Rod ends after Aaron has had a love-experience with an American woman married to a Florentine marchese: this affair does not fulfill Aaron, and when his flute is broken by a bomb explosion in a café, he feels that his life-symbol is shattered. Lilly, whom he has finally overtaken, gives Aaron a long talk about the exhaustion of the love-urge:

And yet we try to force it to continue working. So we get inevitable anarchy and murder. It's no good. We've got to accept the power motive, accept it in deep responsibility, do you understand me? It is a great life motive. It was that great dark power-urge which kept Egypt so intensely living for many centuries. It is a vast dark source of life and strength in us now, waiting either to issue into true action, or to burst into cataclysm. Power—the power-urge. The will-to-power—but not in Nietzsche's sense. Not intellectual power. Not mental power. Not conscious will-power. Not even wisdom. But dark, living, fructifying power.

Lilly says that both men and women must "yield to the deep power-soul in the individual man," and that if Aaron does not yield he will die. When Aaron asks whom he shall submit to, Lilly—his face "dark and remote-seeming . . . like a Byzantine eikon at the moment"—says, "Your soul will tell you."

✦ ✦ ✦ ✦

During the time that he was in Sicily—March 1920 to February 1922, with about six months' sporadic wanderings—Lawrence wrote some of the finest *Birds, Beasts and Flowers* poems. His poetry was now of a different texture, freer and more volatile, full of rhythms that were more conversational than before, yet without sacrifice of good lines and living images. The influence of Whitman is evident, from the personal opening of the first poem, "Pomegranate"—

> You tell me I am wrong.
> Who are you, who is anybody to tell me I am wrong?
> I am not wrong.

—to the last item in the collection, "The American Eagle," written soon after Lawrence's arrival in America in 1923:

> And the bub-eagle that Liberty had hatched was growing a
> startling big bird
>
> On the roof of the world . . .

though the voice is always Lawrence's and, above all, the animals are Lawrence's animals. Some of them are found in the section "The Evangelistic Beasts," and are entitled "St. Matthew," "St. Mark," "St. Luke," "St. John"—symbolic beast envisioned out of Lawrence's private mythology, vitally put down on the page. ("Thud! Thud! Thud!/ And the roar of black bull's blood in the mighty passages of his chest. . . .")

Lawrence's quick eye was responsible for a clever description of bats ("Swallows with spools of dark thread sewing the shadows together"), and there are humorous poems to mosquitoes, kangaroos, fish, he-goats, she-goats and other animals. The "Tortoise" poems and "Snake" show how reptiles fascinated Lawrence.

His gifts also served him ably in his verses about tropical flowers, fruits, and trees. It is significant that he took the name of this volume from a line in one of those Protestant hymns which had so deeply stirred him in childhood.

In pieces such as "Cypresses," quoted here in its original version, he is successful (as he is in "Snake") in effectively blending the doctrinal with the poetic:

> Tuscan cypresses
> What is it?

Folded in like a dark thought
For which the language is lost,
Tuscan cypresses,
Is there a great secret?
Are our words no good?

The undeliverable secret,
Dead with a dead race and a dead speech, and yet
Darkly monumental in you,
Etruscan cypresses.

Ah, how I admire your fidelity,
Dark cypresses.

Is it the secret of the long-nosed Etruscans?
The long-nosed, sensitive-footed, subtly-smiling Estrus-
    cans
Who made so little noise outside the cypress groves?

Among the sinuous, flame-tall cypresses
That swayed their length of darkness all around
Etruscan-dusky, wavering men of old Etruria:
Naked except for fanciful long shoes,
Going with insidious, half-smiling quietness
And some of Africa's imperturbable sang-froid
About a forgotten business.

What business, then?
Nay? tongues are dead, and words are hollow as hollow
    seed-pods,
Having shed their sound and finished all their echoing
Etruscan syllables,
That had the telling.

Yet more I see you darkly concentrate
Tuscan cypresses,
On one old thought:
On one old slim imperishable thought, while you remain
Etruscan cypresses;
Dusky, slim marrow-thought of slender, flickering men
    of Etruria,
Whom Rome called vicious.

They say the fit survive;
But I invoke the spirits of the lost.
Those that have not survived, the darkly lost,
To bring their meaning back into life again,
Which they have taken away
And wrapt inviolable in soft cypress trees,
Etruscan cypresses.

Evil, what is evil?
There is only one evil, to deny life
As Rome denied Etruria
And mechanical America Montezuma still.

Another book of Lawrence's short stories, *England, My England*, was published in 1922. The title story had come out in a magazine during the war; its setting is Greatham, in Sussex, where the Lawrences, as we have seen, had lived for a time in 1915. The central figure in the story is a portrait of E. V. Luca's younger brother Percy, who had married Madeline, one of the daughters of Wilfred and Alice Meynell. Egbert in the story is a good-natured, insouciant young man who does nothing; and although he is the father of children he feels no responsibility and is content to live off the bounty of his father-in-law. Much of the love Egbert's wife has felt for him is crushed out after one of the little girls is badly injured by a scythe he has carelessly left lying about. When the war comes, Egbert dreamily enlists; he is soon killed. The story is not without cruelty in its portraiture, though much of the life at "Crockham" is sympathetically presented, and there are not unfriendly pictures of the younger children. Lawrence's ending was purely imaginary; he had no idea that it would prove prophetic. In a letter to Catherine Carswell he explained what he had intended: "It seems to me, man must find a new expression, give a new value to life, or his women will reject him, and he must die." Lawrence had been shocked to hear that, not long after "England, My England" appeared in the October 1915 issue of the *English Review*, Percy Lucas died in France. Lawrence told Catherine Carswell that he wished the story had gone to the bottom of the sea before it had been printed. Yet he felt that the hero of his story had been a spiritual coward: "But who isn't?" He added, "If it was a true story, it shouldn't really damage," and in a postscript he said, "No, I *don't* wish I had never written that story. It should do good, at the long run." And, when Lawrence's American publisher, Thomas Seltzer, suggested that the story lend its name to the 1922 collection of shorter pieces, Lawrence agreed.

Several of the other stories take wartime England for their settings. "Wintry Peacock," in which a familiar Lawrencean symbol is used once again, takes place in the hills of Derbyshire —above the road known as the Via Gellia—where Lawrence had gone to live after his expulsion from Cornwall. The ex-soldier on one of the neighboring farms, sent home after being wounded, hates the peacock that is fondled and held captive by his wife, a sly, pretty young woman who tries to read the letters he receives from his Belgian sweetheart. We have seen that in Lawrence's earlier tales there is almost always conflict between lovers, whether or not they are married; in Lawrence's later fiction, these conflicts have been intensified by the war.

One of the *England, My England* stories, "Tickets, Please," is about the wartime girl conductors on a Midlands tram-line, and the Don Juanish inspector, John Thomas Raynor, who because of his reputation and the folk-etymology significance of his first two names, is known as Cuddy. The girls he has been flirting with gang up on him one night and beat him savagely and tear his clothes. The girl who instigates the outburst of group sadism is the fiercest of the lot; she is attracted to John Thomas, yet she realizes she will probably never have him on a serious and permanent basis. The story is of course a comic modern version of the Classical myth of Orpheus and the Maenads.

"Monkey Nuts" is a little comedy of the months after the war, before demobilization. A shy soldier named Joe, working at a West Country railway station with Albert, his corporal, attracts a pretty "land girl" who futilely makes love to him. Joe sullenly tries to avoid her; the gayer Albert several times offers himself as a substitute and is rebuffed. Joe finally rejects the girl's advances in a humiliating, public scene, and both men feel jeeringly triumphant. They seem to have fought this male-against-female war more wholeheartedly than the war against the Germans: Joe, when the girl is finally defeated, feels "more relieved than he had felt when he heard the firing cease, after the news had come that the armistice was signed."

"Samson and Delilah" is a story of reunion rather than separation, but it too is characterized by a savage conflict. After more than fifteen years in America, Will Nankervis comes back to Cornwall one night in wartime and reveals himself to his deserted wife, who keeps a tavern. When he refuses to leave, she and some soldiers quartered at the inn tie up Nankervis and leave him out in the road. After he at last works himself free, he returns to the inn and finds—the true Lawrencean touch—that the door is unlocked. His wife, sitting by the fire, is not surprised to see him. When she gets through scolding him, he tells her that he admires her spirit and that he has come back from America with a thousand pounds. She does not resist him when he touches her between the breasts.

Two of the stories not concerned with the war have Midlands settings, with strong beginnings and middle sections and interesting characters, but they are not satisfactorily resolved: "The Primrose Path" and "Fanny and Annie." In "The Primrose Path," a young man meets his ne'er-do-well uncle, recently returned from Australia; separated from his wife, he has a young woman and her mother living with him. This story, which may be rewritten from an earlier draft, seems to be an autobiographical reminiscence: the rather vague young man is typical of Lawrence's early period, and the uncle seems to be the same one who appears in the autobiographical sketch, "Rex," first printed in the *Dial* in February 1921 and included in the posthumous *Phoenix* volume. In "Rex" the uncle is the beloved, spoiled young brother of the boy's mother; he has become "sporting," and he reads the poetry of Browning. These features occur in somewhat the same way in the opening passages of "The Primrose Path," where the young man tells his uncle that his mother died at Christmas time, as Lawrence's mother had in 1910. Perhaps it is the autobiographical element that makes the outcome of the story so flimsy, after the effective scene with the uncle's dying wife and the meeting with the publican who is keeping her, a man named George who seems in many ways to be George Saxton of *The White Peacock*. The story ends with the young man going home with his uncle to meet the youthful mistress and her complying mother. The uncle is surly to the girl, and the young man is shocked.

"That girl will leave him," he said to himself. "She'll hate him like poison. And serve him right. Then she'll go off with somebody else."
And she did.

This is the end of the story, and it is too abrupt and too anecdotal to be appropriate after the elaborate earlier development. The same criticism might be made, more mildly, of "Fanny and Annie," which begins so vividly with the girl looking out of the railway-carriage windows as her train arrives at an industrial town:

Flame-lurid his face as he turned among the throng of flame-lit and dark faces upon the platform. In the light of the furnace she caught sight of his drifting countenance, like a piece of floating fire. And the nostalgia, the doom of home-coming, went through her veins like a drug. His eternal face, flame-lit now! The pulse and darkness of red fire from the furnace towers in the sky, lighting the desultory, industrial crowd on the wayside station, lit him and went out.

The emotional force of this beginning, with its fiery colors, suggests that there will be an explosion of power later in the story, and there is. The girl, who is thirty, has been jilted by the cousin she loved, who has died, and she has returned home to marry her first sweetheart, a foundry worker, whom she does not really love. On the following Sunday he takes her to church, and just after he finishes his solo in the choir, a stout red-faced woman in a black bonnet stands up and begins to shout denunciations of him because her daughter is with child by him. After the dramatic shock of this scene, the rest of the story is anti-climax. Fanny wonders if she dare go to the evening service with her fiancé, and as she listens to his family discussing the shrewishness of the woman who had raved in church, Fanny makes up her mind not to go with him. But when she decides to stay with his mother that night, she indicates that she will remain beside him no matter what trouble lies ahead.

The three other stories in the book have a common theme: the power of touch. This was played upon lightly at the end of "Samson and Delilah"; in "The Blind Man," "You Touched Me," and "The Horse Dealer's Daughter," touch—physical touch—is the most important element in the story.

Lawrence got the idea for "The Blind Man" while visiting Catherine Carswell and her husband at the vicarage where they were temporarily living, in the Forest of Dean, in 1918; he uses the vicarage as the scene of the story, calling it "the Grange." Catherine Carswell served as the model for the portrait of Isabel, though she says it does not resemble her.

Isabel's husband has been blinded in the war, and his forehead has been terribly scarred; it is at his suggestion that she invites her Scottish friend, Bertie Reid, for a visit. He is a barrister and a literary man, and although he is Isabel's oldest and dearest friend, he is terrified of women, of the possibility of physical relations with them. Isabel is extremely fond of him, yet she has a deep contempt for him, and this ambivalent attitude is cleverly depicted. It is ironic that Bertie, so afraid of physical contact, suffers it in this story at the hands of the blind man, which tenderly rove across his face and body. Then, with Bertie nearly fainting, Maurice takes Bertie's hand and puts it into his forehead scar and his "disfigured eye sockets"; and Maurice seeks out Isabel to tell her excitedly of this great new friendship. Isabel watches Bertie, who in his sick terror wants only to escape. The power of touch is here shown working in a negative, reverse direction: the Bertie Reids of life, the neuters, are unfit for touch. Besides this message, "The Blind Man" has an additional importance in that it points to the kind of stories Lawrence was to write years later, toward the end of his last period. "The Blind Man" has a light-comedy satiric tone, or the suggestion of one, not found in Lawrence's subsequent writings (except for "Two Blue Birds" in *The Woman Who Rode Away*) until the stories of the last two or three years of his life that were posthumously collected in *The Lovely Lady*.

Touch in its positive aspect is the motivation of "You Touched Me," in which a demobilized young man returns to the household where he had been reared as a foundling, and is touched in his sleep by one of the women there, who in a daze of night-wandering believes she has come to the bedroom of her sick father. Hadrian is aroused, and thereafter pursues Matilda, who is some ten years older than he; he is eager to marry her. Hadrian gets the help of her dying father, who threatens to disinherit Matilda if she does not agree to the marriage. When Matilda protests to Hadrian, he says "You touched me"—and although Hadrian has not read Freud, he knows (Matilda and her sister think him "sly") instinctively how our unconscious acts reveal our deep, unrecognized intentions. Matilda agrees to marry him.

Touch is also the keystone of the remaining *England, My England* story to be considered, "The Horse Dealer's Daughter." In this, the doctor rescues a girl from drowning and brings her to his home and strips off her clothes—and after she returns to consciousness she embraces him and awakens him into love for her. The situation prefigures a short novel of Lawrence's last period, the posthumously published *The Virgin and the Gipsy*.

Themes similar to those in the *England, My England* collection are handled more deeply and at greater length in the three long stories in the volume published in 1923, called *The Ladybird* in Britain and *The Captain's Doll* in America; these titles are taken from two of those in the collection. The third story, "The Fox," is—like the other two—built around a central symbol; and each of these tales fits Paul Heyse's "Falcon Theory" of the *novella* (discussed later, in the description of "St. Mawr").

The situation in "The Fox" resembles in some degree that of "You Touched Me": in each of these stories, a young man returning to England from Canada insists upon an older woman's marrying him. In "The Fox," matters are complicated by a woman-friend, but the young man destroys her by cutting down a tree in such a way that it takes a sudden curve and kills her.

This young man is fox-faced, and he is identified with the fox that has been killing the fowls on the farm that is the setting of the story, which Lawrence possibly began while living at Hermitage, Berkshire in 1918. He seems to have completed it soon after in Derbyshire; he finished the lengthened version of it in Sicily in November 1921. For the girls in the story, Lawrence used two young women he had known at a farm at Hermitage: Violet Monk became Nellie March, and Cecily Lambert became Jill Banford.

"The Fox," one of Katherine Mansfield's favorites among Lawrence's writings, is notable for the clash of wills that occurs among the three actors: before the young man arrives, the two girls have a tightly emotional relationship that can be broken only when the more manlike and willful of them is murdered. The ending is one of the finest points of the story, because it is not "set": the girl is not resentful over the killing of her friend, but she holds herself back from the young man. She will in time submit to his dominance, she knows that, but as the story ends she is still trying to fight for her independence.

"The Captain's Doll" was written at Taormina late in 1921; in speaking of it in a letter Lawrence told Earl Brewster that if he did not have his stories to amuse himself with he would die of spleen. "The Captain's Doll" begins in occupied Germany, after the war, and ends in the Tyrol, where the Scottish captain tells the war-impoverished German countess who has made a clever figurine after him, "If a woman loves you, she'll make a doll out of you. . . . I feel I've been insulted for forty years: by love, and the women who've loved me. I won't be loved. And I won't love.—I'll be honored and I'll be obeyed: or nothing." She agrees to submit to his will, in a concluding scene that has too much contrivance in it. This is unfortunate, for the tensions in the early part of the story, and the suicide or possibly accidental death of the captain's ageing wife, are deftly handled; and the descriptions of Germany and of the Alps represent Lawrence at his finest as a painter of the surface of things.

"The Ladybird" was written just after "The Captain's Doll"; when the book containing these stories came out in 1923, Lawrence told Murry in a letter: "I think in the long run perhaps 'The Ladybird' has more the quick of a new thing than the other two stories." And the theme of "The Ladybird" is more essentially Lawrencean than even the story of the Scottish captain's attempt to assert his domination over the German countess. The mystic Czech who is a war prisoner in England makes an

Englishwoman fall in love with him; the little captive has a "beyondness" that her Cambridge-voiced husband lacks. Count Dionys tells Daphne that the sunlight we see is only the inside-out of darkness, and that her own beauty is but the whited sepulchre of her real, dark, inner beauty. The ladybird in the title is the symbol of the Count's family, a *Marienkäfer* or Mary-beetle, "descendant of the Egyptian scarabeus, which is a very mysterious emblem." As Professor Tindall says in *D. H. Lawrence and Susan His Cow*, "Clearly the Count is a member of some central European lodge of the Theosophical Society." The husband and wife in the story are plainly modelled after Herbert and Cynthia Asquith.

Lawrence's growing interest in Oriental mysticism took a practical turn at about this time: early in 1922 he and Frieda spent some six weeks on Ceylon with Earl and Achsah Brewster, who were being instructed in Buddhism. Lawrence left little record of his stay there; his published letters deal but briefly with the experience; he found the place too hot and energy-bleeding. But the Brewsters give a good account of Lawrence's visit in their *Reminiscences*, one of the fairest and most selfless of the Lawrence-memoir volumes, a book containing some of the most rewarding material about Lawrence. Earl Brewster says Lawrence while in Ceylon became so weary of the seated Buddha that in later years he would exclaim "Oh, I wish he would stand up!"

One of the few products of Lawrence's Ceylonese visit is the "Elephant" poem in *Birds, Beasts and Flowers*, written at the time of the journey to India made by the future King Edward VIII-Duke of Windsor, then Prince of Wales. There is something prophetic in the way Lawrence mulls over the Prince's motto, *Ich Dien* (I serve), and in the entire picture of the

> Pale, dispirited Prince, with his chin in his hands, his nerves
> tired out,
> Watching and hardly seeing the trunk-curl approach and
> clumsy, knee-lifting salaam
> Of the hugest, oldest of beasts, in the night and the fire-
> flare below.
> He is the white men's royalty, pale and dejected fragment
> up aloft.

And down below huge homage of shadowy beasts, bare-foot
            and trunk-lipped in the night.
. . . . an alien, diffident boy whose motto is *Ich dien.*

I serve! I serve! in all the weary irony of his mien—
            'Tis I who serve!
Drudge to the public.

Lawrence wrote a quite different poem about elephants, some
years later, which appeared in the *Pansies* volume under the
title "The Elephant is Slow to Mate."

✓ ✓ ✓ ✓

After Ceylon, Lawrence went to Australia, to try a "new"
continent. He and Frieda stayed there from May till August
of 1922. The result of this visit was two books which represent the two ways he looked at Australia: *The Boy in the Bush*
(published 1924), which is a rewriting of another person's story,
is about the surface of Australia and is a reconstruction of that
country's adventurous past; *Kangaroo* (published 1923) is a projection of Lawrence's own philosophy and of some of his European experiences into a contemporary Australian setting.

The Boy in the Bush was written later, in 1923, while Lawrence was travelling in Mexico; it is a partial recasting and
complete rewriting of *The House of Ellis,* a manuscript by a
woman Lawrence met in Australia, M. L. Skinner. Lawrence
revised the book with generous personal touches: some of the
horseback and rough-riding scenes were apparently out of his
own later New Mexican experience, and he gave the hero three
women as lovers instead of the one he found in the original version. Lawrence on November 1, 1923 wrote Miss Skinner from
Mexico:

I have been busy over your novel, as I travelled. The only
thing was to write it all out again, following your MS. almost
exactly, but giving a unity, a rhythm, and a little more psychic
development than you had done. I have come now to Book IV.
The end will have to be different, a good deal different.

The Boy in the Bush is a story which has never been properly
appreciated, a zestful adventure narrative that in the right hands

would make an excellent film. It concerns Jack Grant, who has been a bad boy in England and has been packed off to live with some Australian cousins. The Ellis household out in the bush and the assortment of people there provide some lively and amusing pages, and the hatred levelled against Jack by a neighboring cousin, Red Esau, adds a touch of frontier ferocity that reaches a violent climax when at last the two enemies come to death-grips.

Jack has courage and luck: he prospects for gold and is successful. But he meets opposition when he tries to seduce his dark, quiet cousin Mary, who he thought had a strong, unspoken love for him; he reasons angrily with himself that if he had begged her, said he needed her tormentingly, she would have submitted, but that to take him as he was would have been too much for her. All the while he had been true, in his fashion, to his tawny-eyed cousin Monica, and at the end he has a governor's daughter riding out after him to offer herself to him. But the deepest response he feels is from the little red-haired daughter of Esau, whom he is bringing up after killing her father in a fight: she alone accepts Jack absolutely.

Jack at the last has a splendid Lawrencean vision when he dreams of taking his wife and a few friends and getting a huge piece of land in the north and living like Abraham, a lord of the earth. But Jack realizes, as Lawrence finally had to, that it is all impossible: "A little world of my own! As if I could make it with the people that are on earth today! No, no, I can do nothing but stand alone. And then, when I die, I shall not drop like carrion on the earth's earth. I shall be a lord of death, and sway the destinies of life to come."

Dorothy Brett reports, in *Lawrence and Brett: A Friendship*, that Lawrence wanted to have Jack die at the end, but that Frieda made him keep Jack alive: "Let him become ordinary. . . . Always this superiority and death."

Kangaroo was written about a year earlier than *The Boy in the Bush*, chiefly in the bungalow "Wyewurk," on the coast below Sydney, that figures so importantly in the story. *Kangaroo*, the second of Lawrence's leadership novels, is a momentous statement of the predicament of civilized man in the twentieth century. The protagonist, Richard Lovat Somers, is a continuation of Lilly of *Aaron's Rod*, but is even more like Lawrence than Lilly was. A quiet, sensitive, bearded writer whose books are not widely read, Somers has come to Australia after his disillusionment with Europe.

The opening of *Kangaroo* is casual enough on the surface, but there are undercurrents of conflict. The young mechanic sprawling on the grass of the park in Sydney is just a bit too interested in the peculiar-looking strangers whom he immediately classifies as "Bolshies." Somers is not unaware of this interest, and even causes the mechanic a moment of discomfort when he catches him nudging his companion to look at "the queer blokes." Later Somers finds that the young man is his neighbor in the cottage he has taken in another part of town. Somers, sickened with humanity, wants isolation; there is a wryly humorous passage when his wife Harriet makes friends with the Callcotts over the hedge: "Somers, in the little passage inside his house, heard all this with inward curses. 'That's done it!' he groaned to himself. He'd got neighbors now."

The couples become friendly. Jack Callcott, in his direct, colonial way, tries to make a "pal" of Somers, but succeeds only in frightening and embarrassing the Englishman. He tells Somers of an organization called the Diggers; later, after Somers has moved down the coast, Jack brings him to Sydney to meet Ben Cooley, the Jewish attorney known as Kangaroo, who is leader of the Diggers. Some readers of Lawrence have felt that Kangaroo is patterned after S. S. Koteliansky, a Russian friend whom Lawrence once described as being "a bit Jehovahish," but Frieda has said the portrait more nearly resembles Dr. David Eder, with whom the Lawrences planned to go to South America during the First World War. Kangaroo in the story makes an appeal to Somers that is far deeper than the appeal Jack has made. He wants Somers, whose books he has read for years, to come into the movement: the Diggers are a half-secret military organization under the leadership of five "masters," of whom Kangaroo is Number One. The description of the Diggers reveals how thoroughly Lawrence understood the possibilities of Fascism, though he could have seen only a little of Fascism in Italy after the war; actually he had spent most of his time in

Sicily and had left the region altogether and gone out to India some six months before the March on Rome. The Diggers are in any event more like Nazis than Italian Fascists, which makes their appearance in this novel prophetic indeed: in the year *Kangaroo* was written, Hitler was only beginning to muster Storm Troopers for his then small and obscure National Socialist Party. Lawrence was in the spirit of the time, or somewhat ahead of it, as when he had given the first fictional treatment of the newly charted Oedipus Complex in *Sons and Lovers,* and had experimented with techniques for reproducing consciousness-effects in *The Rainbow* and *Women in Love.*

Kangaroo has many lovable human qualities, yet he represents an inhuman will. He is magnetic, as leaders generally are, inspiring personal devotion in masses of men. Kangaroo tempts Somers with love; he wants "generous, passionate men" to be all working together "in the one fire of love." But Somers is mistrustful: "I know your love, Kangaroo. Working everything from the spirit, from the head. You work the lower self as an instrument of the spirit. Now it is time for the spirit to leave us again." So he evades Kangaroo. He also evades the temptations of a rival leader, the socialist Willie Struthers, who wants Somers to edit "a sincere, *constructive* socialist paper, not a grievance-airer, but a paper that calls to the constructive spirit in men. . . . Now Mr. Somers, you're the son of a working-man. You were born of the People. You haven't turned your back on them, have you, now that you're a well-known gentleman?" This appeal is hard to dodge. To get away from Struthers is a relief, "like escaping from one of the medical-examination rooms in the war." Now Somers can discern the outlines of the choices that lie before him. He says to himself, "Why can't mankind save itself. It can if it wants to. I'm a fool. I want neither love nor power. I like the world. And I like to be alone in it, by myself."

Lawrence says a good deal about marriage in *Kangaroo,* and his own marriage is drawn upon for fictional presentation throughout the book. His relationship to Frieda has not been discussed at length in the present volume since the passages dealing with the earlier phases of their association. It has not been dwelt upon because it was stabilizing into a condition that, with a few minor variations, was permanent from about the middle of the war—and the end of the *Look! We Have Come Through!* poems—to Lawrence's death. The relationship had one serious break, when Frieda returned alone to Europe from America in 1923, but this separation did not last long. The picture of the Lawrences' marriage as given in *Kangaroo* is the fullest and truest Lawrence ever painted of it. The marriage of Lilly and Tanny in the preceding novel, *Aaron's Rod,* is a preliminary sketch; the only time the story focuses on it at any length is in the Jim Bricknell episode, previously described, in which Tanny tends to side with Jim. In *Kangaroo,* Somers and Harriet are wandering across the world as Lawrence and Frieda wandered, and they arrive in Sydney with two Gladstone bags and a small hatbox. The moment they enter the bungalow they have rented, Harriet before she has even taken her hat off removes "four pictures from the wall, and the red plush tablecloth from the table," and then she takes out of one of the bags "an Indian sarong of purplish shot color, to try how it would look across the table." The book contains many incidental accounts of the everyday aspects of marriage, the gaiety and companionship, as in the chapter "Bits" when Somers and Harriet take a trip to a little coastal town and Somers gets soaked by a wave when he pursues his wind-blown hat into the sea; Harriet laughs at this then, and again when they are home and Somers is rather ruefully seated on a barrel by their grate-fire. The book also contains some of the quarrels and misunderstandings inevitable in marriage, as when Somers begins to conspire politically with Jack Callcott and will not let Harriet in on their secrets; she calls Somers' reticence "A bit of little boy's silly showing off," but she is hurt:

Then at evening he found her sitting on her bed with tears in her eyes and her hands in her lap. At once his heart became very troubled: because after all she was all he had in the world, and he couldn't bear her to be really disappointed or wounded. He wanted to ask her what was the matter, and to try to comfort her. But he knew it would be false. He knew that her greatest grief was when he turned away from their personal human life of intimacy to this impersonal business of male activity for which he was always craving. So he felt miserable, but went away without saying anything.

The later chapter, "At Sea in Marriage," deals with modern marriage in general and Somers' marriage in particular: and of course this is Lawrence's own. He repeats some of the principles he had enunciated in regard to marriage in *Fantasia of the Unconscious*, here presented in terms of an elaborate metaphor in which marriage is seen as a ship over whose control two people contend, each wanting to steer in a different direction. In *Fantasia,* Lawrence has mentioned the differences between male and female activity; in "At Sea in Marriage" he still acknowledges the differences but admits that the male must strive for mastership. Somers had nothing but Harriet, "and that was why, presumably, he wanted to establish this ascendancy over her, assume this arrogance. . . . And she could *not* stand these world-saviours" like Jack Callcott and Kangaroo, whom her man would go prancing off with, expecting her to be there to soothe him when he came home disillusioned. Somers needed, Lawrence indicates, to communicate with his own "dark god" before Harriet or anyone would admit his true mastery; this is repeated, as will be seen, throughout *Kangaroo*.

Frieda Lawrence said in her memoir that "It was a long fight for Lawrence and me to get at some truth between us; it was a hard life with him, but a wonderful one. . . . Whatever happened on the surface of everyday life, there blossomed the certainty of the unalterable bond between us, and of the everpresent wonder of all the world around us."

In *Kangaroo*, this marriage is counterpointed against the male activity of the Diggers and against various other phases of modern society. In a lengthy flashback, the marriage is seen in operation during the upheavals and dislocations of war. This flashback occurs after one of the interviews with Kangaroo from which Somers flees in a tangible terror that makes him think of the terror he felt during the war. Somers goes to a hotel to be alone; the long chapter called "The Nightmare" recapitulates his wartime experiences in England, particularly the period when he was living on the Cornish coast and was under suspicion. Norman Douglas has said that in this chapter Lawrence committed "an artistic outrage" by "infecting Australian surroundings with this exotic taint." Perhaps Norman Douglas would also object to Aeneas' visit to the Afterworld, or to Ivan Karamazoff's story of the Grand Inquisitor. The point is that "The Nightmare" has a great deal to do with the central theme of the book *Kangaroo*. Somers' experiences during the war are completely those of Lawrence: being hounded out of Cornwall, having to report regularly to the police, being summoned to medical examinations for possible conscription—Lawrence had lived through all this, and in *Kangaroo* he wrote of it in a vivid and bitter poetry full of a nostalgia for the Cornish coast, a nostalgia greater even than Lawrence's hatred for the furtive, spying Cornishmen.

Although "The Nightmare" was written by a man who had not been exposed to the battlefields, it is one of the severest indictments of the First World War: it is a sharp analysis of the mass-bullying that went on during those years, which disgusted Lawrence-Somers with his own country forever. The recounting of that wartime ordeal is vital to the novel *Kangaroo*, for it explains the attitude and deepens the characterization of the protagonist. Twice the draft-men had called Lawrence-Somers while he was in Cornwall, and twice the doctors had rejected him. After his expulsion from Cornwall he was summoned yet again, this time in his own Midlands region.

The doctors handled him harshly: "Somers knew his appearance had been anticipated and they wanted to count him out." If by this time he had something resembling a persecution complex, these doctors did nothing to assuage it. He began to loathe his native Midlands. His own people seemed even worse than the Cornish—"These horrible machine people, these iron and coal people. They wanted to set their foot absolutely on life, grind it down and be master. . . . they had looked into his anus, they had put their hand between his legs. That athletic young fellow, he didn't seem to think he ought to mind at all. He looked on his body as a sort of piece of furniture, or a machine, to be handled and put to various uses. Somers laughed, and thanked God for his own thin, underweight body. He hoped the athletic fellow would enjoy the uses they put him to."

Lawrence-Somers tried to get out of England, but the authorities would not grant a passport to "one of the most intensely English men England ever produced, with a passion for his country, even if it were often a passion of hatred. But no, they persisted he was a foreigner. Pah!"

Toward the end of the novel, Kangaroo is badly wounded in a street-fight in Sydney between his Diggers and the socialists. At the hospital Kangaroo tells Somers it is he and not the wound that is killing him. And Somers *was* killing him, just as Lawrence was in his own consciousness killing the impression of what Kangaroo stood for. Lawrence and Richard Lovat Somers had to be free men.

"It is the collapse of the love-ideal," said Richard to himself. "I suppose it means chaos and anarchy: in the name of love and equality. The only thing one can stick to is one's own isolate being, and the God in whom it is rooted. And the only thing to look to is the God who fulfills one from the dark. And the only thing to wait for is for men to find their aloneness and their God in the darkness. Then one can meet as worshippers, in a sacred contact in the dark."

This is not, as some would have it, Nazi mysticism, which would be tribal: the "dark God" bears a superficial resemblance to some of the early Nazi symbols, but only superficial reasoning would attempt to link them. Lawrence's "God" comes out of the mine-darkness and out of Indian concepts of the chakra and the Kundalini. An answer to those who have accused Lawrence of Fascist sympathies is contained in the subsequent discussion of *The Plumed Serpent*.

The people in *Kangaroo*, even the somewhat allegorized figure of the name character, are all livingly presented: Jack Callcott, with his alternations between eagerness and bitterness, his wife Victoria who is "impressed" by Somers, the émigré brother-in-law Jaz, whom Jack calls a "Cornish whisper," and Somers' German wife Harriet—all are excellent foils for Somers with his monologues on the lonely shore and his clashes with Kangaroo. Parts of the book repeat one of the faults of *Aaron's Rod*—the author's tendency to stop and chat colloquially with the reader—but this is inconsequential beside the writing-power displayed throughout most of the novel. Perhaps books of this kind should not technically be called novels, any more so than

the work of Carlyle or Nietzsche. These books of Lawrence
are above most "novels"—they make important statements about
life and are superbly written.

Somers, in spite of his affection for Kangaroo, sees the menace
of the man; "Kangaroo wants to be God himself." Somers' rejection of the opposing political theory is not quite so harsh: "Bol-
shevism is at least not sentimental." Somers also tells himself
that it is a choice of evils and he chooses neither—the romantic
retreat was still fairly easy to make in those days, before the
remotest and the most harmless little republics or quiet islands
might at any moment become military targets. A few years after
Kangaroo, Lawrence wrote in a literary article, "Once be disillusioned with the man-made world, and you can still see the
magic, the beauty, the delicate realness of all the other life." The
German poet Rilke had in 1919 an experience not unlike the
one Lawrence imagined in *Kangaroo.* Rilke's letters from
Switzerland, where he had gone from Munich after the Bavarian
revolution—particularly the magnificent letter of August 6 to
Countess Aline Dietrichstein—reflect this experience. In the
August 6 letter, Rilke discusses the necessarily ambivalent rôle
of the poet in a revolution, and in this and subsequent letters he
too finds a return to nature—in a specialized, subtilized, Rilkean
fashion—the poet's solution. *Kangaroo,* despite its intense concern with the man-made world, is also full of all that "other
life" of nature—the stony, druidical atmosphere of Cornwall,
the strange little Australian coast-towns, the changing moods of
the southern ocean, the mystery and terror of the bush, Sydney's
"many-lobed" harbor, Hampstead Heath in a wartime autumn—
all done by Lawrence at the height of his power as a descriptive
writer. Here is an example that will show some of the wonder
of *Kangaroo:*

Lights were beginning to glint out: the township was deciding it was night. The bungalows scattered far and wide, on the
lower levels. There was a net-work of wide roads, or beginnings
of roads. The heart of the township was one tiny bit of street
a hundred yards long: Main Street. You knew where it was,
as you looked down on the reddish earth and grass and bush,
by the rather big roof of pale zinc and a sandy-coloured round
gable of the hotel—the biggest building in the place. For the rest,

it looked, from above, like an inch of street with tin roofs on either side, fizzling out at once into a wide grass-road with a few bungalows and then the bush. But there was the dark railway, and the little station. And then again the big paddocks rising to the sea, with a ridge of coral-trees and a farm-place. Richard could see Coo-ee with its low, red roof, right on the sea. Behind it the rail-fences of the paddocks, and the open grass, and the streets cut out and going nowhere, with an odd bungalow here and there.

So it was all round—a far and wide scattering of pale-roofed bungalows at random among grassy, cut-out streets, all along the levels above the sea, but keeping back from the sea, as if there were no sea. Ignoring the great Pacific. There were knolls and pieces of blue creek-hollow, blue of fresh-water lagoons on the yellow sands. Up the knolls perched more bungalows, on very long front legs and no back legs, caves of dark underneath. And on the sky-line, a ridge of wiry trees with dark plume-tufts at the ends of the wires, and these little loose crystals of different-coloured, sharp-angled bungalows cropping out beneath. All in a pale, clear air, clear and yet far off, as it were visionary.

So the land swooped in grassy swoops, past the railway, steep up to the bush: here and there thick-headed palm-trees left behind by the flood of time and the flood of civilization both: bungalows with flame-trees: bare bungalows like packing-cases: an occasional wind-fan for raising water: a round well-pool, perfectly round: then the bush, and a little colliery steaming among the trees. And so the great tree-covered swoop upwards of the tor, to the red fume of clouds, red like the flame-flowers of sunset. In the darkness of trees the strange birds clinking and trilling: the tree-ferns with their knob-scaly trunks spreading their marvellous circle of lace overhead against the glow, the gum-trees like white, naked nerves running up their limbs, and the inevitable dead gum-trees poking stark grey limbs into the air. And the thick aboriginal dusk settling down.

✓ ✓ ✓ ✓

When Somers told the wounded Kangaroo that he and Harriet were going to America next, the dying leader hissed an angry prophecy: "They'll kill you in America." This possibility must have been in Lawrence's mind as he and Frieda took a ship going to San Francisco. They landed on September 4, 1922; their destination was Taos, New Mexico, where they had been invited by Mabel Dodge Sterne, later Mabel Dodge Luhan, who felt that Lawrence was particularly destined to "express" New Mexico. He spent the greater part of three years there, and wrote numerous stories and poems about the place. The vivid sections at the end of *Birds, Beasts and Flowers* were written there; the opening of the poem "Men in New Mexico"—

> Mountains blanket-wrapped
> Round a white hearth of desert

—is typical of the imagery in the New Mexican poems. In "Autumn at Taos," Lawrence in projecting a New Mexican setting ("The aspens of autumn/Like the yellow hair of a tigress brindled with pine") nevertheless remembers symbols from another continent and another age ("the golden hawk of Horus").

The volume contains several animal poems that also came out of New Mexico: "Mountain Lion," "The Red Wolf," "Bibbles." The last is Lawrence's dog,

> Little black snub-nosed bitch with a shoved-out jaw
> And a wrinkled reproachful look . . .

This is one of Lawrence's most amusing poems, for besides being a living sketch of a comic little black dog, it is also used to depict that part of humanity which is soggily and indiscriminately affectionate. Long after Lawrence's death there was a squabble, in the *New Mexico Sentinel*, among the former campfollowers, as to whether or not Lawrence had been cruel to Bibbles and kicked her.

Lawrence had a symbolic relationship with another animal in New Mexico, the cow Susan; he felt a certain balance between his individuality and hers; and she certainly came far closer than the straying dog to the ideal relationship Lawrence was looking for in humanity. Susan appears in an essay, "Love Was Once A Little Boy," which came out in 1925 in the volume *Reflections on the Death of a Porcupine*. The title-essay describes another New Mexican experience, and several of the pieces are concerned with Lawrence's views on sex. "The Crown" is reprinted in a revised version.

Lawrence's New Mexican years were spent partly in the hysterical atmosphere of Mabel Luhan's ranch, usually full of captive and quarreling celebrities and arrivistes, or in escapes from this atmosphere—escapes to the near-by mountains, to Old Mexico, once even to Europe. Mrs. Luhan (then Mrs. Sterne) and her Indian-buck lover had sat up nights "willing" the Lawrences to Taos. When at last the wished-for guests arrived, they were given a new little adobe house on Mrs. Luhan's premises, but by winter they had moved to a cabin at Del Monte ranch in the Sangre de Cristo range.

Mabel Luhan's *Lorenzo in Taos* says that Frieda broke up the beautiful friendship that was developing between Lawrence and Mabel; Lawrence, whose letters through this period stand out in clear sanity against Mrs. Luhan's desperate report, doubtless told the complete truth of the matter in a letter to Catherine Carswell: "Taos too much. Mabel Sterne and suppers and motor drives and people dropping in." Two Danish painters whom Mrs. Luhan disliked, Merrild and Gøtzsche, also moved up to Del Monte, and Lawrence rejoiced because they effectively kept her away.

By March the Lawrences were in Mexico, by the end of July in New York; when Frieda sailed for England in August, Lawrence went to California, visiting Mexico again in late September and two months later sailing for England from Vera Cruz. Then he and Frieda revisited Germany and returned to Taos a year after they had left. But now they were accompanied by the Hon. Dorothy Brett, a further screen against Mabel Luhan. They all stayed at Mrs. Luhan's place, however, until she presented Frieda with a ranch near Del Monte. When Frieda reciprocated by giving Mrs. Luhan the manuscript of the final version of *Sons and Lovers*, Mrs. Luhan's feelings were hurt. Lawrence rechristened the ranch; it had been called Lobo and he changed the name to Kiowa. Dorothy Brett moved up there too, but this time the escape from Mrs. Luhan was not so effective, for she and her guests sometimes ascended the mountain to badger the recalcitrant prophet.

The Lawrences remained at the ranch until October 1924,

when with "the snow . . . dropping wet off the pine trees" and the desert seeming to decompose in the distance, they set off again for Mexico. It was there, in Oaxaca in February 1925, that Lawrence was gravely ill of tuberculosis—which he called "malaria and flu." When he was well enough to travel, he and Frieda returned to Kiowa ranch. After six months there, they left America, in September, and Lawrence never returned, though his ashes were brought back several years after his death.

Most of Lawrence's writing in and about America was either travel-descriptive or fictional. One of the exceptions is his volume of American-literature studies, mostly revised from essays written in England during the war; another exception is the play *David*, which takes its theme from the story of David and Jonathan and Saul: it is written in a rich language that is sometimes Lawrence's own and sometimes the Bible's, though there is never a clash of styles; Lawrence could adapt his rhythmic prose to that of the Old Testament.

Several of Lawrence's travel sketches of his American sojourn were printed in *Mornings in Mexico* in 1927—"Indians and Entertainment," "The Dance of the Sprouting Corn," and "The Hopi Snake Dance" appear in that volume along with some pieces about Old Mexico. In "Indians and Entertainment," Lawrence defines the contrast between the Indians' consciousness and ours. Aside from the essay's fine interpretation of animism and its interesting suggestions about the difference between Indian "entertainment" and Greek drama, it is an excellent statement of Lawrence's theories about contrasting ways of consciousness. He sees the blind-faced, singing Indian as motivated by "the consciousness in the abdomen"; this is far different from the songs of the wild Hebridean fisherman, which are still essentially human. But the Indian's consciousness is in his blood-stream and it is something the white consciousness, Lawrence admits, cannot approach—there can never be a bridge of connection between the two: one way of consciousness annihilates the other. Yet Lawrence can be felt wishing himself across the gulf. His next big novel, *The Plumed Serpent*, represents his yearning to get over that void, and records his actual failure to do so.

Discussion of *The Plumed Serpent* should rightly be preceded by an examination of some of Lawrence's other work leading up to that book. He had originally been attracted to America during the First World War, and before that war was over he had written the first versions of most of the *Studies in Classic American Literature,* which began to appear in the *English Review* in late 1918 and early 1919. In 1920 he had written an essay for the *New Republic*—"America, Listen To Your Own"—in which he advised Americans to take up life where the Indians, the Mayas, the Incas, the Aztecs had left off: America's real continuity, he argued, is with these races, not with superimposed European life-forms. Walter Lippmann answered with a neat literalness, in the same issue of the magazine, that "America is a nation of emigrants who took possession of an almost empty land," and that there is no true continuity with Montezuma. Mary Austin, later to meet Lawrence in New Mexico, answered Lippmann in turn in the *New Republic.*

Studies in Classic American Literature, first published in 1923, deals with "the old people, the little thin volumes of Hawthorne, Poe, Dana, Melville, Whitman." And although the book uses Lawrencean scales to weigh values, it is an important commentary upon American literature and life that has much to say even to the most un-Lawrencean readers. One of the most ingenious theories about the essential mythology of *Moby Dick* is found here; Lawrence sees the hunted whale as "the deepest blood-being of the white race," which our fanatical mental consciousness wants to hunt down and make subject to our will: and in this mad pursuit we even get the other races, black, yellow and red (the crew of the *Pequod*), to help us. Lawrence discusses Melville's early years among the Polynesians, the child-people of ancient races. But his idyllic life there was ruined because of Home and Mother, and he had to escape. "The truth of the matter is, one cannot go back. Some men can: renegade. But Melville couldn't go back: and Gauguin couldn't really go back: and I know now that I could never go back. Back towards the past, savage life. One cannot go back. It is one's destiny inside one."

Lawrence traces the intentions and fate of various other earlier Americans—Franklin, de Crèvecoeur, Cooper, Poe, Hawthorne and Whitman—viewing their accomplishments either in the light of his own life or of his own prejudices, but casting new beams of revelation upon many aspects of these figures that might otherwise remain obscure. He loathes Franklin's practical maxims and sets up a passionate list of his own to cry them down; he sees Hawthorne's books as parables of the conflict between blood-knowledge and the atrophying mind-knowledge of the Puritans and, while he praises much in Whitman, he attacks the poet's "ache of amorous love" side. In the "Spirit of Place" chapter he indirectly expresses his own yearning for a homeland: "Men are free when they are in a living homeland, not when they are straying and breaking away. Men are free when they are obeying some deep, inward voice of religious belief. Obeying from within. Men are free when they belong to a living, organic, *believing* community, active in fulfilling some unfulfilled, perhaps unrealized purpose."

Lawrence's two short novels of New Mexico, "St. Mawr" and "The Princess," were published in the same volume in England in 1925; the former appeared separately in America in that same year. St. Mawr is a magnificent stallion, a Freudian image of wild life that has much in common with two similar figures in modern literature, Robinson Jeffers' Roan Stallion in the narrative poem (1925) of that name, and the horse in Kay Boyle's long story (1940), "The Crazy Hunter." Each of these tales is an interesting example of the working out of Paul Heyse's "Falcon Theory" of the *novella:* Heyse said that the short novel should have a symbol or "silhouette" (as in the *Decameron* falcon story, Day Five, Novella Nine) that will be the dominant and remembered thing in the story. St. Mawr is an untameable horse purchased in London by Lou Carrington, an unfulfilled American woman married to an Englishman. Lou and her mother, Mrs. Witt, take St. Mawr to the American southwest, where the landscape has a stirring effect upon the two women. Lawrence here described his own ranch, Kiowa, which lies twenty miles above Taos in the Rockies: the setting, convincingly presented in some of Lawrence's finest spontaneous prose, is one of the important actors (or motivators of action) in the story. But it is the horse that is dominant: he is, among other things, the symbol of the unconquerable maleness Lawrence was celebrating.

One of the significant passages in "St. Mawr" describes the proposal of marriage made by Mrs. Witt to her groom, Morgan Lewis. Mrs. Witt is a Mabel Luhan-like woman who, as she rigidly goes riding in Hyde Park, seems "to be pointing a pistol at the bosom of every other horseman or horsewoman, and announcing: *Your virility or your life! Your femininity or your life!*" Lewis is a quiet little Welshman who refuses to cut off his beard because it is a part of him. He dislikes people because he dislikes the aunt and uncle who brought him up; and because they were religious, he dislikes religion. When Mrs. Witt, who cannot break through his inscrutability, makes her fantastic proposal, Lewis says such a marriage "would never do." He has to work for women now, be their servant, but the woman he marries would have to respect his body—and Mrs. Witt respects no man. He would feel shame to have a woman mocking and shouting at him as he has seen married women do: "But if I touch a woman with my body, it must put a lock on her, to respect what I will never have despised: never!" When she asks what it is that he "will never have despised," he tells her, "My body! And my touch upon the woman." This passage suggests something in the work of another author—the memoir of Lawrence written after his death by Mabel Luhan (*Lorenzo in Taos*), in which she says that Lawrence did not attract her physically, but that she wanted to "seduce his spirit"; and because "the strongest, surest way to the soul is through the flesh," she wanted to touch him although she did not want to touch him. The little, bearded Lawrence-man, Morgan Lewis, feels that something like this determines the attitude of Mrs. Witt, who insists that she loves him. He loves her, "in an odd way," but holds back and feels insulted by her approach: and she privately attributes his refusal to conventional male self-conceit. The entire episode is a social commentary as caustic as it is amusing. And it is, among other things, a prelude to *Lady Chatterley's Lover:* the bearded little groom, uttering Lawrence philosophy and fascinating the upper-class women, is a preliminary sketch of the gamekeeper Mellors—or Parkin, as he was called in the first version of the *Chatterley* book.

"St. Mawr" has a gallery of interesting characters besides Mrs. Witt and the stubborn little groom. Lawrence uses Dean

Vyner and his wife to represent not only the repressive attitude
of the Church but also Grundyism in all its forms: the Vyners
think St. Mawr should be killed. There is also Lewis's fellow-
groom, the American Indian named Phoenix, who in England is
homesick for the Southwest. Lawrence uses this character for
something more than a rather wry jest at his favorite bird-
symbol: he is gently making fun of the domesticated, semi-
westernized Indian, of which he saw more than one example
around Mabel Luhan's corner of New Mexico. Lawrence also
lampoons a quite different type, the country-house English girl;
there is one in particular, Flora Manby, who is trying to ensnare
Mrs. Witt's son-in-law, Rico. After Rico has been injured by
St. Mawr, Flora Manby wants to buy the stallion, and Lou
Carrington hears that she wants to geld him. Mrs. Witt advises
her daughter to say, "Miss Manby, you may have my husband,
but not my horse. My husband won't need emasculating, and my
horse I won't have you meddle with. I'll preserve one last male
thing in the museum of this world, if I can." Lawrence later
explained exactly what the horse-symbol meant to him, in a passage in his last book, *Apocalypse:*

How the horse dominated the mind of the early races, especially of the Mediterranean! You were a lord if you had a horse.
Far back, far back in our dark soul the horse prances. He is a
dominant symbol: he gives us lordship: he links us, the first
palpable and throbbing link with the ruddy-glowing Almighty
of potence: he is the beginning even of our god-head in the
flesh. And as a symbol he roams the dark underworld meadows
of the soul. He stamps and threshes in the dark fields of your
soul and of mine. The sons of God who came down and knew
the daughters of men and begot the great Titans, they had "the
members of horses," says Enoch.

Within the last fifty years man has lost the horse. Now man
is lost. Man is lost to life and power—an underling and a wastrel.
While horses thrashed the streets of London, London lived.

The horse, the horse! the symbol of surging potency and
power of movement, of action, in man.

Mrs. Witt and her daughter bring St. Mawr to the American
West, which is contrasted with the London drawing rooms and

country estates. The magic influence of the New Mexican land-scape upon the characters has already been mentioned: it was an influence that Lawrence himself felt very strongly, and it was one that he was frequently and functionally to use in his writings.

"The Princess" also draws upon the New Mexican landscape, particularly upon its mountains. Again, as in "St. Mawr," "Things," and some of his other stories, Lawrence in "The Princess" reveals a Jamesian talent for portraying "international" people—those caught between two cultures. In "The Princess," Dollie Urquhart, half Scottish and half Bostonian, has gone out to New Mexico after her father's death; she is thirty-eight, virginal, with an equally virginal companion. Dollie has lived chiefly in Europe, where even as a child she was wise and knowing; early in life she read Maupassant and Zola, but always shrank away from *touching* life. Now, in New Mexico, she feels the effect of the landscape, and of one of the guides at the dude ranch, Domingo Romero. He is the last *paisano* remnant of a once great local family of landowners. In the midst of his heavy, Mexican despair there is a spark of dauntlessness and pride that sets him apart from the mass of men.

A quiet sympathy grows between him and the Princess—as Dollie was always called by the father who adored and spoiled her. She is pretty, and looks only twenty-five; in her groping out for new experience, she arranges for Romero to take her and her companion on a long trip over the Rockies, to a place where she can see the animals in their wilderness. On the way up, when Miss Cummins' horse is injured, the Princess sends her back, and she and Romero go on alone. Then the scenery becomes one of the actors.

This story, like "St. Mawr," was written at Lawrence's New Mexico ranch in 1924, before the autumn chill came down; when composing these stories, Lawrence could sit out among the trees and "take down" the scenery as freshly as a painter work-ing outdoors. And "The Princess" is full of rich scenery: Law-rence was not only describing the landscapes and sky that he could see at the moment, but was also remembering horseback rides through the mountains as he wrote of Dollie Urquhart and Romero ascending the cold slopes through forests of aspen and spruce. Setting becomes symbol in no overt way, but gradually and masterfully. The countryside itself, as seen from the lower foothills, had moved the Princess to seek new experience, and as she goes up with Romero to the remotest heights, the hard masculine scenery becomes the symbol of what she is seeking.

In the cabin, she sleeps in the bunk while Romero beds down on the floor. She wakes up in the middle of the icy night, sees that the fire has gone out, and calls to Romero, who asks, "You want me to make you warm?" She says "Yes," though when he touches her she wants to scream; he is passionate and wild, and she is numbed and terrified. We have previously been told that she understood the Maupassant and Zola she had read, and even the *Decameron* and the *Nibelungenlied,* but that Dostoyevsky had been beyond her.

The next day, when she wants to go back, Romero says Americans "always want to do a man down," and she insists she is not an American. He is afraid of what she will tell when they return, but mostly he is puzzled by her admission that she hadn't enjoyed his love-making: "I don't care for that kind of thing." He keeps repeating, "You don't like last night? . . . You don't?" When finally it becomes clear to him that she had not enjoyed herself, he says "I make you," and takes away all her clothes except the pajamas she is wearing: the old, male vanity, futile but hopeful against the insurmountable barrier of frigidity.

The story works intensely toward its savage wild-west climax. Romero has a passionate time—"You sure are a pretty little white woman, small and pretty. . . . You sure won't act mean to me—you don't want to, I know you don't"—and when she stonily submits to him, he says "I sure don't mind hell fire . . . after this." And once he tells her that he will not let her go, that she called to him in the night, "and I've some right." It is the Lawrencean male, Hadrian of "You Touched Me," but this time a man closer to earth, the dark man wishing to possess the white princess. Lawrence docs not idealize Romero, whose half-civilized vulgarity is realistically shown, but he does recognize that Romero, who behaved with propriety until summoned and indeed until coldly rebuffed, has some rights. And although the Princess is not a satirized figure, she is not sympathetically drawn either: she is the latest in the Helena-Hermione series. And she has *willed* this sexual experience. She will not marry Romero, will not let him "conquer" her. When, in the succeeding days, she sometimes feels a bit roused while the man is slaking his passion, she hates him and wishes herself once more cool and intact. And after the Forest Service men kill Romero in a gun battle and find her in the cabin in pajamas, she tells them he had gone out of his mind. And that is the explanation she gives herself and others during her convalescence at the dude ranch:

The real affair was hushed up. The Princess departed east in a fortnight's time, in Miss Cummins' care. Apparently she had recovered herself entirely. She was the Princess, and a virgin intact.

But her bobbed hair was grey at the temples, and her eyes were a little mad. She was slightly crazy.

"Since my accident in the mountains, when a man went mad and shot my horse from under me, and my guide had to shoot him dead, I have never quite felt myself."

Later she married an elderly man, and seemed pleased.

✔ ✔ ✔ ✔

One of Lawrence's primary reasons for going to Taos was to learn the rituals of the Indians. He saw the festivals described in *Mornings in Mexico,* and Mrs. Luhan's Indian husband Tony told him much besides. All this went into *The Plumed Serpent*; Mabel Luhan has even complained that Lawrence "stole" the Taos experience and dramatized it in a Mexican setting. Professor Tindall casts an important light on the question by showing how much Mexican lore must have been taken by Lawrence from various books he is known to have read, including Prescott, Bernal Díaz, and—most significant of all—*Fundamentals of Old and New World Civilizations,* by Zelia Nuttal, whom the Lawrences had met in Mexico (she is caricatured in the minor rôle of Mrs. Norris in *The Plumed Serpent*). Professor Tindall shows how Lawrence borrowed from Mrs. Nuttal's work some of the gods of his pantheon and many of the designs and symbols in the novel: Professor Tindall thinks that Lawrence drew upon both Frazer and Mrs. Nuttal for the chapters "The First Water" and "The First Rain"; Mrs. Nuttal believed that the union "of above and below" was symbolized by the rainy season, that it was "the time of fertility and spiritual rebirth," as signified by the marriage of Kate and Cipriano in the rain. Professor Tindall further hypothesizes that Lawrence also read Lewis Spence's *Gods of Mexico,* which contains Aztec hymns resembling those in *The Plumed Serpent.*

Lawrence's book was begun early in 1923, apparently when he was living on the shores of Lake Chapala, and was finished early in 1925, during the Lawrences' second visit to Oaxaca. It is a curious comment upon *The Plumed Serpent* that when the book first came out in 1926, its American publisher listed it as a novel. Later that publisher, Alfred Knopf, put it under the category of *belles-lettres.*

Kate, the heroine of *The Plumed Serpent,* is the widow of an Irish politician whose fervent work for his cause brought about his early death; this is reminiscent of the Polish patriot who was Lydia Lensky's first husband in *The Rainbow.* Professor Tindall says in his *Susan* book that Dr. George Vaillant, Curator of Mexican Archeology at the American Museum of Natural History, told him that Kate is modelled after "the widow of a famous Harvard radical"—obviously John Reed. Frieda, in her indignant attack upon Tindall in the Easter 1940 issue of the short-lived and fantastic *Phoenix* magazine, denied this; she did not claim that she was herself Kate, but that she is Kate is apparent to anyone who knew Frieda Lawrence. Middleton Murry assumed that Lawrence does not appear in the novel because he had already resigned himself to death. This is a lurid assumption, although Lawrence strongly felt an aura of death in the air of Mexico, as his letters demonstrate, and he was critically ill during part of his stay there. But he is not unrepresented in the book, for he gives himself a Mexican incarnation as the revolutionary general, Cipriano. Frieda Lawrence has denied the Vaillant-Tindall story that Cipriano was actually "a prominent Indian general."

The other leading masculine character, Don Ramón, is generally believed to be José Vasconcelos, one-time follower of the revolutionist Carranza and later Minister of Public Education under Obregón. Carleton Beals, in his *Glass Houses,* indicates that Lawrence knew Vasconcelos. This mystic politician attempted, as Waldo Frank says, "to reintegrate the two wills of the Revolution by political means: his aim was to free the will of bread-and-power from North American obsession by linking it, for the first time, with the religious impulse of the people." This description would serve for the activity of Don Ramón Carrasco, as seen through Lawrence's imaginative vision. It is interesting to note that, like Russell and Murry and many other men Lawrence knew, Vasconcelos changed sides; he became one of the leaders of the clerical Sinarquista faction with the rather menacing official name of National Action Party.

Lawrence's severe Mexican illness is memorialized in the unfinished story, "The Flying Fish," which has been published in *Phoenix:* later, in Europe, Lawrence told the Brewsters that he would never finish it because it was written so close to the borderline of death. The story is a valuable commentary on *The Plumed Serpent* by virtue of its extreme difference from the novel; it presents another Mexico. The protagonist, who is lying ill there, gets a cablegram that summons him back to his ancestral estate in Derbyshire, a home full of legend that is described in a curiously beautiful version of Elizabethan English. Mexico dominates the first part of the fragment, and "the fatal greater day" of the dark races is contrasted with "the fussy, busy, lesser day of the white people"—but it is all presented as through a dream, or through the fever of a sick man's consciousness.

A different atmosphere pervades *The Plumed Serpent*—not the dreamy Mexico the man in "The Flying Fish" sees, but two quite different Mexicos: that of *Mornings in Mexico*, with a bright-colored painting of all the surface beauty of the place, and that of the mystic dark interior of the people and their ancient religions.

As for Lawrence's feeling himself dead or beyond reach—he appears rather flamboyantly in *The Plumed Serpent* as Don Cipriano, General Viedma, who works beside Don Ramón Carrasco in the religious revolution brought on by Don Ramón's determination to revive the ancient gods. Don Ramón is at the last the idealization of what Gerald Crich and Kangaroo, in their different ways, were not—the perfect friend, the successful leader, the individual who points the way to betterment.

When Kate comes to Mexico she first sees its horror, the blood and grime and filth of its surface. She goes to a bullfight. The two Americans who accompany her are as sickened as she is, but in American fashion stick it out for the "thrill," while she must flee. Kate meets the bearded little Cipriano and, subsequently, Don Ramón: they take her at once into the heart of their movement. The chief god in their pantheon is the plumed serpent Quetzalcoatl, whose name Lawrence originally intended to use as the title of the novel. When Kate goes down to Jalisco province, where Ramón has his hacienda, she sees the people under the spell of their new leaders: the peons stand in the courtyard, stand rigid with dilated eyes as they listen to Ramón chant the Quetzalcoatl hymns. The day finally comes when the people march into the churches and carry out the Christian paraphernalia.

Kate has one more experience of the physical horror so often found in Mexico when, in an unusually gruesome chapter, Don Ramón's hacienda is attacked by bandits and she helps fight them off. Later she is married to Cipriano in an ancient mystical ceremony, but does not deeply feel herself his wife. Half the time her rational, civilized soul is pulling away from all this weirdness and nonsense. Yet, partly because she is under the spell of Cipriano, she stays. In another ceremony Ramón and Cipriano in bright robes become gods of Mexico, and Kate in green becomes the goddess Malintzi.

The book is soaked in the actual Mexico, but the other Mexico, the Mexico of Lawrence's mind, is always present too. Oddly enough, two of Lawrence's most antipodal critics, Catherine Carswell and Professor Tindall, unite in declaring this Lawrence's greatest work. Lawrence himself had thought so when the book was finished, but his opinion soon changed. Mrs. Carswell finds *The Plumed Serpent* the greatest novel of Lawrence's generation because it creates a life-system. Professor Tindall thinks that the book is "art if not sense," and that in the Quetzalcoatl symbolism Lawrence at last found what T. S. Eliot says the true artist must find, an "objective correlative."

But at the last this is a question on which the reader must make up his own mind; the book will of course have to be weighed against all the rest of Lawrence's work.

It must be remembered that the revolution of Don Ramón and Cipriano—who, among other things is an Oxonian—is endowed with living qualities: Lawrence had such a passionate, emphatic feeling for the little dark man of his pantheon that Cipriano has a fairly consistent vitality, but Don Ramón is sometimes stodgily unbelievable. And in spite of the author's partial identification with Cipriano, Kate's struggle is Lawrence's own. He felt pulled toward the dark way of consciousness, and he also felt the resistance of his Europeanized mind. Kate is jealous of the mystic relationship between Don Ramón and Cipriano, but nevertheless stays with them after some feeble protests. Lawrence himself got out.

Professor Tindall has said he believes the book is "proto-fascist." The question of Fascism has been repeatedly raised in connection with Lawrence's work, and many critics besides Tindall have objected to Lawrence's absorption with ideas about leadership and "blood-knowledge." This question must be faced in any full evaluation of Lawrence's writing because it concerns the possible values of the way of life he, as a prophetic writer, was trying to establish.

And it must be said that some of Lawrence's doctrines certainly appear to resemble some of those of Fascism, though Lawrence himself would certainly never have become a Fascist in philosophy or in action. The first principle of Fascist action, suppression of civil liberties, would have been violently opposed by Lawrence in actual life. And the important racial and nationalistic dogmas of Nazi-like philosophies find no parallel in Lawrence's work. The brand of mystic leadership that held Lawrence's imagination in thrall for a time was a religious concept of a different kind from the *Führerprinzip* either in motive, as outlined in *Mein Kampf*, or in actuality, as history has seen it work out. Fascist sympathizers of course tried to claim Lawrence: there was, for example, a curious article in the *New Mexico Quarterly Review* not long before Pearl Harbor, in which a history instructor at New York University, Stebleton H. Nulle, not only said that Lawrence was like Hitler but also

congratulated him on the supposed resemblance. A rather ineffective rejoinder to this article appeared in a later issue. The
best answer to those who, sympathetically or not, call Lawrence
a Fascist, was made by a man equipped to be an authority on
Nazism—Franz Schoenberner, editor until 1933 of the famous
German liberal weekly, *Simplicissimus*. Schoenberner, who knew
Lawrence personally, pointed out in his *Confessions of A European Intellectual* (1946) that, as the present volume has already
indicated, the resemblance of some of Lawrence's doctrines to
Fascism was only on the surface: although *The Plumed Serpent*
and some of Lawrence's other books at times "came dangerously
near to that kind of 'myth' which in a much cheaper edition was
so eagerly exploited by the Nazi prophets," Lawrence, unlike
Knut Hamsun and other authentic European Fascist-intellectuals,
"was not a nihilist and defeatest, a bitter, disappointed detractor
of life and mankind. He had faith and flame, an immeasurable
spiritual passion, an ardent belief in life and man and all the
great forces in nature, of which he felt himself a part." This is
a different picture from those Franz Schoenberner paints of the
Nazis whom he watched as they gradually took over Germany.
He believes that it will be a good thing when Lawrence's works
become a regular part of the British school curriculum, for
"aside from his artistic values and his somewhat dubious philosophy, D. H. Lawrence always will remain an outstanding example of the highest moral courage, of the purest sincerity and of
untrammeled inner freedom"—hardly the attributes of a Fascist.

After *The Plumed Serpent*, Lawrence got beyond his interest
in the power-urge; this was his last novel idealizing it. Two
years after publication of that book, he said in a letter to Witter
Bynner, "The leader of men is a back number. After all, at the
back of the hero is the militant ideal: and the militant ideal or
ideal militant seems to me also a cold egg . . . the leader-cum-
follower relationship is a bore. And the new relationship will be
some sort of tenderness, sensitive, between men and men and
between men and women, and not the one up one down, lead
on I follow, *ich dien* sort of business. So you see I'm becoming
a lamb at last. . . ."

It must be remembered that Lawrence had for a long time
looked upon himself as a potential leader of men, pointing

toward a new way of life. He had hoped to make a beginning with the joint lectures he and Bertrand Russell had once planned, and it will be recalled that Lawrence and Murry and others had discussed the founding of a colony. Lawrence had at last felt that this could be established in New Mexico, but of all his English friends, only one (Dorothy Brett) was willing to follow him there. *The Plumed Serpent* was the last manifestation of a ten years' dream. The leadership idea became indeed a cold egg.

So far as primitivism is concerned, it should be remembered that Lawrence was a man disgusted with the mechanism of civilization, a man who would not have used its instruments as even the most mystical Nazis have done. His extolling of "blood knowledge" was not an advocation that what he called "mind knowledge" should be annihilated; on the contrary, he merely felt that civilization had gone too far in the direction of cerebral activity and needed a strong dose of its opposite to help restore the balance. Fascists hate knowledge, intellectual activity, and enlightenment, because these things make for freedom of the mind and create difficulties in the way of holding their followers and victims in check. However wrong Lawrence might have been, he never went to this extreme: it was not the acquisition of knowledge or the activity of the intellect that he hated, but the *perversion* of these processes.

Yet *The Plumed Serpent* confronts many of its readers with an experience that is often found in Lawrence: although the idea of the novel, and the people in it, may not be satisfactory to the reader, he may find the writing superb.

What is the secret of Lawrence's vision, and how is it that in spite of frequently unsympathetic subject-matter, Lawrence can touch his pages so brightly to life? Once he gives an inkling of his secret, in the chapter called "The Novel," in *Reflections on the Death of a Porcupine*. He reveals there his sense of the "quickness" of living things. This is a feeling for "the God-flame in things" as opposed to the deadness in them; quickness "seems to consist in an odd sort of fluid, changing, grotesque or beautiful relatedness." A table in the room where he is writing is dead: "It doesn't even weakly exist. And there is a ridiculous little iron stove, which for some unknown reason is quick . . .

and there is a sleeping cat, very quick. And a glass lamp that, alas, is dead." Lawrence believed that the man in the novel "must have a quick relatedness to all the other things in the novel: snow, bed-bugs, sunshine, the phallus, trains, silk-hats, cats, sorrow, people, food, diphtheria, fuchsias, stars, ideas, God, tooth-paste, lightning, and toilet-paper. He must be in quick relation to all these things. What he says and does must be relative to them all."

With Lawrence's explanation in mind, it is possible to understand how his writing, as writing, can charm in places where the subject-matter does not. To take an example of his writing power from *The Plumed Serpent*, there is the description of Kate sitting alone on a verandah—a visiting European woman who feels an essential mystery in Mexico:

Morning! Brilliant sun pouring into the patio, on the hibiscus flowers and the fluttering yellow and green rags of the banana trees. Birds swiftly coming and going, with tropical suddenness. In the dense shadow of the mango grove, white-clad Indians going like ghosts. The sense of fierce sun and almost more impressive, of dark, intense shadow.

The "feel" of Mexico is there, in Lawrence's loose and hastily written but essentially living prose. Life as we know it moves about Kate as she sits on that verandah, and when, a few sentences later, "silently appears an old man with one egg held up mysteriously, like some symbol," we know that the old man, his gesture, and the atmosphere surrounding him have been given to us in an unforgettable way.

Though *The Plumed Serpent* may be in some ways a diffused and obscurantist story, it gives its readers Mexico—all Mexico's vibrant colors, its thick heat, its smashing rains, its population drifting as in a dream through the almost sinister vegetation or along the shores of the chalk-colored lakes. Here is Lawrence's power: almost any passage picked from the book has the gleaming magic that is style in the truest sense—not merely individuality, though that is part of great writing when it is not purely eccentric—not merely individuality, but also wonder, and vision, and a poetry capable of kindling life on the printed page.

PART FOUR

THE LAST SCENE IS EUROPE, A EUROPE MIDWAY between two exhausting wars.

Lawrence left America for the last time when he and Frieda sailed from New York on the S. S. *Resolute* on September 24, 1925. They were in England by the end of the month. Lawrence once again found that he could not bear his native land, and within a few weeks he and Frieda were in Baden-Baden. In the middle of November they settled at the Villa Bernarda at Spotorno, near Genoa, which remained their home until the following April. In May 1926 they rented the Villa Mirenda at Scandicci, in the hills above Florence. They stayed at the Villa Mirenda for two years, with occasional visits to nearby countries—visits which will be mentioned later at appropriate places in the text.

After leaving the Villa Mirenda, the Lawrences never again had a place suggesting permanence. During the last two years of Lawrence's life they lived for brief spells in various countries—in Switzerland, Austria, and Germany and in the Balearic Islands. Lawrence died in France, at Vence near the southern coast, on March 2, 1930.

During that last phase of his life and of his writing career, he produced several of his most remarkable works, including *Lady Chatterley's Lover, The Escaped Cock,* and such poems as "Bavarian Gentians" and "The Ship of Death." He was ill oftener than he had been before, and he was subject to the exasperation of having the manuscript of a volume of poems seized in the mails and of having the London exhibition of his pictures depleted when Scotland Yard directed a dozen policemen to take away thirteen of the paintings.

His disgust with mankind manifested itself from time to time as it had during the war. In a mood of discouragement in July 1926, he told his British publisher that he did not wish to write any more books: "There are so many, and such a small demand for what there are. So why add to the burden and waste one's vitality over it." He was doing no work at this time except for "an occasional scrap of article," and he could live cheaply in Italy. Yet it was after this statement that he wrote *Lady Chatterley's Lover* as well as a good many stories and poems.

The leadership ideal of his third phase as a writer had proved to be a disappointment, as we have seen—"a cold egg"—and Lawrence no longer sought exalted male comradeship. It was at this period, incidentally, that he realized the best of friendship in the steady, unemotional relationships with such men as Earl Brewster, Aldous Huxley, and Richard Aldington. These men had known him for a long while and had remained his good friends; they did not always agree with his ideas, any more than he agreed with theirs; but they were friends. They saw his worth and they valued him, as man and artist.

Frieda was still with him, more necessary than ever. It is significant that his two most important fictional pieces during this period—*Lady Chatterley's Lover* and *The Escaped Cock*—showed how the man who was disillusioned with the world could find his fulfillment in a woman.

The stories Lawrence wrote during the last phase of his New World sojourn and after his final return to Europe, those collected in *The Woman Who Rode Away*, emphasize the man-woman relationship. This in its various aspects is the dominant theme in the book, which was published in both New York and London in May 1928.

The title story, "The Woman Who Rode Away," was written in New Mexico in 1924, during the summer in which "St. Mawr" and "The Princess" were also composed. In those two stories, the landscape of the Southwest had a powerful effect upon the women who came to it; in "The Woman Who Rode Away," the heroine has already lived for years in Old Mexico and goes questing for a remoter landscape and experience. The American woman, partly suggestive of Mabel Luhan, leaves the little outpost of civilization where she lives, and goes out to a mystic "lost" tribe of Aztec descendants who take her, not against her will, as a sacrifice. These Indians, hidden in a valley behind almost inaccessible rock barriers, feel that her coming is a sign that the magic and mastery the whites have taken from them will be restored. The moon will come back to the Indians' grasslands and the sun will follow, and the Indians will again have the sun on their right hand, the moon on their left. The white woman goes in a dream-like state to a blood-sacrifice that is piercingly described: the glittering-eyed naked priests in the cave watch the sun descend as they await the moment to kill the woman who has ridden away from the white men.

Lawrence did not always combine fable and philosophy so smoothly. The story, written while *The Plumed Serpent* was in progress, is an epitome of the central theme of that novel. And although it lacks the magnificent orchestration of *The Plumed Serpent*, "The Woman Who Rode Away" is not without stylistic power, and within the world created in this story, the outcome is more believable than that of *The Plumed Serpent*, with its realistic European woman in a semi-realistic Mexico; in the short story, the magic atmosphere of fable is dominant throughout.

Several tales in *The Woman Who Rode Away* reflect the Lawrence-Murry conflict of 1924-25. The two men had been virtually estranged for several years after the war, but Murry's enthusiasm for *Fantasia of the Unconscious* drew them together again. Murry in 1923 founded the *Adelphi* for Lawrence: he regarded himself as merely a *locum tenens*, a place-holder, until Lawrence should arrive and take over the magazine and make it into an organ for *Fantasia* doctrines. Lawrence, in Mexico, was now warm, now cold, to the idea; he had not been too enthusiastic about the previous venture of the sort in which he and the "lieutenant" had been involved, with Katherine Mansfield, during the war—the magazine which lasted for three issues and was called the *Signature*. But Lawrence was at last lured out of the New World, preceded by Frieda, with whom he had quarreled violently.

Murry reports that when Lawrence arrived in London in the early winter of 1923, his face "had a greenish pallor" and his first words were "I can't bear it." Murry interpreted this greenness of countenance and despair of expression to mean that Lawrence was sickened by the sight of "nightmarish" London: Catherine Carswell indicates in *The Savage Pilgrimage* that Lawrence's greenish look and bitter statement were caused by revulsion over the signs of "chumminess" between Murry and Frieda, and it is now known, from parts of Murry's diary which have been published posthumously, that Frieda wished to become Murry's mistress at this time, but that out of loyalty to Lawrence he rejected her (they became lovers for a while in France after Lawrence's death).

Lawrence insisted that the *Adelphi* should blast and attack everything, and when Murry refused to consider this seriously, Lawrence tried to persuade him to come to New Mexico. Whether or not Murry promised to go, and the extent of his possible commitment, has been the subject of a good deal of debate, including the debate Murry carried on with himself in his books and articles. In any event, the Lawrences went to Strasbourg and Baden-Baden and then to Paris, before returning to America in March 1924. And after a period of fairly amicable correspondence between the two men, Lawrence sent Murry a vitriolic letter from Mexico the following January, about the time he was completing *The Plumed Serpent* and was on the edge of an almost fatal illness. He recalled the famous, repulsive "last supper" at the Café Royal the year before, when Murry in the presence of most of Lawrence's London friends had said he loved Lawrence, but could not promise never to betray him; now Lawrence wanted to put an end to the Jesus-Judas condition the two men found themselves in. They met once more, during Lawrence's next visit to England later in 1925, and Murry told Lawrence (this is Murry's own admission) that Judas was the only disciple who understood Jesus. Judas, he said, killed himself because the crucifixion proved futile; the "betrayal" was an invention of men "who did not understand" what was between Jesus and the Judas who was "the broken-hearted lover." Murry thinks this "impressed" Lawrence, but shortly afterward he was again irritated with Murry for not visiting him in Italy at the time when, on doctor's orders, the second Mrs. Murry could not travel.

The foregoing information is necessary to a complete understanding of four of the stories in *The Woman Who Rode Away:* "The Border Line," "Jimmy and the Desperate Woman," "The Last Laugh," and "Smile."

"The Border Line," first published in a magazine in the fall of 1924, is based upon the Lawrences' trip to Germany earlier that year. Katherine Farquhar, the German woman who has been married to two Englishmen, is distinctly Frieda, and the two men in the story are phases of Lawrence and Murry. Katherine's first husband, a "red-haired fighting Celt," has been killed in the war, and Katherine has married his friend Philip, who could "give off a great sense of warmth and offering, like a dog when it loves you. . . . And Katherine, after feeling cool about him and rather despising him for years, at last fell under the spell of the dark, insidious fellow." But as she crosses the Channel to the Continent, she comes to believe that her first husband, Alan, is not really dead and that she is going to meet him. She is filled with horror as her train crosses the dismal Marne country; she wearily goes to sleep, and upon waking realizes that whatever feeling she has for her second husband is only an illusion. That night in Strasbourg she walks the icy streets, seeing the overhanging, high-gabled houses she had known as a child, and the cathedral rising ghost-like in the darkness, "built of reddish stone, that had a flush in the night, like dark flesh. . . . And dimly she realized that behind all the ashy pallor and sulphur of our civilization, lurks the great blood-creature waiting, implacable and eternal, ready at last to crush our white bitterness and let the shadowy blood move erect once more, in a new implacable pride and strength. Even out of the lower heavens looms the great blood-dusky Thing, blotting out the Cross it was supposed to exalt."

She sees a man standing in the cathedral square and knows at once it is Alan. He says nothing, but puts his hand on her arm, as he used to do, with the air of authority she had always fought against. He is a stranger, his face more duskily ruddy than Alan's, yet he is Alan. She sees him again in Baden-Baden, after she has been joined by her second husband, who now looks yellowish and defeated. Philip cannot get warm; he stays in bed, chattering, while Katherine goes out to the edge of the Black Forest to look for Alan, whose presence she has felt there. After his appearance one day, "among the rocks he made love to her, and took her in the silent passion of a husband, took a complete possession of her." The next night, with Philip dying, Alan silently returns and takes Philip's hands from around Katherine's neck:

> Philip unfurled his lips and showed his big teeth in a ghastly grin of death. Katherine felt his body convulse in strange throes under her hands, then go inert. He was dead. And on his face was a sickly grin of a thief caught in the very act.
> But Alan drew her away, drew her to the other bed, in the silent passion of a husband come back from a very long journey.

This was Lawrence's first ghost story, and it is not surprising that, like his subsequent ghost stories, it is sexual. The supernatural is of course used only in a symbolic way: Lawrence in this story asserts the reunion with his wife, and the dominance of his blood-consciousness theories as symbolized here by the Germanic old cathedral, and he once more "kills off" what Murry stood for.

But he was not altogether finished with Murry, whom he lampooned in the three other stories previously referred to. "Jimmy and the Desperate Woman" makes Murry look the most ridiculous, and "Smile" prods him the most cruelly; he does not escape being satirized in "The Last Laugh," a laugh of course at Murry's expense. (After reading the first edition of the present book, John Murry wrote to the author about Lawrence's satiric anti-Murry stories: "These, at the time, seemed to me just an outrage. And I still think they sprang from the worst and most *dishonest* part of L. Considering what the real situation had been, they strike me still as a very shabby sort of revenge"— a cryptic reference to Murry's loyalty to Lawrence in rejecting Frieda's advances.)

In the first of these other anti-Murry stories, "Jimmy and the Desperate Woman," Jimmy is the editor of a highbrow magazine whose personalized, extremely candid editorials bring him hosts of admirers. Women say of him, "He is very fine and strong somewhere, but he does need a level-headed woman to look after him." He has a face "like the face of the laughing faun in one of the faun's unlaughing, moody moments," and he thinks of himself as "a sort of Martyred Saint Sebastian." The portrait resembles that of Dennis Burlap, the unctuous little editor with the enigmatic smile in Aldous Huxley's *Point Counter Point*, a character also based on Murry. In Lawrence's story, Jimmy publishes some poetry by an ex-school teacher unhappily married to a collier. He arranges to visit her after giving a lecture in a city near her home, a lecture on Men in Books and Men in Life—"Naturally, men in books came first." When Jimmy meets the embittered Mrs. Pinnegar, he suggests that she and her little girl leave the husband, who is carrying on with another woman, and come to live with him in London; after the divorce, he and Emily can be married. Jimmy says this "more to himself than to the woman"; it is as if the whole thing "were merely an interior problem of his own." He is brought up against external reality when Pinnegar comes home from the pit. There is another of those unforgettable Lawrencean scenes in which the man strips himself to the waist and the woman washes the coal grime off him: it is the collier's ritual, and Jimmy sits by, "excluded." Later, Pinnegar discusses his domestic affairs with Jimmy: his wife may go, if she wishes to, and take the child. Pinnegar is an Aaron Sisson who stayed at home—he wants at all costs to have a woman who will give in to him. If he can't find such a woman at home, he'll find her elsewhere. Jimmy arranges with Mrs. Pinnegar to meet him in London in a few days, and he returns home. A friend in whom he confides tells him he is a fool, and Jimmy quakes. He sends Mrs. Pinnegar a letter saying that perhaps they have been precipitate and that she had better not come if she feels any reservations. Her telegraphed answer is that she and the child will arrive on the scheduled day. Jimmy greets them with a sickly grin, but when he feels the presence of her husband about her, this goes to his head like neat whisky. "Which of the two would fall before him with a greater fall—the woman, or the man, her husband?"

"The Last Laugh" is not easy to explicate. It may be taken, on the surface, as a story with supernatural elements whose elucidation is not strictly necessary to the enjoyment of the story, or it may be studied for its Lawrencean meaning. Lawrence himself appears at the beginning of it, without disguise, with his red beard and his nickname "Lorenzo," bidding two guests farewell after a party in Hampstead that breaks up at the witching hour. He might almost be the sorcerer who magically causes the strange subsequent events, and indeed, as the author who sets and keeps the story in motion, he is. The two people Lorenzo is bidding goodnight, Miss James and Mr. Marchbanks, are obviously Dorothy Brett, with the listening-machine she carried because of her deafness, and Murry, described as "a sort of faun on the Cross, with all the malice of the complication." Lorenzo, seeing new-fallen snow, ironically says "A new world," and Marchbanks-Murry typically imposes his artificial standards: "It's only whitewash!" As he and the cool, virginal Miss James, who have a platonic relationship, walk downhill in the fresh snow, Marchbanks—with "a curious, baffled grin on his smooth, cream-coloured face"—insists that he can hear someone laughing. She puts on her machine, but cannot hear this, though later she sees or hallucinates a figure in some nearby holly bushes. Miss James and Marchbanks have meanwhile been joined by a young policeman; Marchbanks now and then laughs wildly, and he goes in "quick, wolf-like" pursuit of the source of the laughter he has been hearing. He talks for a few moments to a woman at the door of a strange house; she extends a sexual invitation and he immediately enters, leaving the policeman to escort Miss James home. On the way, she hears voices and sees the laughing, dark face of the figure in the pagan holly bush; and lightning twitches through the falling snow. The policeman is frightened: a window has been broken in a nearby church, and Miss James can hear laughter coming from the interior. She sees pieces of paper, leaves of books, and at last the altar-cloth come flying out the window. Even the policeman can hear wild, gay music from the organ, and Miss

James smells almond blossoms on a sudden, warm, spring-like wind. She lets the policeman, who is cold with terror, come into her house to warm himself at the fire; she tells him not to go upstairs, and she ascends, to retire. In the morning she laughs as she examines the pictures she has painted before her occult experience, and she discovers that she can hear perfectly when the servant comes up to tell her that the young policeman is still in the parlor, unable to move. When Marchbanks arrives, he and Miss James question the young policeman, one of whose feet has become "curiously clubbed, like the weird paw of some animal." Miss James hears the laughter again, and then Marchbanks is caught in it once more, he cries out "like a shot animal," and his face becomes fixed in a grin "chiefly agony but partly wild recognition," and he says "I knew it was he!" and falls writhing on the floor and dies. "There was a faint smell of almond blossom in the air."

Students of the occult will recognize some familiar symptoms, both of lycanthropy and of the poltergeist influence. Obviously, the three people involved have been brushed by a supernatural experience: in some ways this is reminiscent of E. M. Forster's "The Story of a Panic," in which a boy becomes possessed of the Pan spirit during a conventional English picnic in Italy, and it is also like some of the horror stories by Arthur Machen. In Lawrence's tale, Marchbanks is possessed and killed by the demon that has broken loose in Hampstead that night, while Miss James is strangely exalted by the whole experience. The young policeman who has come into their orbit has been only touched by the demon in passing; his transmogrification is but partial. Miss James appears to recognize the spirit that is causing all the trouble, and seems pleased, and Marchbanks before he dies says "I knew it was he!" Since this is the kind of story that most tormentingly invites conjecture, it is difficult to avoid speculation as to the "he" that has caused the turbulence: is it the red-bearded Lorenzo to whom the aspect of the night was, ironically, "a new world"? It is quite possible that Lawrence playfully wrote this story as a fable symbolizing his relationship to the people involved, and to the Church, whose effects he fluttered—as, in *The Plumed Serpent*, he marshalled the followers of Don Ramón and Cipriano and had them denude the Mexican churches of their Christian furniture. A further clue might be found in the almond-blossom odors that blow through the story. The almond has a phallic significance in Frazer, from whom, as we have seen, Lawrence frequently borrowed his symbols. In the discussion of "The Myth and Ritual of Attis" in *The Golden Bough,* Frazer mentions that, in one of the Phrygian myths, Attis was born to a virgin "who conceived by putting a ripe almond or pomegranate in her bosom. Indeed in the Phrygian cosmology an almond figured as the father of all things, perhaps because its delicate lilac blossom is one of the first heralds of spring, appearing on the bare boughs before the leaves have opened." Perhaps Marchbanks has to be killed because he refuses to recognize the great natural powers; he sees the snow as whitewash, an artificial thing, and he betrays the phallic mysteries by giving himself too readily to mechanical sexual usage.

"Smile" was Lawrence's cruelest caricature of Murry. "Smile" is quite short, and the central character is not so fully developed as that of "Jimmy and the Desperate Woman," but the story is more incisive. The situation, like that of "Jimmy," derives in part from an actual incident, in this instance from a painful experience in Murry's life. In the story he appears as Matthew, first seen on a train crossing Europe after receiving a telegram to the effect that his wife is critically ill: "His dark, handsome, clean-shaven face would have done for Christ on the Cross, with the thick black eyebrows tilted in the dazed agony." When he arrives at the retreat of the Blue Sisters, in Italy, he learns that Ophelia has died. When he sees her laid out, he wants to laugh: an "extraordinary" smile breaks out on his face, and the nuns involuntarily reflect it on their own faces. Later they see him, "in a melancholy overcoat," forlornly pacing the corridor, and he says he has mislaid his hat: "He made a desperate, moving sweep with his arm, and never was man more utterly smileless."

This story is in part a fictionalized version of the death of Katherine Mansfield at the Gurdjieff Institute at Fontainebleau in 1923. Like the woman in the story, Katherine Mansfield had left her husband several times and had at last found a retreat. Murry had made several appeals to her to allow him to visit Fontainebleau, and at last she granted him permission when the

Institute was to have a formal inauguration ceremony. Katherine Mansfield, whose health had apparently been improving, died the night of Murry's arrival: she and Murry had just said good-night to the other members of the colony and were going upstairs to her room when she began to cough; as she arrived at her room she coughed blood, and in half an hour she was dead. When Lawrence had first heard of her death he had written Murry a letter of condolence without sentimentalism: "The dead don't die. They look on and help." Three years later, Lawrence turned Katherine Mansfield's death into fiction, after the final break with Murry—when Murry in early 1926, did not come out to Italy. The story "Smile" appeared in a magazine the following June, but it must have been written early in the year; the setting suggests the Genoa region where the Lawrences lived until they moved to Florence in April. After this last break, there was only occasional correspondence between Lawrence and Murry, usually acrid on Lawrence's side. The exchange ended at last in May 1929, when Murry, after hearing that Lawrence had not long to live, proposed visiting him in Mallorca; Lawrence replied that he had no idea of dying yet, and that he and Murry were too dissonant to carry on a friendship: "It is no good our meeting—even when we are immortal spirits, we shall dwell in different Hades."

Murry, whose twitchings from doctrine to doctrine and whose continual public disrobing of the soul made him fair game for satire (Huxley and Lawrence) as well as for serious censure (J.W.N. Sullivan and Hugh I'Anson Fausset), was not the only one of Lawrence's acquaintances to be lampooned in *The Woman Who Rode Away*. Sir Compton Mackenzie, a man who loves islands, is the central figure in "The Man Who Loved Islands." This is a simple story of a man who isolates himself more and more from humanity, going from island to island until at last he is left alone with the overwhelming and murderous elements. It is really more of an idea of Mackenzie than a character study, but after it appeared in the *London Mercury* of August 1927, it caused Lawrence some difficulty. He and Mackenzie were both published in England by Martin Secker; Lawrence told Mabel Luhan, "Compton Mackenzie, after swallowing one story in which he appeared as a character, was mortally offended by another more recent one in which I used him, and Secker wants me not to print it in a book." And although Secker omitted it from the English edition (Knopf included it in the American), he did not leave it out of the posthumous volume of short stories, *The Lovely Lady*, which he brought out in 1933, when he was no longer Mackenzie's publisher. Compton Mackenzie, who found Lawrence likable but often difficult, has told the author of the present volume that Lawrence's stories give a distorted view of many of his acquaintances because "he had a trick of describing a person's setting or background vividly, and then putting into the setting an ectoplasm entirely of his own creation." Norman Douglas and other victims of Lawrence's method have made similar complaints. Sir Compton says that those who know these victims can see the stories only as falsifications, though the stories may have artistic validity for the reader who comes to them afresh. (The other story Lawrence referred to which Mackenzie "swallowed" was "Two Blue Birds.")

As to the story "Glad Ghosts," Lawrence Clark Powell in his "descriptive catalogue" of *The Manuscripts of D. H. Lawrence* (1937) identified the principal characters as the Hon. Herbert Asquith (whom Powell wrongly called "Sir Herbert") and Lady Cynthia Asquith; the name Lathkill is indeed so suggestive of Asquith that it is no wonder Lawrence felt the story would perhaps be unsuitable for Lady Cynthia's anthology, *The Ghost Book*. When this anthology appeared in October 1926, it contained instead Lawrence's "The Rocking-Horse Winner."

"Glad Ghosts" is a first-person tale, whose narrator is a signally independent man: "As for me, I knew that, like a sansculotte, I should never be king till breeches were off. . . . Most people are just another species to me. They might as well be turkeys." He has known at the Twaithe [Slade] art school an aristocratic girl named Carlotta Fell, who has married Lord Lathkill, of a family noted for ill-luck. The narrator, Mark Morier, sees the pair of them over the years, as he comes back to England now and then on his travels. The couple is not unsimilar to Lady Daphne and her husband in "The Ladybird"— and, like Basil Bingham in that story, Lathkill comes from the war wounded. The Lathkill bad fortune hagrides him and Carlotta: two of their children are killed in an accident, and another dies of illness. The next time Morier is in England he goes to visit the Lathkills, somewhat reluctantly, but upon their strong urging, at their Derbyshire estate. Carlotta, to whom Morier is strongly attracted, is not eager to live; she "needs help." The place has an aura of death, and Morier is put in the ghost room. He is told that he may tempt the family apparition to visit him, and that her visits are always followed by an upturn in the family fortunes—not meaning money. At dinner there is a rather mad colonel with a somnambulistic young wife; that evening the colonel tries to evoke the spirit of his former wife, in vain. But the Lathkill ghost, described in advance as "gratifying," is wandering that night, and there is a pervading scent, as of plum-blossom: "I know she came. I know she came, even as a woman, to my man. But the knowledge is darkly naked as the event. I only know, it was so. In the deep of sleep a call was called from the deeps of me, and answered in the deeps, by a woman among women. Breasts or thighs or face, I remember not a touch, no, nor a movement of my own. It is all complete in the profundity of darkness. . . . I shall never know if it was a ghost, some sweet spirit from the innermost of the ever-deepening cosmos; or a woman, a very woman, as the silkiness of my limbs seems to attest; or a dream, a hallucination!" In the morning Morier leaves, with Lord Lathkill telling him he will never really go away from them, and Carlotta saying "At last it was perfect!" She seems again so beautiful, "as if it were the ghost again, and I was far down the deeps of consciousness." And the next autumn, when Morier is again overseas, he receives a letter from Lord Lathkill; Carlotta has had a son, and one of the young plum trees has come into bloom out of season— and the colonel's wife has had a daughter. Lathkill says, "I have peace upon my bones, and if the world is going to come to a violent and untimely end, as prophets aver, I feel the house of Lathkill will survive, built upon our ghost."

Once again a Lawrence ghost story—if this really is a ghost story—is also a sex story. Lawrence congratulated the Brewsters for letting their daughter read it, because it "treats sex *honestly.*" It is noteworthy that the plum-blossom scent is used as a kind of substitute for the almond-blossoms of "The Last Laugh."

Richard Aldington, in his introduction to a Penguin edition of *The Woman Who Rode Away*, says that "if the identification [by Powell] of the main characters [in "Glad Ghosts"] is correct, the finale of the story was a piece of reckless impudence."

In contrast with the occult tales in *The Woman Who Rode Away*, "None of That" is a naturalistic story, a variant of the "Princess" theme: Ethel Cane in the story is a wealthy American girl in Mexico, and like many of Lawrence's heroines she is sexless—she wants none of *that*. When she sees Cuesta in the bull ring, dressed in pink and silver and playing skillfully with the bull, she is fascinated, as the woman in Hemingway's *The Sun Also Rises* is fascinated by a younger matador: once again Lawrence and Hemingway, whose "The Prussian Officer" and "A Simple Enquiry" have certain resemblances, indicate that they have elements of vision in common as they see modern men and women acting out the themes of love and death. The woman in the Hemingway story and the one in the Lawrence story react in the same way to the grace and skill of the bullfighter as he makes those athletic gestures that in the face of possible death are supremely functional. But the woman in the Lawrence story has been attracted by a man who long ago has lost the innocence of Hemingway's neophyte; Cuesta in "None of That" lures Ethel Cane to his house one night and turns her over to his bullfight gang, telling them not to bruise her. Yet bruises are discovered on her body at the inquest held after she poisons herself. But, the Mexican who is telling the story says, "there was another revolution, and in the hubbub this affair was dropped." Ethel left Cuesta half her fortune in a will made ten days before her death, and the will was declared valid.

Lawrence kept himself out of this story, which is as objective as a tale by Maupassant, yet in the long line of Lawrence characters who have been destroyed because they denied or mechanized the forces of sex, Ethel Cane has a definite place.

Two light-comedy pieces are also contained in *The Woman Who Rode Away*, "In Love" and "Two Blue Birds." The first is a trivial story of a young girl who shrinks away from the physical love-making of her fiancé and then decides she will have to put up with it. The story as it appears in its final form was considerably revised from a manuscript entitled "More Modern Love," which suggests the possibility that it was written at an earlier period.

"Two Blue Birds" is a satiric little story of the jealousy of a rather sexless wife over her rather sexless husband and his rather sexless secretary. It has the tone of the shorter pieces Lawrence was to write hereafter, those collected in *The Lovely Lady*. "Two Blue Birds" makes no demands upon Lawrence's prose skill—indeed, it is told in a rather chirping, blue-bird style— but it is an entertaining little episode.

"Sun" tells of a bored American woman who learns to love the sun by lying naked on the rocky ledge of a Mediterranean island. Like so many American women, she has found life in a city apartment deathlike; the doctors have recommended that she leave New York and get into the sun. Her business-man husband solemnly lets her and their little boy depart. On the Mediterranean island, amid almond trees blossoming like pink snow, a new life begins for Juliet. She finds a place to lie naked under the sun, her new lover, and all nature collaborates; there is some wonderfully phallic scenery, particularly "one cypress tree, with a pallid, thick trunk, and a tip that leaned over, flexibly, up in the blue. It stood like a guardian looking to sea; or a low, silvery candle whose huge flame was darkness against light: earth sending up her proud tongue of gleam." Juliet feels the sun penetrate her, pulse inside her, fill her with warmth. When she returns to the house she has rented, she makes her little boy take off his clothes on the terrace, and this frightens him. Then, in one of those passages that continually lift Lawrence above his contemporaries, she rolls an orange to the child "across the red tiles, and with his soft, unformed little body he toddled after it. Then immediately he had it, he dropped it because it felt strange against his flesh. And he looked back at her, querulous, wrinkling his face to cry, frightened because he was stark."

Juliet's life cannot remain idyllic: one day her husband appears, pale, and smelling of the city, abashed before her gold nakedness. He has taken a month's vacation. She tells him she cannot go back to East Forty-Seventh, and he says she may stay on the island as long as she wants; he will join her on his vacations. She privately contrasts her husband with a peasant she has seen on the island, with whom she has exchanged some intense looks:

Ripe now, and brown-rosy all over with the sun, and with a heart like a fallen rose, she had wanted to go down to the hot, shy peasant and bear his child. Her sentiments had fallen like petals. She had seen the flushed blood in the burnt face, and the flame in the southern blue eyes, and the answer in her had been a gush of fire. He would have been a procreative sun-bath to her, and she wanted it.
Nevertheless, her next child would be Maurice's. The fatal chain of continuity would cause it.

"Sun" was written at the villa the Lawrences were living in at Spotorno, near Genoa, at the end of 1925. The story is a repository of many important Lawrencean symbols. First, he uses the Sicily-like island as opposed to New York, to show the advantage of being up at a villa rather than down in a city. Second, and most central, the sun is the giver of life and the nourisher of the mysteries of sex. This is not only the dark-hearted sun Count Dionys told the beautiful, pale English-woman about in "The Ladybird," but it is also the sun that was the preserver of life in Lawrence himself, a tuberculous man who needed to live in its radiance. Lawrence in his last phase adopted the sun-worship of the ancients: the conclusion of his last completed book, *Apocalypse*, is a hymn to the sun. And the story called "Sun" has other symbols—the almond blossoms that figured so importantly in "The Last Laugh"; the cypress tree which Juliet lies under, the nearby "contorted" cactus plants, and the snakes she occasionally sees. Above all, there is the peasant: Lawrence in his last period glorified the Mediterranean peasants, with whom he had felt a kinship since *Twilight in Italy*, as the men and women who were best living out the sentence of civilization. "Sun" has all these elements, brought together with imaginative power and superior writing skill. The version published in *The Woman Who Rode Away* was somewhat milder, in its sexual references, than the expanded text published as a limited-edition book by the Black Sun Press in 1928.

Lawrence wrote a short novel during this period, *The Virgin and the Gipsy*, and although it was completed early in 1926, it was not published until after his death. When it came out in 1930, the book carried a publisher's note which stated, "This work lacks the author's final revision, and has been printed from the manuscript exactly as it stands."

The Virgin and the Gipsy resembles the fable at the center of *Lady Chatterley's Lover:* the relationship of the vicar's daughter and the gipsy is essentially that of Connie Chatterley and Mellors. The flood scene in *The Virgin and the Gipsy* has correspondences with an earlier story, "The Horse Dealer's Daughter" in *England, My England;* in each instance there is a girl who narrowly escapes drowning and is rescued by a man who gives her the touch of love.

Lawrence turned back to the Midlands for the setting of *The Virgin and the Gipsy:* the stony hill-country of Derbyshire frames the story. The vicar's daughter and the gipsy have known each other slightly and have, in the Lawrence tradition, indulged in an intense ocular intercourse before the perilous flood brings them together forever and separates them forever. The background of the story is filled in with family sketches of the cleverly humorous kind Lawrence could strike off with ease. And while the book is not an important one, it has a good deal of Lawrencean charm and, like *Lady Chatterley's Lover*, a nostalgia for the country he knew so well in his youth.

✦ ✦ ✦ ✦

In *Lady Chatterley's Lover*, Lawrence wrote fuller descriptions of the manifestations of love than had ever been written before in serious literature in English, and he put into the mouths of his characters words that are not used in the genteel society he had hated from the time when he was a miner's little boy.

It is ironic that one of the elder intellectuals to whom Lawrence had become cool, Edward Garnett, should have played so important a part in the gestation of *Lady Chatterley's Lover*. Garnett's son David had enjoyed the book, and Lawrence wrote to ask him whether his father, who had found *The Rainbow* too strong, would like to have a presentation copy of *Lady Chatterley*: "In my early days your father said to me, 'I should welcome a description of the whole act.'—which has stayed in my mind till I wrote this book."

Lawrence publicly explained his intentions in *Pornography and Obscenity* (1929), which he wrote after the criticisms of *Lady Chatterley* and the censorship troubles over the *Pansies* poems. In *Pornography and Obscenity*, Lawrence indicated the difference between the "mob" use of taboo words and the private, individual definitions of them. He believed that word-prudery was a mob-habit people needed to be shaken out of—he was against genuine pornography, which never came out into the open, which rubbed humanity's "dirty little secret." Some of these premises were repeated and deepened in the preface to the authorized Paris edition of the novel. This preface ("My Skirmish with Jolly Roger"), reprinted in expanded form as the book *A Propos of Lady Chatterley's Lover* (1930), surprisingly contained some praise of the Church because it had fostered the sense of the intrinsic rhythms of living and because it had established the idea of marriage for life. Lawrence again spoke for the "blood-stream" kind of sex, and spoke against its opposite, the destructive personal-nervous type of sex:

The mind has an old grovelling fear of the body and the body's potencies. It is the mind we have to liberate, to civilize on these points. The mind's terror of the body has probably driven more men mad than ever could be counted. The insanity of a great mind like Swift's is at least partly traceable to this cause. In the poem to his mistress Celia, which has the maddened refrain "But—Celia, Celia, Celia s***s," (the word rhymes with spits), we see what can happen to a great mind when it falls into panic. A great wit like Swift could not see how ridiculous he made himself. Of course Celia s***s! Who doesn't? And how much worse if she didn't. It is hopeless. And then think of poor Celia, made to feel iniquitous about her proper natural function by her "lover." It is monstrous. And it comes from having taboo words, and from not keeping the mind sufficiently developed in physical and sexual consciousness.

In contrast to the puritan hush! hush!, which produces the sexual moron, we have the modern young jazzy and high-brow person who has gone one better, and won't be hushed in any respect, and just "does as she likes." From fearing the body, and denying its existence, the advanced young go to the other extreme and treat it as a sort of toy to be played with, a slightly nasty toy, but still you can get some fun out of it, before it lets you down. These young people scoff at the importance of sex, take it like a cocktail, and flout their elders with it. These young ones are advanced and superior. They despise a book like *Lady Chatterley's Lover*. It is much too simple and ordinary for them. The naughty words they care nothing about, and the attitude to love they find old-fashioned. Why make a fuss about it. Take it like a cocktail! The book, they say, shows the mentality of a boy of fourteen. But perhaps the mentality of a boy of fourteen, who still has a little natural awe and proper fear in fact of sex, is more wholesome than the mentality of the young cocktaily person who has no respect for anything and whose mind has nothing to do but play with the toys of life, sex being one of the chief toys, and who loses his mind in the process. Heliogabulus, indeed!

So, between the stale grey puritan who is likely to fall into sexual indecency in advanced age, and the smart jazzy person of the young world, who says: "We can do anything. If we can think a thing we can do it," and then the low uncultured person with a dirty mind, who looks for dirt—this book has hardly a space to turn in. But to them all I say the same: Keep your perversions if you like them—your perversion of puritanism, your perversion of smart licentiousness, your perversion of a dirty mind. But I stick to my book and my position: Life is only bearable when the mind and the body are in harmony, and there is a natural balance between them, and each has a natural respect for the other.

Pornography and Obscenity and *A Propos of Lady Chatterley's Lover* are important documents in the incessant war between art on the one side and official or unofficial censorship on the other. The former essay is reprinted in *Phoenix* and has been reissued in a separate volume together with some of Lawrence's other writings on attitudes toward sex, in the volume, *Sex, Literature, and Censorship* (now in America a Viking Compass paperback). In Lawrence's letters to various friends at the time *Lady Chatterley's Lover* was being printed in Italy, he repeatedly explained that this was a nakedly phallic book, and that it had in it much tenderness. For a while he considered calling the novel *Tenderness*. He told Harriet Monroe that he wanted to restore "the other, the phallic, consciousness into our lives: because it is the source of all real beauty, and all real gentleness." The phallic consciousness was "not the cerebral sex-consciousness, but something really deeper, and the root of poetry, lived or sung." A letter to the Brewsters reveals how emphatically *Lady Chatterley's Lover* belongs to the main stream of Lawrencean philosophy:

It's a novel of the phallic Consciousness: or the phallic Consciousness versus the mental-spiritual Consciousness: and of course you know which side I take. The *versus* is not my fault: there should be no *versus*. The two things must be reconciled in us. But now they're daggers drawn.

In the story, Constance Chatterley is among the legions of modern women who have not been awakened in the phallic Consciousness. And when her husband, Sir Clifford, comes home paralyzed from the First World War, Connie's sex-life must be carried on surreptitiously. Her husband's friend, the playwright Michaelis, is unable to fulfill her—and then she meets the gamekeeper.

It is a restating of themes suggested earlier, as we have seen, in *The Virgin and the Gipsy*, "The Ladybird," and "Glad Ghosts." Here the experience is more complete, and the phallic ecstasy becomes at the last a purification:

She had often wondered what Abélard meant, when he said that in their year of love he and Heloïse [sic] had passed through all the stages and refinements of passion. The same thing, a thousand years ago: ten thousand years ago! The same on the Greek vases, everywhere! The refinements of passion, the extravagances of sensuality! And necessary, forever necessary, to burn out false shames and smelt out the heaviest ore of the body into purity. With the fire of sheer sensuality.

In the short summer nights she learnt so much. She would have thought a woman would have died of shame. Instead of which, the shame died. Shame, which is fear: the deep organic shame, the old, old physical fear which crouches in the bodily roots of us, and can only be chased away by the sensual fire, at last it was roused up and rooted by the phallic hunt of the man, and she came to the very heart of the jungle of herself. She felt, now, she had come to the real bed-rock of her nature, and was essentially shameless. She was her sensual self, naked and unashamed. She felt a triumph, almost a vainglory. So! That was how it was! That was life! That was how oneself really was! There was nothing left to disguise or be ashamed of. She shared her ultimate nakedness with a man, another being.

And what a reckless devil the man was! really like a devil! One had to be strong to bear him. But it took some getting at, the core of the physical jungle, the last and deepest recess of organic shame. The phallus alone could explore it. And how he had pressed in on her!

And how, in fear, she had hated it. But how she had really wanted it! She knew now. At the bottom of her soul, fundamentally, she had needed this phallic hunting out, she had secretly wanted it, and she had believed that she would never get it. Now suddenly there it was, and a man was sharing her last and final nakedness, she was shameless.

What liars poets and everybody were! They made one think one wanted sentiment. When what one supremely wanted was this piercing, consuming, rather awful sensuality. To find a man who dared do it, without shame or sin or final misgiving! If he had been ashamed afterwards, and made one feel ashamed, how awful! What a pity most men are so doggy, a bit shameful, like Clifford! Like Michaelis even! Both sensually a bit doggy and humiliating. The supreme pleasure of the mind! And what is that to a woman? What is it, really, to the man either! He becomes merely messy and doggy, even in his mind. It needs sheer sensuality even to purify and quicken the mind. Sheer fiery sensuality, not messiness.

Ah God, how rare a thing a man is! They are all dogs that trot and sniff and copulate. To have found a man who was not afraid and not ashamed!

Lawrence wrote three drafts of *Lady Chatterley's Lover*. The third of these is the unexpurgated Florentine edition of 1928; the second has not been printed except in an Italian translation; the first was published in America in April 1944, with some fanfare, under the title *The First Lady Chatterley*. Charles S. Sumner of the Society for the Suppression of Vice seized four hundred copies of the book at the Dial Press offices (New York City) on May 9, 1944, and on May 29 a magistrate declared the book "clearly obscene" in violation of the State Penal Code. But on November 2, two of the three justices in the Court of Special Sessions found "reasonable doubt" as to the obscenity, and the case against the book was dismissed.

The First Lady Chatterley was in many ways different from Lawrence's final version—the gamekeeper, Parkin (he is called Mellors in Lawrence's third working-over of the text), has an almost comic quality at times, and there is considerably more class-warfare in this edition than in the final one, where the plangent erotic hum drowns out all other themes.

Frieda Lawrence reports that because Lawrence felt the tenderness and gentleness of the first version "hadn't enough punch and fight in it, it was a bit wistful," he reworked the novel; "he wanted to make the contrast between the cynicism and sophistication of the modern mind and the gamekeeper's attitude sharper. To give a glimpse of the living spontaneous tenderness in a man and the other mental, fixed approach to love."

The First Lady Chatterley retains a kind of inchoate flavor like that other posthumously published novel which lacked Lawrence's final revision—*The Virgin and the Gipsy*. There is a sketchiness about *The First Lady Chatterley* which throws it into poor contrast with the final version, that is richer, deeper and, in the best Lawrencean sense, "darker." The second version, as yet unpublished in English, is synopsized by E. W. Tedlock, Jr., in *The Frieda Lawrence Collection of D. H. Lawrence Manuscripts;* this second draft, in which the gamekeeper is still named Parkin, seems in this account as if it might be better than the first, but still not so vital as the third.

Yet the *Lady Chatterley's Lover* which was printed in Lawrence's lifetime is in several ways not up to the standard of his finest writing. The prose, except for occasional ecstatic passages containing something of his old power, is less sharp, less strong, than that of his preceding novel, *The Plumed Serpent*, which was his last successful effort at imaginative prose sustained at book-length. And the plot of *Lady Chatterley* has mechanical elements not usually found in Lawrence.

In *Lady Chatterley's Lover* the situations—unusual as they may be in themselves—and the way they are worked out, follow generally along the accepted lines of the conventional novel.

Consequently Lawrence is open to criticism when parts of the plot, certain motivations in the story, seem mechanical, or when a leading character such as Clifford appears to be merely a symbolic figure set up by the author to convey an idea. Lawrence discusses this aspect of Clifford in *A Propos of Lady Chatterley's Lover*:

As to whether the "symbolism" is intentional—I don't know. Certainly not in the beginning, when Clifford was created. When I created Clifford and Connie, I had no idea what they were or why they were. They just came, pretty much as they are. But the novel was written, from start to finish, three times. And when I read the first version, I recognized that the lameness of Clifford was symbolic of the paralysis, the deeper emotional or passional paralysis, of most men of his sort and class today. I realised that it was perhaps taking an unfair advantage of Connie, to paralyse him technically. It made it so much more vulgar of her to leave him. Yet the story came as it did, by itself, so I left it alone. Whether we call it symbolism or not, it is, in the sense of its happening, inevitable.

If Lawrence actually depended this much on his daimon, the daimon had become less reliable than he had been in the past. For the physical crippling of Clifford greatly weakens the story—it would have been far more effective if he could have been ostensibly potent yet at the same time actually representative of the sexlessness which, in Lawrence's view, characterized the group of shallow young aristocrats and artists Lawrence was lampooning.

The clever and successful Irish playwright Michaelis, who proves to be an ineffectual lover to Connie, is more truly symbolic of what Lawrence was hitting at through Clifford than Clifford himself is. Michaelis, in his contact with Connie, has failed to awaken her. This is an important point, for so many of Lawrence's heroines need awakening; and *Lady Chatterley's Lover* is a variation of the sleeping-beauty myth, in folklore often called the little-briar-rose theme: the man has to break through a barrier of thorns to awaken the sleeping girl.

Lawrence himself may be somewhat indentified, personally and doctrinally, with Mellors the gamekeeper. Mellors' early love experiences partly resemble those of his prototype Annable in *The White Peacock,* and some of them are a restatement of Lawrence's own youthful love affairs. Mellors, like Lawrence, is a man who has pushed beyond the bounds of his class. He has been an army officer and can speak the language of educated people, though he often uses Midland dialect, which Lawrence himself would sink into when he felt anyone was snobbish. The sensitive, educated side of Mellors corresponds to that of other Lawrencean male characters who are aware of the magnificence of nature. But there has never before been in any of these men so complete a blending of sensibility and competent proletarian maleness. Lawrence must have felt that he was doing through his writing what Mellors was doing amid the created life of the novel: Lawrence was attempting to be a regenerator of the sex-impulse, and in his own way also a protector of wild life.

But in spite of all philosophic implications, and the distortions of plot and character they require, the book remains a compelling love story, a warm, phallic song of love. It has been explained that Lawrence once thought of calling the novel *Tenderness,* and there is much tenderness in this story of a man and a woman finding fulfillment in one another amidst a ruining world.

Lawrence was prepared for the storm that greeted *Lady Chatterley's Lover:* the prudish criticisms of the book did not irritate him half so much as the fact that it was pirated extensively in America. His publishers wanted him to bring out a bowdlerized edition but he could not cut the book down to fit the public taste: "I might as well try to clip my own nose into shape with scissors. The book bleeds."

The black-market circulation of *Lady Chatterley's Lover* continued until the Grove Press courageously published the unexpurgated text in New York in 1959; soon after, the New American Library followed suit in Canada, and Penguin Books in England. Attempts to ban the book were defeated in the courts of each of these countries in the early 1960s.

The effect of this novel upon the men and women who have read it does not seem to be corrupting, but rather what Lawrence predicted: and as Norman Douglas—one of Lawrence's harshest critics—said in his autobiographical *Looking Back,* Lawrence's "work is in the nature of a beneficent, taboo-shattering bomb. An American friend tells me that Lawrence's romances have been of incalculable service to genteel society out there. The same applies to genteel society in England. . . . Lawrence opened a little window for the bourgeoisie." Horace Gregory, in his *Pilgrim of the Apocalypse*, is less condescending: "No novelist (or poet) living today finds it necessary to continue the half-century fight for sexual liberation in English writing. After *Lady Chatterley's Lover* all subsequent uses of the sex symbol are anticlimactic. It had been a long fight from the publication of Whitman's Song of the Body, through the Oscar Wilde trial, through twenty years of Freud to this last writing of a novel printed in Italy and Paris; the fight was won in 1928."

The statements of both Douglas and Gregory were made in books published in 1933, and the passing of time has emphasized their truth. It will never be quite possible for those who have come after the first appearance of *Lady Chatterley* to know how effectively it helped break through the screen that Puritanism had so long held before western eyes. The novel in English had either ignored the phallic or hidden it behind pruderies and hypocrisies. Consider the results when the middle section of an anatomy chart is not shown or the sex organs are omitted from it; consider the ancient statues which moderns have tried to neutralize with leaves as codpieces—in every case the sexual is given false emphasis. And this is the way things stood in the world Lawrence was born into, nineteenth-century society with its repressions, its sly adulteries, its unrecognized Oedipus complexes, its drawing-room pretense of universal eunuch-hood. Now Lawrence in writing *Lady Chatterley's Lover*, and in defending it, was not demanding that every book should be principally concerned with the phallic. He repeatedly indicated that he was trying to bring about a balance—and to do so, he had to go to an extreme. If society had been in balance, *Lady Chatterley* would not have been necessary; if it had been written nevertheless, it would have been a different kind of book. As it stands, *Lady Chatterley* is one of the triumphs of naturalism, but it is a good deal more than this. The story is not limited to sexual descriptions—though, as Lawrence saw, the book is dead without them; *Lady Chatterley's Lover* touches the entire consciousness.

And it has left its mark upon the consciousness of mankind.

It has not only helped to destroy many inhibitions in its reader, as Norman Douglas asserted, but also in Lawrence's fellow-writers, as Horace Gregory pointed out. Of course there will always be cheap books of the *Forever Amber* and *By Love Possessed* type—the poor in taste always ye have with you—but one of the further benefits of the Lawrencean liberation is that is helps to make such tawdriness look tawdrier than it used to look. Lawrence was a Puritan, and he was offended by the kind of suggestiveness that gives lace-edged innuendoes to so many books and films, and by little obscenities such as the smoking-room story: he wanted the cleanness of the direct.

Lawrence's intention in *Lady Chatterley's Lover* was sympathetically understood by Henry Williamson, who wrote (apparently to T. E. Lawrence "of Arabia") about the book:

What D. H. Lawrence means by *Lady Chatterley's Lover* is that the idea of sex, & the whole strong vital instinct, being considered indecent causes men to lose what might be their vital strength and pride of life—their integrity. Conversely, the idea of "genitals being beauty" in the Blakian sense would free humanity from its lowering and disintegrating immorality of deed and thought.

Lawrence wilted & was made writhen by the "miners-chapel-dirty little boy, you" environment: he was ruined by it: and in most of his work he is striving to straighten himself, and to become beautiful. Ironically, or paradoxically, in a humanity where "genitals are beauty" there would be a minimum of "sex" and a maximum of beauty, or Art. This is what Lawrence means, surely.

✓ ✓ ✓ ✓

After *Lady Chatterley's Lover*, Lawrence wrote only short pieces, except for *Apocalypse*, and he turned them out prolifically despite his gaining illness. They require detailed treatment here because they summarize or connect with so much that went before; and most of the stories have backgrounds so literal that antecedent facts are even more important than previously, for complete understanding.

Seven of Lawrence's last stories were published in *The Lovely*

Lady in 1933; a satiric tone pervades the collection, of which "Mother and Daughter" is typical. When Mrs. Bodoin interviews the elderly Armenian who wants to marry her daughter, she asks him if he "really" prefers "to smoke a hookah."

"What is a hookah, please?"
"One of those water-pipes. Don't you all smoke them, in the East?"
He only looked mystified and humble, and silence resumed.

The domineering Irishwoman, who has in the past been able to "squash" her daughter's suitors by ridicule, loses to "that Turkish carpet gentleman": the maternal spell over the thirty-year-old daughter is broken. The wealthy Armenian makes a good marriage settlement but asks for the London apartment and all its trappings—the spoils of Bodoin. The old woman submits, with restrained fury, and moves out, telling her daughter "sinisterly" that she hopes she will be happy, and adding "You're just the harem type, after all."

"I suppose I am! Rather fun!" said Virginia. "But I wonder where I got it. Not from you, mother . . ." she drawled mischievously.
"I should say *not*."
"Perhaps daughters go by contraries, like dreams," mused Virginia wickedly. "All the harem left out of you, so perhaps it all had to be put back into me."
Mrs. Bodoin flashed a look at her.
"You have *all* my *pity!*" she said.
"Thank you, dear. You have just a bit of mine."

Here is another statement of familiar Lawrencean themes: the breaking, by the intrusion of an outsider, of the domination of one person over another. Sometimes the relationship involved is parental: in *Sons and Lovers*, the outcome was obverse in that the intruding girl, and even death, could not break the mother's dominance over her son. But the situation is reversed in much of Lawrence's later fiction: in *Women in Love*, when Loerke comes between Gerald and Gudrun; in "The Fox," when the young soldier smashes the partnership between the two girls; and in *Lady Chatterley's Lover*, where there is one more exam-

ple, among many, of the successful invasion of a weakened relationship. In "Mother and Daughter," Lawrence uses as the
instrument of his bombardment another Lawrencean theme—
the triumph of the "dark" people—and does so in a slyly comic
way, with the elderly Armenian as "hero," rescuing the daughter from her too-close and jagged-nerved relationship with her
mother.

The same elements are found in "The Blue Moccasins," written in Switzerland the summer of 1928; Mrs. Brewster remembered Lawrence reading it aloud as he sat among the harebells
on a steep hill. "The Blue Moccasins" tells of the break-up of a
marriage between a young man and an older woman. No synopsis could do justice to Lawrence's weaving together of the relationship of the young bank clerk and the older woman, with
the scarlet thread of complication—a younger woman—stitched
in skillfully. The jealousy of the wife, and the rather stupefied
reaction of the husband, are masterfully dramatized. As in
"Mother and Daughter," character and conflict are the basis of
the story; there are no Lawrencean landscapes, no influence of
nature upon the people, but only the people themselves, modern, complicated, and intense. "The Blue Moccasins" has a
greater range than most of these stories, because it traces a
relationship over a number of years and because it has a dramatic ensemble scene in which an entire village is made witness
to an incident in a domestic quarrel. The account of the little
Christmas play is Lawrence at his comic best, with Percy Barlow
in blackface as a Moor, and the female complication as a
houri—wearing Mrs. Barlow's missing blue moccasins. And then,
in one of the climactic love scenes, with Percy virtually being
seduced before the whole town, his elderly little wife appears
at the edge of the stage and says, "Percy will you hand me my
moccasins?"—which the houri had previously kicked off in one
of the play's high moments, saying, "Away, shoes of bondage,
away!"

The pert, managing little wife is mockingly sketched, yet she
is a sympathetic figure. Lawrence originally intended to have
her triumph in the end, as the earliest version of the story in
manuscript indicates; Percy was to tell the complication-houri
that he loved his wife, who was perfect and who put "the final

touch to life." Before Lawrence read to his friends in Switzerland the ending he finally gave to the story, he asked them how they would close it, and they were all on the side of Mrs. Barlow. But he would not let her be victorious: the pattern of the broken relationship was too strong in his consciousness. He has Percy at the end of the story being drawn to the younger woman, telling her that his wife has curdled his inside—he does not know how he is even going to be civil to her again.

An aging woman losing her dominance is also the theme of the title story, "The Lovely Lady." This was published by Lady Cynthia Asquith in her "murder book," *The Black Cap,* in 1927; as noted earlier, she had used Lawrence's "The Rocking-Horse Winner" for *The Ghost Book* in the preceding year. "The Lovely Lady" is concerned with a parental relationship, a mother-and-son affair in which the seventy-two-year-old Mrs. Attenborough, who looks as if she were only thirty, has cowed her son Robert. He is an ineffectual barrister who can make only five hundred pounds a year; he cannot earn more, though he finds it easy to earn less. Here is an epitome of *Sons and Lovers,* with the modish setting of a suburban house in the 1920s: "But as her sons grow up, she selects them as lovers— first the eldest, then the second"—as Lawrence wrote to Edward Garnett in 1912, about the earlier story. There has been an elder son in "The Lovely Lady" whose fate is exactly that of William in *Sons and Lovers* (and of Lawrence's own brother Ernest): Henry "had died suddenly when he was twenty-two, after an awful struggle with himself, because he was passionately in love with a young and very good-looking actress, and his mother had humorously despised him for the attachment. So he had caught some ordinary disease, but the poison had gone to his brain and killed him, before he ever regained consciousness."

The Miriam of this story is Mrs. Attenborough's niece Cecilia, a member of the household; she is "safe" because her aunt has expressed disapproval of cousins' marrying. Cecilia tries once or twice to make love to Robert, but he is either too afraid or too diffident to be responsive. Cecilia, taking sun baths on the roof—Lawrence is assuredly on her side—hears the guilty old woman talking to herself during the afternoon rest period; Mrs. Attenborough is in the room below, and the voice of her troubled conscience comes eerily up the rain-pipe. Once Cecilia hears the old woman say that Robert's father was not her husband but a clever and passionate Italian priest: "I am disappointed in you, Robert. There is no poignancy in you. Your father was a Jesuit, but he was the most perfect and poignant lover in the world. You are a Jesuit like a fish in a tank. And that Ciss of yours is the cat fishing for you. It is less edifying than even poor Henry." Cecilia puts her mouth to the tube and pretends to be Henry: she tells the mother not to kill Robert as she has killed Henry. The old woman is shocked and horrified, and when she comes down to dinner that evening she is no longer the youthful-appearing Mrs. Attenborough: despite her make-up she is now "haggard with a look of unspeakable irritability, as if years of suppressed exasperation and dislike of her fellow-men had suddenly crumpled her into an old witch." Robert is astonished and repelled. And his mother goes into her last illness after telling Robert that he should marry Cecilia, that they are not actually cousins; she jeers at them, hoping to drive them apart, but they draw closer together, though Cecilia does not dare tell him about the rain-pipe and what she has done. Robert hates his dying mother, and passionately asserts that he knows he has a heart: "But it's almost sucked dry. I *know* people who want power over others." His mother leaves the unsuccessful barrister "the noble sum of one thousand pounds; and Ciss one hundred. All the rest, with the nucleus of her valuable antiques, went to form the 'Pauline Attenborough Museum.' "

In the struggle in *Sons and Lovers*, the mother and the boy and the girl had torn one another apart, but their contest and their suffering were sympathetically presented. Even the destructive mother was portrayed with tenderness, though as the result of her intervention the young man and the young woman could never find fulfillment in each other, even after death had removed their antagonist. Lawrence had in his own life ultimately shaken free of the mother-grasp and formed a union with a woman; poor Robert Attenborough in "The Lovely Lady" is too far gone; he wants to love Cecilia but cannot let himself go. His emotions have so long been nullified by his mother that they have atrophied from disuse. Robert is the kind of young man Lawrence frequently mocked at in the stories and poems of his later work: Rico Carrington in "St. Mawr" and Bertie Reid in "The Blind Man" were the first members of the expanding group of sexual cripples. Robert is not presented in such a cruel light as most of the others, and his domestic circumstances are shown in some detail, and this helps create a little sympathy for him—the type is usually not granted any justifying background facts. Yet Robert is never a fully sympathetic figure, and if he is doomed to emotional defeat it is, to a great extent, his own fault. Paul Morel at the end of *Sons and Lovers* is ready to fight his way back to the light. But Paul is a good deal younger than poor Robert Attenborough, whom Paul in time would have become.

Cecilia is on the other hand capable of acts of will. Lawrence generally dislikes women who are, but here Cecilia is regarded without disfavor: she breaks the tyranny of the lady who on the surface has been lovely too long. Cecilia is poor, dependent upon Mrs. Attenborough even as Robert is, but she is not passive; she fights against Mrs. Attenborough's enchainment. She defeats the old woman, though she is not truly victorious, for the consuming matriarchy was so well established that any conquest of it could only be Pyrrhic. The old woman has none of Lawrence's sympathy: she is a composite of all the domineering women he has known and hated. The Brewsters report that he had become somewhat embittered against his mother by 1922, less than ten years after the completion of *Sons and Lovers*, for all that she had subjected the children to: "She had brought down terrible scenes of vituperation upon their heads from which she might have protected them. . . . Lawrence could never forgive his mother for having dragged them into those unnecessary scenes. Shaking his head sadly at the memory of that beloved mother, he would add that the righteous woman martyred is a terrible thing." She remained the "beloved mother," of course, and his later references to her often have a throb in them, yet he had developed a critical attitude to her that manifested itself now and then. His antagonism to the dominating type showed itself in story after story, and never more strongly than in "The Lovely Lady."

It is of course unfair to compare this little tale with *Sons and Lovers* on an aesthetic level: the intention was far different. The scope of "The Lovely Lady" is deliberately restricted, and the development is speeded along by means of the rain-pipe trickery, a really sorry bit of claptrap. *Sons and Lovers* has been mentioned in connection with this story merely to indicate the change in Lawrence's attitude across the years. The essential *Sons and Lovers* situation, squeezed into a smaller frame, has no longer the rich Nottinghamshire background but rather a suburban garden, and the characters instead of being passionate working-class types are thin-souled city people. Tragedy has been succeeded by satire.

The satiric tone that pervades the stories in *The Lovely Lady* is weakest in "The Overtone," where it fades before a rising poetry. The tale starts to be a comic little triangle, one of Lawrence's favorite situations, with a young girl ready to break up the marriage of two people in their fifties. The husband is a blond, youthful-looking man, and the girl yearns toward him. As he steps out of his parlor into the moonlight, he thinks of the failure of his marriage, which everyone on the outside of it thinks a success. He remembers his honeymoon, and the night he had begged his wife to give herself to him on a hilltop, which she had refused to do. Later she had told him she thought a man's body ugly—"all in parts with mechanical joints," and over the years their sex relations had diminished to nothing. While he is remembering all this in the moonlight, and the tale seems to be developing into another of Lawrence's bitter little stories about a sexless but continuing relationship, his wife is indoors talking trivialities to another woman, and her underlying despair keeps coming into her voice as she remembers how she had waited for the rays of her husband's love to pierce through the clouds of fear and mistrust, and to open the flowers of her heart. The girl, listening to the women's conversation and hearing the despair in Mrs. Renshaw's voice, gets up and goes out to weep in the moonlight. Renshaw sees and hears her and calls out for her not to be alarmed, for Pan is dead. The girl realizes that Pan is dead inside Renshaw, and this is sad for her because she is "a nymph." While she is talking to Renshaw, the wife joins them, and the girl utters a long paean to Dionysus and Christ. After this the tale ends, and the three people walk back to the house, with the girl "glad to get away from them."

The story has a various symbolism—rose-petals and moonlight and the gods—but it leaves the reader unsatisfied. The girl's chant that closes the story is not of the quality Lawrence could sometimes attain to, as in the hymns in *The Plumed Serpent* or the man's soliloquy at the end of *The Escaped Cock*. Lawrence in "The Overtone" seems to have neglected his formula: for once the invasion of an unhappy marriage was unsuccessful.

Of the remaining three stories in *The Lovely Lady*, "Rawdon's Roof" is the slightest: a satirical anecdote. First published in 1928, in London, as one of the Woburn Books, this story is extremely slight—and it is also, as Lawrence Clark Powell has called it, "amusing" and "Gallic." Rawdon, who has vowed that no woman shall ever again sleep under his roof, refuses to take in a woman willing to leave husband and family for him. It is not that he does not love her, but that he must make sure his vow is kept. But his manservant has smuggled in a woman of his own for the night.

"The Rocking-Horse Winner" is a horrible commentary on today's money-madness—horrible because its evil forces crush the child in the story.

"The Rocking-Horse Winner" has some unusual elements: it is surprising to find in a Lawrence story even a partial knowledge of horse-racing and of the sporting world. It is one of the phases of life Lawrence usually ignored. Now and then there is mention of a "sporting" uncle, as in the autobiographical sketch "Rex" or the story "The Primrose Path," but there are no details of betting procedures or other related matters, as there are in "The Rocking-Horse Winner." And throughout Lawrence there is virtually no recognition of the football and cricket and boxing activities that take up so much of the time of modern man. There is, however, the description of the bullfight in *The Plumed Serpent*, and in the story "None of That" a bullfighter is one of the leading characters. But this is a different world from that of baseball or tennis or Rugby, or even of horse-racing: death is courted in the bull ring. "The Rocking-Horse Winner" presents a quite different picture of another corner of another kind of sporting world.

Its satiric element occurs in connection with the family that is always grasping for money and always living beyond its means: the mother with her expensive tastes and the father who is described, with apposite vagueness, as going "in to town to some office." The mother does not love her children, but makes such a show of loving them that people say she adores them. The family's house is haunted by the phrase, "There must be more money!" The children hear it continually, though it is never spoken aloud; they hear it particularly at Christmas time as they play among their expensive toys.

The little boy, Paul—the only instance outside *Sons and Lovers* when Lawrence gives this name to a leading character—asks his mother why the family has no money, and she tells him it is because they have no luck. He says he is lucky, that God has told him so—and then he begins his uncanny rides on the toy horse that magically conveys to him the names of the winning race horses.

With the help of the gardener and of a sports-minded uncle, Paul without his parents' knowing it makes them increasingly richer. The story fills with the names of the great races and of the winning horses, providing a lurid and frantic background. And in the foreground there is the boy fiercely riding his rocking-horse, cajoling it, tearing his nerves apart, in the wild journey that can end only in death.

Lawrence has here written a study not only of the gambling neurosis—even the winners are destroyed—but also of the entire money neurosis that destroys so many modern families, often crushing the children. "The Rocking-Horse Winner," with its contagious excitement and its air of inescapable doom, is an important contribution to the literature of the uncanny. It is, in the truest sense, a horror story.

"Things" is straight satire on Americans abroad: a later-day Henry James couple, after years of residence in Europe, have to return home; the man must go to work. The Melvilles paint in Paris and palpitate in Italy; for a while "Indian thought" uplifts them, but it lets them down. They return to America once, "for the child's sake," but have to live in an apartment, without the bric-à-brac they have collected abroad; they have become so deracinated that they are unhappy in America, but on returning to Europe they are unhappy there too. Erasmus is finally offered a job at "Cleveland University," teaching

Romance literature, and his wife urges him to accept. The dilettante of forty feels baffled, like a cornered rat, but when he sees the great industrial furnaces of Cleveland, he is impressed—the modern world has nothing bigger to show:

And when they were in their up-to-date little house on the campus of Cleveland University, and that woebegone débris of Europe, Bologna cupboard, Venice bookshelves, Ravenna bishop's chair, Louis Quinze side-tables, "Chartres" curtains, Sienna bronze lamps, all were arrayed, and all looked perfectly out of keeping, and therefore very impressive; and when the idealists had had a bunch of gaping people in, and Erasmus had showed off in his best European manner, but still quite cordial and American; and Valerie had been most ladylike, but for all that "we prefer America"; then Erasmus said, looking at her with queer sharp eyes of a rat:

"Europe's the mayonnaise all right, but America supplies the good old lobster—what?"

"Every time!" she said with satisfaction.

And he peered at her. He was in the cage, but he was safe inside. And she, evidently, was her real self at last. She had got the goods. Yet round his nose was a queer, evil scholastic look, of pure scepticism. But he liked lobster.

Lawrence's dislike of Americans was never more sharply expressed. He wrote to the Brewsters about this story, "You'll think it's you, but it isn't"—yet it *is* the Brewsters, in part. Lawrence, who seems genuinely to have liked them, uses some of their external circumstances—the painting and their involvement with "Indian thought"—though the essential psychology of the story, and its outcome, are drawn from Lawrence's wide knowledge of wandering Americans. He is making fun of not any one or any pair of them, but of a whole generation. It is as if, like Addison, he recognizes that satire is most effective when it can "pass over a single foe to charge whole armies."

Lawrence had known Americans abroad before he had known them in their own country: early in his literary career, he had met one of his first expatriated Americans at Ford Madox Ford's home. This was Ezra Pound, who is reported as behaving obstreperously as long ago as 1909. Lawrence had dealt with expatriate Americans in 1920, when he sent the *New Republic* an essay that has already been mentioned—"America, Listen to Your Own"—in which he stated that Americans, invading Europe like Goths, were too naïvely impressed by European monuments: "Italy fairly trembles with the shock of their dropping knees." By the time he wrote "Things," about two years before his death, Lawrence was well acquainted with Americans and their behavior, in every part of their own country and in most corners of Europe. He saw the schizoid condition of those who were educated and sophisticated to the point where America would always seem crude and provincial—they loved Europe, but never quite belonged there, were never able to become an organic part of it. Lawrence's penetrating observation of such people, plus his dislike of them, give the story "Things" its special pungency.

Like most of the tales in *The Lovely Lady*, all written during the last few years of Lawrence's life, "Things" is not stylistically orchestrated. It was as if Lawrence, as he drew near the end of his life, became too weak to use the drums and brass he had played upon so effectively in the past, and had to depend upon the thin, high sounds of some of the instruments in the strings section. This condition is matched in narrative by successions of scherzo passages that advance the stories and present the characters with light rapidity. Few themes are developed beyond a tune-clue or leitmotif suggestion; and there is no complication of themes. In many of the stories there is very little conversation—an occasional snatch of it will indicate direction, but there is no gradual building of scenes, with one growing out of the other; all is hasty, summarizing narrative. It is neatly adapted to the purpose for which Lawrence intended it: the stories are light and it is appropriate that the style is likewise. All this serves to give Lawrence's work a range, though to those who read all of it, these last-phase stories are at times jarring because they restate in thin, nervous language much that has previously been uttered in a rich, plangent style. It is not that the later work is less interesting—it is actually in a more popularized vein—but that its quality is slighter. A comparison of the passage quoted from "Things" with some of the sections quoted in discussions of the earlier work should indicate the difference. Consider part of a sentence from the "Things" quotation: ". . . All were arrayed, and all looked perfectly out of keeping, and therefore very impressive; and when the idealists had had a bunch of people in, and Erasmus had showed off in his best European manner, but still quite cordial and American. . . ." The cacophony, the slovenliness of grammar and of style, do not indicate a master of English prose; the passages quoted from *The Rainbow, Women in Love, Sea and Sardinia,* and *Kangaroo* show what writing power had been at Lawrence's command in his second and third periods.

This loss of vitality in his writing may in part be measured by the extent of his loss of touch with nature. In reviewing H. M. Tomlinson's *Gifts of Fortune* in 1926, Lawrence made a statement which has been mentioned earlier, in relation to *Kangaroo*: "Once be disillusioned with the man-made world, and you still see the magic, the beauty, the delicate realness of all the other life." Lawrence's work up to his last period had been so deeply concerned with nature that in those final stories it is surprising not to find more manifestations of nature—as if night had come over a magnificent landscape and then one corner of it had been artificially lighted to reveal a little group of people arguing among themselves in shrill tones. Once again, what they say is interesting, sometimes fascinating—the scenario is good. But all this belongs to a different world than that of *Sons and Lovers*, "The Prussian Officer," *The Rainbow, Women in Love*, "The Fox," *Sea and Sardinia, Aaron's Rod*, the Introduction to Magnus's *Memoirs, Kangaroo*, "St. Mawr," "The Princess," *The Plumed Serpent*, "The Woman Who Rode Away," and "Sun."

Lawrence was disillusioned with the man-made world, but he did not turn back to nature; instead he remained absorbed in types of people he chiefly disliked, and wrote little, nasal-voiced satires about them. He was like a man in a parlor full of people he loathed, and who, instead of going outdoors to nature, which he loved, stayed inside to bicker and vituperate. The satires he wrote are good—let it be said again—they are sharp, they are penetrating, but they belong to a different order from the novels and stories mentioned above, and they are less important, for they do not challenge comparison with the finest of their genre; they do not, like the earlier novels and stories,

give Lawrence an important place in twentieth-century literature.

Lawrence did not, of course, get altogether away from nature
in his last works. It flares up now and then, greatly enriching
the quality of the material. Nature appears fairly frequently in
Lady Chatterley's Lover, though not so effectively as in previous
novels; if Lawrence's descriptive powers had been at their height
when he was writing *Lady Chatterley*, it would have made a
far more forceful book. In the subsequent writings, the passages
involving nature are generally the most vital—this is true of *The
Escaped Cock*, of *Etruscan Places*, and even of *Apocalypse;* and
in the verse, an occasional piece like "Bavarian Gentians" comes
up with a wonderful freshness among the sharp little stones of
the later poetry.

One of Lawrence's finest descriptive pieces, "Mercury," was
written in this last period. It was published in the *Atlantic
Monthly* in February 1927 and in the *Nation and Athenaeum*
in the same month, and later reprinted in *Phoenix;* it was apparently written during the preceding summer, at Baden-Baden. It
is the account of a visit to the hill of Mercury, where the
Romans are supposed to have worshiped the god, and it is an
unforgettable account, for once again it is a master who impro-
vises at the keyboard. It is a pastoral, a day in the country with
all the landscape agleam; then there is the sound of thunder,
the flare of lightning, the smashing of rain; and then the hush
after the storm, the shock of death, and the return of the sun.
Lawrence's old magic is here, notably in the passage describing
the emergence of a Blakean figure out of the storm-darkness
when the crowd is huddled on the verandah of the restaurant:

Then suddenly the lightning dances white on the floor, dances
and shakes upon the ground, up and down, and lights up the
white striding of a man, lights him up only to the hips, white
and naked and striding, with fire on his heels. He seems to be
hurrying, this fiery man whose upper half is invisible, and at
his naked heels white little flames seem to flutter.

Here again Lawrence uses many of the effects of poetry, such
as "the continual, slightly modified repetition" he mentioned

in the Preface to *Women in Love* as being characteristic of his style. The kind of repetition used in the foregoing quotation is not the kind of writing ordinarily found in a business report or a scientific treatise, but here a different result is desired: Lawrence wants to make the reader *see* this Mercury symbol emotionally, and the movement of the writing, with the near-repeating of tune-phrases, helps to accomplish this. Lawrence is not prolix; his impressionistic gift enables him to condense into a quick, vital image what more deliberate writers would take far greater space to describe, without the living and kinetic qualities of Lawrence: as in such a phrase as "the white striding of a man." Lawrence could compress much in a short space—Marchbanks, in "The Last Laugh," is "a sort of faun on the Cross, with all the malice of the complication"—and whatever flowing, repetitious effects are found in his prose, they are not a mark of carelessness. They were introduced deliberately: not, of course, with Lawrence coldly deciding that at a certain point he needed another long-rhythmed sentence; rather, the entire effect was part of a larger method. Lawrence knew in general what he wanted, had certain general principles, and then wrote spontaneously what he pleased. Aldous Huxley in his famous essay on Lawrence says, "It was characteristic of him that he hardly ever corrected or patched up what he had written. I have often heard him say, indeed, that he was incapable of correcting. If he was dissatisfied with what he had written, he did not, as most authors do, file, clip, insert, transpose; he re-wrote. In other words, he gave the *daimon* another chance to say what it wanted to say. . . . He was determined that all he produced should spring direct from the mysterious, irrational source of power within him. The conscious intellect should never be allowed to come and impose, after the event, its abstract pattern of perfection." Tedlock, in his book on Lawrence's manuscripts, says that the printed text of "Mercury" follows Lawrence's holograph in ink in a notebook, "written on both sides, [with] little revision and correction."

"Mercury" then provides us with an example of Lawrence's method at its best. And while the piece cannot be technically called anything more impressive-sounding than a travel sketch, it is an important contribution to twentieth-century writing.

It focuses for a few moments on a little group of people of that century and swings around for a panorama view of an enduring landscape, and in a few thousand words gives us a picture of life and death, a picture that becomes an unforgettable experience.

An author who did not have Lawrence's type of vision, and who wrote with chill deliberateness, was the kind of author Lawrence disliked—and by whom he was usually disliked in turn; for example John Galsworthy, on whom Lawrence wrote an essay in 1928.

Galsworthy was at that time the reigning Pooh-Bah of the British novel. An English patrician with liberal instincts and a notable sense of social justice, Galsworthy wrote a series of plays and novels chiefly critical of prevailing society. He was far more successful in the marketplace than Lawrence ever was. Now that the passing of time has reduced the stature of Galsworthy and increased that of Lawrence, the essay on him by Lawrence is of special interest, particularly because of the personal contrast between the men, and their dislike of one another. Lawrence spoke out many truths about Galsworthy which were either unnoticed or at least not mentioned at the time. Part of the criticism is an overflow from *Lady Chatterley's Lover,* and in some places even the phrasing is similar, as in the passage condemning Galsworthy for the "shameful" way in which he treats passion: "The whole thing is doggy to a degree. The man [in the story] has a temporary 'hunger'; he is 'on the heat' as they say of dogs. The heat passes. It's done. Trot away, if you're not tangled. Trot off, looking shamefacedly over your shoulder." It is interesting to remember that this was probably written at the time *Lady Chatterley's Lover* was under construction, for it indicates the connection between Sir Clifford in that story and some of Galsworthy's men of property. Lawrence's criticism develops into a social instrument for attacking all the Forsythes in Galsworthy's "saga."

If this is more billingsgate than authentic criticism, it at least demarcates the differences between Lawrence and Galsworthy: after the two men met in 1917, Galsworthy made a note (published after his death) to the effect that he found Lawrence unpleasant, and Lawrence wrote in an essay that he had been offended by Galsworthy's telling him, "ex cathedra," that *The Rainbow* was "a failure as a work of art." The situation is a little reminiscent of that in Galsworthy's 1920 play, *The Skin Game*, in which a gentleman and a parvenu morally ruin themselves and their families as they battle each other; one of the implications of the play is that, although the man of low birth behaved like a man of low birth, all the trouble could have been avoided if the man of higher birth had displayed a decent tolerance and a little kindness.

Lawrence in this last phase was at times a desperately sick man, and those who knew him say they feel it was miraculous that he lasted as long as he did. His illness doubtless increased his tendency to bitterness and drove him to write harsh polemics. Now and then he was full of his old sense of gaiety and life, and now and then he wrote as magnificently as he ever did. Poems such as "Bavarian Gentians" and "The Ship of Death," and the short novel, *The Escaped Cock*, are Lawrence at his finest. They have in them an awareness of death but they are not full of complaint and despair. They have a strange, haunted beauty that sets them apart from the invective work of the period, and indeed from all the rest of Lawrence's writings.

The Escaped Cock was Lawrence's title for the story which since his death has been given the smoother and less sensational name of *The Man Who Died*. Earl Brewster has told of the genesis of the story; he and Lawrence were on an Etruscan pilgrimage when, on Easter morning 1927, they saw in a shop-window a toy white rooster that was escaping from its egg. Brewster told Lawrence that it suggested a title to him: "The Escaped Cock—a story of the Resurrection." Lawrence said he had been intending to write a Resurrection story; and when some time later, *The Escaped Cock* was published, Lawrence wrote in the copy he gave to Brewster: "To Earl this story, that began in Volterra, when we were there together."

The first version of this novella was published in the *Forum* magazine in America in 1928, under its original title, and it stirred up the protests of various readers. Only the first part of the story appeared in the *Forum*—the resurrected man had not even met the priestess at the point where the narrative broke off. The expanded version—as a short novel—was first published during the next year, with its original title, by Harry and Caresse Crosby's Black Sun Press in Paris.

The Escaped Cock is an imaginative presentation of the life of a prophet after resurrection from the tomb. The prophet is not named except as "the man"; there is nothing supernatural about his rising, for although he was almost dead in the tomb he explains later that he has lived because he was taken down too soon. His symbol is a barnyard cock which is tied by one leg; he buys it and later gives it freedom. The man is a prophet who has passed beyond his mission; he will now wander the earth and say nothing. He finds a new kind of salvation with a virgin priestess on the Syrian coast. She is the votary of

Isis Bereaved, Isis in Search. The goddess, in painted marble, lifted her face, and strode one thigh forward through the frail fluting of her robe, in the anguish of bereavement and of search. She was looking for the fragments of the dead Osiris, dead and scattered asunder, dead, torn apart, and thrown in fragments over the wide world. And she must find his hands and his feet, his heart, his thighs, his head, his belly; she must gather him together and fold her arms round the re-assembled body till it became warm again, and roused to life, and could embrace her, and could fecundate her womb. And the strange rapture and anguish of search went on through the years, as she lifted her throat and her hollowed eyes looked inward, in the tormented ecstasy of seeking, and the delicate naval of her bud-like belly showed through the frail, girdled robe with the eternal asking, asking of her search. And through the years she found him bit by bit, heart and head and limbs and body. And yet she had not found the last reality, the final clue to him, that alone could bring him really back to her. For she was Isis of the subtle lotus, the womb which waits submerged and in bud, waits for the touch of that other inward sun that streams its rays from the loins of the male Osiris.

The priestess is a woman who "had known Caesar and shrunk from his eagle-like rapacity," and the glowing maleness of Antony had not attracted her. An old philosopher had told her that she was a night-blooming lotus, and that the hot, bright, day-sun would not lure her out. Altogether, what the philosopher says to her repeats many of the principal, recurring Lawrencean symbols: the mine-darkness, the rising flowers, the identification of blossoming with sex-expression, the contrast between superficial power and the deeper "dark" power. And all is sanctified by the power of touch, when the man who had died comes to the temple and the priestess restores his living-ness as she rubs his wounds with oil and wakes his sex-life, and her own, for the first time. Lawrence in one of his letters defended the sexual aspects of the story: "Church doctrine teaches the resurrection of the body; and if that doesn't mean the whole man, what does it mean?"

The materialistic Roman world comes between the stranger and the priestess, and the man has to flee, escaping in the boat of the Roman captain who had come hunting him. The former prophet rows away, laughing softly to himself, and saying that he has sowed the seed of his life and his resurrection.

Completed in August 1928, this story is Lawrence's last important fictional prose. He could still bring his setting vividly to life: "The sea was dark, almost indigo, running away from the land, and crested with white. The hand of the wind brushed it strangely with shadow, as it brushed the olives of the slope with silver"—Lawrence's "quick" poetry is there; it has an almost feathery softness at times. There are fewer jarring colloquialisms, and fewer Whitman-like insertions of foreign words and phrases from the languages Lawrence had picked up on his travels. The style is exactly right for bringing that particular phase of the past into life. *The Escaped Cock* is one of Lawrence's few attempts to write about the past, and it is a supreme re-creation.

✓ ✓ ✓ ✓

Lawrence's last travel book is the posthumously published *Etruscan Places*, a record of his visits to the cemeteries of Etruria. His observations and descriptions are, as always valuable, but because so little is known about the Etruscans, his intuitions were also allowed free play. Lawrence had for a long time thought sympathetically of this people, and in March 1926 he visited the Etruscan museums at Perugia and other Umbrian towns. He had left the villa at Spotorno on a six-weeks' break-away after a period of illness and screeching fights—Frieda's two daughters and Lawrence's sister Ada, accompanied by a friend, had been house guests, and there had been much turbulence. In Capri, where he had fled to join the Brewsters, Lawrence met his old friend, the Scottish painter Millicent Beveridge, and she and another woman painter, Mabel Harrison, returned with him to the mainland for the Umbrian tour that lasted about ten days. Lawrence, back at Spotorno by April 4, could write his mother-in-law in Germany that he was "the Easter-lamb" for Frieda and her daughters: he had been cross when he went away, "but one must be able to forget a lot and go on." In this letter he mentioned for the first time that he might write "about Umbria and the Etruscans, half travel-book, also scientific." And the next day he wrote his agent that he was contemplating such a book and might live in Perugia for a few months while gathering material. But it was a different part of the Etruscan culture that he finally wrote of, for in early April of 1927 he and Earl Brewster spent a week along the Tyrrhenian coast near Rome, visiting the Etruscan sites from Cerveteri to Volterra. The pieces Lawrence wrote about this trip, which at the time he thought of as only his first series on the subject, appeared as articles in 1927 and 1928; and these were made into the book, *Etruscan Places*, two years after Lawrence's death.

The surface of the early Etruscan culture, the wooden buildings with terra cotta decorations, has been swept away, and what remains is the under-earth greatness: the tombs. There was an ancestral symbolism in Lawrence's visiting them, though as he descended into one burial-cavern after another, instead of confronting walls of coal he found frescoes left by a "dark" people that was also a sun people. The Etruscans had no false literary culture, but lived in the phallic consciousness: to the man of ancient Etruria, "the universe was alive, and in quivering *rapport*. To him, the blood was conscious; he thought with his heart." But the Roman conquered him, the Roman who hated the ark (the womb symbol, "the womb of the world, that brought forth all the creatures") and the phallus, the principal decoration-motif in so many of the Etruscan tombs. The Romans, who were not saints, though they thought they should be, "called the Etruscans vicious" and "hated the phallus and the ark, because they wanted empire and dominion and, above all, riches: social gain. You cannot dance gaily to the double flute and at the same time conquer nations or rake in large sums of money. *Delenda est Cartago.* To the greedy man, everyone that is in the way of his greed is vice incarnate."

Here is Lawrence's anti-civilization philosophy again, with the Romans and the Etruscans as value-symbols. Lawrence at this time frequently thought of the Romans in terms of modern civilization; theirs was a materialistic social order that, like the scientific and industrial world of the nineteenth and twentieth centuries, crushed the instinctual faculties of man. In *The Escaped Cock* Lawrence spoke of the eagle-like Caesar and the golden Antony as being men of the day-sun who could not affect the night-blooming priestess of Isis; and when the wandering prophet who could affect her at last arrived, and awakened her as he was in turn awakened, it was the intruding Roman world that drove them apart. Likewise, in the poem "Attila" written toward the end of this period, and published in *Pansies,* Lawrence says he "would call Attila, on his little horse/a man of peace." Attila, after all, had "helped to smash a lot of old Roman lies." The Romans, with their money-lust and their aqueducts and their sewers, had spoiled the *wonder* of the ancient world. They had destroyed the Etruscans not outwardly but inwardly, turning their knowledge into superstition and corrupting their princes, who "became fat and inert Romans. The Etruscan people became expressionless and meaningless. It happened amazingly quickly, in the third and second centuries B.C."

And only the wonderful tombs are left, with their stuccoed walls painted in reds and blacks and yellows showing dancers and hunters and bulls and lions. Lawrence, going down into tomb after tomb, led by a guide carrying a lamp or a candle, saw these impressive survivals and from them re-created a compelling picture of Etruscan life. He consulted a few authorities but did not always agree with them. Historians and sociologists may in turn disagree with many of Lawrence's intuitions, yet he has given us a marvelous imaginative reconstruction and some stimulating descriptions of the ancient tombs. And there is a Lawrencean travelogue quality in *Etruscan Places,* with interesting glimpses of the malaria-ridden peasants of the twentieth-century provinces of Roma and Tuscany.

Lawrence wrote his Etruscan essays during the period in

which he was at work on *Lady Chatterley's Lover*, when he was using the Villa Mirenda, near Florence, as a semi-permanent base. He and Frieda made various trips—England (for the last time), Scotland and Germany in 1926, Austria and Germany in 1927, Switzerland early in 1928—but never stayed away for very long at a time. Lawrence's last visit to the Midlands is described by his lifelong friend, W. E. Hopkin, who wrote to the author of this volume: "When [Lawrence] was last in Eastwood he and I went over the old ground. When we reached Felley Dam he stood looking over at the Haggs. I sat down by the pool and when I turned to look at him he had a terrible look of pain on his face. When we got back I asked him when he would come again, and he said 'Never! I hate the damned place.' He never glanced once at the house in The Breach as we passed."

The Lawrences' trips were sometimes made, like the Switzerland sojourn, for Lawrence's health: he now had an incessant cough and occasional hemorrhages. His letters bear witness to the fact that he would never name his disease, for they contain frequent references to a cold, an attack of influenza, a spell of bronchitis, or a sore chest. But the man who was so outspoken, so insistent that unpleasant things be called by their right names, never spoke of his affliction as tuberculosis. Catherine Carswell says that in this respect alone he resembled the Christian Scientists. "He preferred not to name an illness precisely, disliking the jargon and finding it unhelpful in the fight for health. But he never denied the existence of the illness, nor ignored the nature of the fight." Sometimes it was difficult to induce him to see doctors: two of the physicians who attended him during these last years were noted German literary men, Max Mohr and Hans Carossa.

Lawrence's illnesses did not cut down his writing activity. Sometimes they increased his exasperation, or made him more susceptible to it—as when the *Pansies* poems were seized and his paintings taken by the police—but most of the time he went on working. This continuity of effort is one of the traits that at the last makes him seem so clearly sane despite the turmoil that always raged around him, and despite his own manifestations of bitterness. He worked.

Organized humanity seemed little inclined to let him have much peace of mind, though the friendship of such men as Richard Aldington and Aldous Huxley in this last period was, as previously pointed out, compensation for a good deal of the hostility of the outside world. And they provided a better association than the will-motored women of England and New Mexico.

Yet Lawrence was continually beset by annoyances of all kinds. Much hatred was directed toward him because of *Lady Chatterley's Lover,* such hatred as that embodied in the *John Bull* article which came out in the autumn of 1928, when he was ill in southern France. "Famous Novelist's Shameful Book— A Landmark in Evil" was devoted to an attack which called the novel "the most evil outpouring that has ever besmirched the literature of our country. The sewers of French pornography would be dragged in vain to find a parallel in beastliness." And Lawrence was attacked as being sex-obsessed and having a diseased mind. This article and others like it were sent to Lawrence by his publisher when he was at the island-fortress of Port Cros, in the Mediterranean, where he and Frieda were visiting Aldington. In his autobiography, Aldington says of these clippings: "I have never seen such an exhibition of vulgarity, spite, filth, and hatred as was contained in those innumerable diatribes. Every editor and peddling reviewer had eagerly seized the opportunity to vilify and if possible crush into ignominy and poverty a man who had done—what? Publish a book whose obvious intention was to rescue sex from prudery and nastiness. Now, we writers may be fools, but we are not such utter fools as to be taken in by such stuff. I had lived with men, and I knew what their talk and lives were, I knew the cynicism and depravity of journalists, I knew some of the men who had written this malevolent twaddle; and I knew they were not worthy to black Lawrence's boots."

While Lawrence was at Port Cros, some French officers came over "to investigate the suspicious alien character, Lawrence," but because of Lawrence's illness, Aldington wouldn't let them see him. Lawrence, it will be remembered, was arrested by the Germans as a possible spy at Metz in 1912, and was put out of Cornwall in 1917 by the British authorities: a strange treatment of the man who would never in any circumstances have served any government as an informer.

The Lawrences had left their Florentine villa for the last time in June 1928, and before going to Port Cros had spent the summer in the Swiss Alps. Many of the *Assorted Articles* essays were written there, according to the Brewsters, who reported that Lawrence had a new one to read to them "almost every day." The composition of these short pieces went on until the next year, when Lawrence assembled them for the book that was published in April 1930, the month after his death.

The articles appeared in various magazines and newspapers—in London chiefly in the *Evening News* and the *Sunday Standard*, in America principally in *Vanity Fair*—in 1928 and 1929. The essays made Lawrence's ideas familiar to a good many people who previously knew only his name. And, since these articles appeared so soon after *Lady Chatterley's Lover*, that name could command special attention. Most of the articles, moreover, were about the perennially interesting subject of sex, and some of them had kindling titles: "Sex Versus Loveliness," "Cocksure Women and Hensure Men," "Enslaved by Civilization," "The Risen Lord," "On Being a Man," "Master in His Own House," "The 'Jeune Fille' Wants to Know," "Matriarchy," "Give Her a Pattern," "Do Women Change?" and "Is England Still a Man's Country?"—to mention eleven of the twenty-three *Assorted Articles*, several of which had slightly different titles when they appeared in the journals.

Some of these have a tone similar to some of the stories later published in *The Lovely Lady*, a few of which were being written at the same time as the articles. Like the stories, the essays are often satirical and colloquial; and there is little of the world of nature in them.

Assorted Articles presents no new phase of Lawrencean philosophy, but rather offers popularized versions of what had been demonstrated in treatises and dramatized in novels. Much of the material is trivial, but that is what gave it a particular value at the time, for by using a popular medium and a popular style, Lawrence could deliver his message to an unusually wide audience. And it was not the more individualized aspects of his doctrine, the personalized mysticism, that he developed in these articles, but rather those with the commonest basis of interest and appeal. The essays were valuable because Lawrence at the end of the 1920s was a wise man for the end of the 1920s, and what he offered was a counsel of common sense. There always had been common sense amid the farrago of mysticism in his work, but it had not always been recognized, partly because it was often given exalted utterance. But the common sense came through straight in *Assorted Articles*.

Of course more people need more sunlight on their bodies, of course young people are hobbled by inadequate sex instruction, of course human beings must be delivered from the repulsion they feel toward one another and toward themselves, of course modern money-worship is bad, of course women should fulfill their individual natures rather than try to adapt themselves to some falsely conceived masculine image of womanhood—most of the points Lawrence made in the book are axiomatic or even indisputable. They are to a great extent dated now, except for the small part of humanity that still clings to the wreckage of the pre-1914 world.

It should not be deduced from the foregoing paragraphs, however, that the articles making up the volume are necessarily poorly written or done in deplorable journalese. It is true that they are often colloquial, even slangy, but they have a vitality beyond the ordinary range of the medium. If Lawrence was not writing in the style of *Women in Love* or *The Plumed Serpent*, he was at least writing warmly and persuasively, and at times brilliantly.

Several of the articles are personal reminiscence. "Hymns in a Man's Life" tells how the old Protestant songs of Lawrence's childhood influenced his imagination; "Autobiographical Sketch" provides some interesting details of his early life, seen from Lawrence's point of view, and gives important clues to his basic attitude:

And now I know, more or less, why I cannot follow in the footsteps even of Barrie and Wells, who both came from the common people also and are both a success. Now I know why I cannot rise in the world and become even a little popular and rich.

I cannot make the transfer from my own class into the middle class. I cannot, not for anything in the world, forfeit my passional consciousness and my old blood-affinity with my fellowmen and the animals and the land, for that other thin, spurious mental conceit which is all that is left of the mental consciousness once it has made itself exclusive.

In other essays also, Lawrence expresses his perceptions and convictions with persuasive simplicity. In "Is England Still a Man's Country?" and in "Matriarchy," Lawrence discusses matters on which he was a seasoned authority and on which he was one of the first to write effectively. In "Dead Pictures on the Walls," Lawrence suggests a circulating library for pictures, not of the museum classics—which have an immortal value, or even of the work of Matisse or Picasso or Braque, which are beyond the interest of most people—but rather the paintings of the "hundreds and hundreds of men and women with genuine artistic feeling, who produce quite lovely works that are never seen. They are lovely works—not immortal, not masterpieces, not 'great'; yet they are lovely, and will keep their loveliness a certain number of years; after which they will die, and the time will have come to destroy them." This is another idea of Lawrence's which has been put into practice, at least on a small scale. He tells of his own amateur painting experiences in another of the essays, "Making Pictures."

Assorted Articles has really very little to do with Lawrence the novelist and Lawrence the poet. The sketches were written for a ready market, by a man who had all his life stood at the edge of poverty and who at last, a year and a half or two years before his death, was beginning to make what was to him a reassuring amount of money. Lawrence told Dorothy Brett in November 1928 that he was not thinking of more books but of little articles—"the papers want them now." The *Sunday Dispatch* would give him twenty-five pounds for a 2,000-word article that could be written in an hour and a half—"and nobody would even publish a story like *None of That*." Money was also coming in from the thousand-copy edition of *Lady Chatterley's Lover* at two pounds a copy: by July 1929, more than

£1,600 were on hand. And this—minus ten percent for commission—was a large amount of money for Lawrence.

He was also at this time selling his old manuscripts to Harry and Caresse Crosby, whose Black Sun Press in Paris was issuing some of his work in private editions. The Crosbys were among the few expatriate Americans whom Lawrence liked. He wrote a friendly, interpretive introduction to Harry Crosby's volume of verse, *Chariot of the Sun,* which he praised with a careful enthusiasm. He found a great deal of chaos throughout the poetry. Lawrence and Harry Crosby had in common their sun worship: to both of them, the sun had a heart of darkness.

Malcolm Cowley has in *Exile's Return* used Harry Crosby as a compelling symbol of the entire Lost Generation, a young man who underwent a "violent metamorphosis" in the First World War that led him to the Paris of the 1920s and to his self-destruction in December 1929. Lawrence had warned Harry Crosby in a letter in the spring of 1928: "Don't lose your delicacy and your sun-sensitiveness, and become Parisy, or look too much at hotels and Cook-tourists." Crosby's suicide at thirty-one upset Lawrence greatly in the last winter of his life: "Did you read that Harry Crosby, the rich young American in Paris who printed *Escaped Cock* for me, shot himself and his mistress in New York? Very horrible! Too much money—and *transition surréalisme—*."

Lawrence was at Bandol during most of that last year of his life, except for a trip to Mallorca and a last voyage to Germany—Bandol, where Katherine Mansfield had lived from time to time during her long and fatal illness. It was an exacerbating year for Lawrence: the manuscript of *Pansies* which he had mailed to his publisher was seized by the British authorities, who confiscated some of the poems, and the exhibition of his paintings at Dorothy Warren's gallery in London was raided by the police.

Pansies, which is not so much authentic poetry as thoughts crystallized in verse-form, was written for the most part toward the end of 1928. Lawrence had composed virtually no poetry since the New Mexican part of *Birds, Beasts and Flowers* six years before; the Quetzalcoatl hymns in *The Plumed Serpent* were an exception, and indeed the whole text of that book is Lawrence's last truly poetic effort—with, again, a few exceptions such as the resurrection of his poetic talents in the prose of *The Escaped Cock* and in at least two of the poems subsequent to or coeval with *Pansies*: "Bavarian Gentians" and "The Ship of Death."

Pansies does not lack expressional force, but it is not poetry even in the sense of Lawrence's earlier free verse. In December 1928 he wrote Aldous and Maria Huxley from Bandol that he had been working on "a book of Pensées, which I shall call pansies, a sort of loose little poem form; Frieda says with joy: real doggerel—But meant for Pensées, not poetry, especially not lyrical poetry." In January he sent the manuscript to his agent in London, and this is when his troubles with official censorship began. Lawrence in a Foreword to the expurgated edition, that omitted some dozen items, tells the story of the censoring of *Pansies*, with several amusing Lawrencean conjectures: "When Scotland Yard seized the MS in the post, at the order of the Home Secretary, no doubt there was a rush of detectives, postmen, and Home Office clerks and heads, to pick out the most lurid blossoms. They must have been very disappointed. When I now read down the list of the omitted poems, and recall a dozen amusing, not terribly important bits of pansies which might have had to stay out of print for fear a policeman might put his foot on them, I can only grin once more to think of the nanny-goat, nanny-goat in-a-white petticoat silliness of it all."

Pansies contains much bitterness, as in these lines from "Dead People:"

When people are dead and peaceless
they hate happiness in others
with thin, screaming hatred,
as the vulture that screams high up, almost inaudible,
hovering to peck out the eyes of the still-living creature.

Pansies also contains plenty of strong social satire, as in "What Is He?" The questioner is told that "he" is a man, but this answer isn't accepted; the man must "do" something, have a job of some kind, since he obviously doesn't belong to the leisured classes:

—I don't know. He has lots of leisure. And he makes quite
beautiful chairs.—
There you are then! He's a cabinet maker.
—No no!
Anyhow a carpenter and joiner.
—Not at all.
But you said so.
—What did I say?
That he made chairs, and was a joiner and carpenter.
—I said he made chairs, but I did not say he was a carpenter.
All right then, he's just an amateur.
—Perhaps! Would you say a thrush was a professional
flautist, or just an amateur?—
I'd say it was just a bird.
—And I say he is just a man.
All right! You always did quibble.

Lawrence has not in his bitterness against men lost his feeling
of admiration for wild life, as "Self-Pity" shows; he has never
seen a wild thing that knew self-pity:

A small bird will drop frozen dead from a bough
without ever having felt sorry for itself.

He can still epigrammatize his attitude to demonstrative
women, as in "To Women, As Far As I'm Concerned":

The feelings I don't have I don't have.
The feelings I don't have, I won't say I have.
The feelings you say you have, you don't have.
The feelings you would like us both to have, we neither
    of us have.
The feelings people ought to have, they never have.
If people say they've got feelings, you may be pretty
    sure they haven't got them.
So if you want either of us to feel anything at all
you'd better abandon all idea of feelings altogether.

He still has hope, as the poem "Sun-Women," in the vein
of his old prophetic writings, reveals. He says it would be
strange if some women came forward saying they were sun-
women, belonging not to men or their children or even themselves:

And how delicious it is to feel sunshine upon one!
And how delicious to open like a marigold
when a man comes looking down upon one
with sun in his face, so that a woman cannot but open
like a marigold to the sun,
and thrill with glittering rays.

Pansies comprised more than three hundred poems. *Nettles*,
issued in March 1930, the month of Lawrence's death, contained only twenty-five, yet this little book seems to have as
much bitterness in it as its larger predecessor. *Nettles* was well
named.

The themes of these "poems" are not new for Lawrence:
the spinsterism and hypocrisy of the British, the official castra-
tion of those who write for the British public, the doom that
hangs over factory cities, the murder of the masses by civilization, the delusion of freedom.

"Editorial Office" is the story of a young man who applies
for a position as literary critic and says he doesn't understand
when the editor asks him if he has been "fixed," if he has bio-
logical credentials:

> Editor (sternly): Have you been
>   made safe for the great British
>   Public? Has everything objectionable
>   been removed from you?
>
> Applicant: In what way, quite?
>
> Editor: By surgical operation.
>   Did your parents have
>   you sterilised?
>
> Applicant: I don't think so,
>   Sir. I'm afraid not.
>
> Editor: Good morning! Don't
>   trouble to call again. We
>   have the welfare of the
>   British Public at heart.

Lawrence's rage over the seizure of *Pansies* in January 1929 is reflected in the bitter comedy of this little verse, but most of the *Nettles* items were probably inspired by the police raid on Lawrence's exhibition of paintings at the Warren Gallery in London in July. In a letter to Earl Brewster on the 13th of August, Lawrence says he has not "done much work lately— a few 'nettles' to follow my *Pansies*." The exacerbation he felt during the *Nettles* period is expressed in a passage of this letter, which is a typical section of his correspondence at the time: "All this persecution and insult, and most of all the white-livered poltroonery of the so-called 'free' young people in England puts me off work. Why should one produce things, in such a dirty world! If one leaves them to themselves they will accomplish their own destruction so much the quicker. Far be it from me to hinder them."

The paintings which had caused the trouble at the Warren Gallery were mostly of ecstatic nudes; one was of a naked Holy Family, one was of Leda and the Swan, one was of Boccaccio's story of the gardener who feigned deafness—the gardener lay half-naked in the foreground, with bonneted nuns in the background and distant trees painted with something like "that subtle rush of cool grey flame" Lawrence wrote of in one of his early poems ("Corot"). These pictures and others in the exhibition had been admired by Lawrence's Italian-peasant friends and other simple people, who had not been shocked, but the paintings were not appreciated by the British authorities, particularly not by Lord Brentford, the Home Secretary, who was "out to get" Lawrence. After the exhibition had been on for several weeks, some London policemen appeared one day and solemnly carried away thirteen of the paintings: they wanted to take some items of Blake, but desisted when they were told that Blake had been dead for a century. The canvases were moved to the basement of a police station and were threatened with destruction by fire.

Frieda, who had gone to London for the exhibit, had to rush back to Florence, where her husband had become grievously ill while visiting Giuseppe Orioli, who had published *Lady Chatterley's Lover;* Frieda took Lawrence to Baden-Baden to recuperate. One of the *Nettles* poems—"13,000 People"—cries out Lawrence's sick rage at the time:

Thirteen thousand people came to see
my pictures, eager as the honey bee

for the flowers; and I'll tell you what
all eyes sought the same old spot

in every picture, every time,
and gazed and gloated without rhyme

or reason, where the leaf should be,
the fig-leaf that was not, woe is me!

And they blushed, they giggled, they sniggered, they leered,
or they boiled and they fumed, in fury they sneered

and said: Oh boy! I tell you what,
look at that one there, that's pretty hot!—

And they stared and they stared, the half-witted lot
at the spot where the fig-leaf just was not!

But why, I ask you? Oh tell me why?
Aren't they made quite the same, then, as you and I?

—and the poem goes on in this vein for another page.

Lawrence was eventually told that the confiscated paintings
would be sent back to him on condition that he would not try
to exhibit them in England again. The bitter *Nettles* verses had
already been written.

The other poems of these years, almost 300 of them collected
by Richard Aldington and Giuseppe Orioli and published in
1933 as *Last Poems*, are mostly of the same sort—one section of
Last Poems is even called "More Pansies" by the editors. Some
of the "More Pansies" poems were written at Mallorca; this
places them in the spring of 1929, and the one called "Forte
dei Marmi" was obviously written while Lawrence was visiting
the Huxleys at that place in July. Some of the poems are coeval
with *Nettles*—and like them in tone—for they were written after
the July police raid on Lawrence's picture exhibit. One of the
verses attacks J. C. Squire, then editor of the *London Mercury*,

who is also scolded in *Nettles;* and one of the sharply amusing
poems in the "More Pansies" section is a riposte to the article by
T. W. Earp, "Mr. D. H. Lawrence on Painting," in the August
17 *New Statesman:*

> I heard a little chicken chirp
> My name is Thomas, Thomas Earp!
> And I can neither paint nor write
> I only can set other people right.
>
> All people that can write or paint
> do tremble under my complaint.
> For I am a chicken, and I can chirp,
> and my name is Thomas, Thomas Earp.

Aldington has wisely commented that most of the *Pansies*
and *Nettles* verse seems to come out of Lawrence's nerves and
not out of his deeper self. Yet toward the end of his life Lawrence also wrote a few of his finest poems, such as "The Ship
of Death" and that piece which contains so many of the essential Lawrence symbols, magnificently woven together, "Bavarian
Gentians"; he had once thought of calling this poem "Glory of
Darkness."

Not every man has gentians in his house
in soft September, at slow, sad Michaelmas.

Bavarian gentians, big and dark, only dark
darkening the day-time torch-like with the smoking blueness
        of Pluto's gloom,
ribbed and torch-like, with their blaze of darkness spread blue
down flattening into points, flattened under the sweep of white
        day
torch-flower of the blue-smoking darkness, Pluto's dark-blue
        daze,
black lamps from the halls of Dis, burning dark blue,
giving off darkness, blue darkness, as Demeter's pale lamps give
        off light,
lead me then, lead me the way.

Reach me a gentian, give me a torch!
let me guide myself with the blue, forked torch of this flower

down the darker and darker stairs, where blue is darkened on
  blueness
even where Persephone goes, just now, from the frosted
  September
to the sightless realm where darkness is awake upon the dark
and Persephone herself is but a voice
or a darkness invisible enfolded in the deeper dark
of the arms Plutonic, and pierced with the passion of dense
  gloom,
among the splendour of torches of darkness, shedding darkness
  on the lost bride and her groom.

This was written in Germany, which the Lawrences left toward the end of September, in Michaelmas season, 1929; they went back to the Mediterranean coast of France, where Lawrence was to die in less than six months.

At Bandol, Lawrence summoned his strength for one last book, *Apocalypse*. This work apparently grew out of his interest in the speculations and astrological designs of the British mystic, Frederick Carter, whom Lawrence had used as a minor character (Cartwright) in "St. Mawr"; Achsah Brewster and the London publisher of Carter's *The Dragon of Revelation* (1932) have both said that *Apocalypse* developed out of an introduction Lawrence began to write for Carter's book, and Lawrence's letters of the time show this to be true. Lawrence's own working out of the matter is mostly a restatement of old Lawrencean ideas, not always put together with thematic coherence. Lawrence in his last glow of writing forgets that in *The Escaped Cock* he had renounced his mission and his rôle of prophet: a dying man on a sunny coast, he writes out his febrile vision of the most Hebraic, most Old Testament-like book of that newer gospel which even in childhood had never moved him as the savage older writings had. But Revelation is attractively full of symbolic beasts and prophetic utterance. Though Lawrence begins with an attack upon it as not being representative of the better aspects of Christianity, he later writes about it with some friendly warmth. It becomes a significant Lawrencean autobiographical extension. And like his own life it ends with a paean to the sun, and to those who feel the deep inner radiance of the sun.

Lawrence sees the Apocalypse itself as originally the great cry of the weak to put down the strong: he finds in Christianity a dualistic conflict between the strong commands and the counsels of meekness. Christianity, like the other great religions of renunciation (Buddhism and Plato's philosophy), is "for aristocrats of the spirit." But the mass of people do not have the aristocratic souls demanded by these prophets. Lawrence explains why the Gospels are so dependent upon images: although the images have little emotional value for us today, ancient sense-knowledge was based upon them, and the Book of Revelation was written in the way of the old pagan civilizations—the four horsemen and the red dragon and the seven seals have to be interpreted with this in mind.

Apocalypse closes with Lawrence's last life-statement:

What man most passionately wants is his living wholeness and his living unison, not his own isolate salvation of his "soul." Man wants his physical fulfillment first and foremost, since now, once and once only, he is in the flesh and potent. For man, the vast marvel is to be alive. For man, as for flower and beast and bird, the supreme triumph is to be most vividly, most perfectly alive. Whatever the unborn and the dead may know, they cannot know the beauty, the marvel of being alive in the flesh. The dead may look after the afterwards. But the magnificent here and now of life in the flesh is ours, and ours alone, and ours only for a time. We ought to dance with rapture that we should be alive and in the flesh, and part of the living, incarnate cosmos. I am part of the sun as my eye is part of me. That I am part of the earth my feet know perfectly, and my blood is part of the sea. My soul knows that I am part of the human race, my soul is an organic part of the great human soul, as my spirit is part of my nation. In my own very self, I am part of my family. There is nothing of me that is alone and absolute except my mind, and we shall find that the mind has no existence by itself, it is only the glitter of the sun on the surface of the waters.

So that my individualism is really an illusion. I am a part of the great whole, and I can never escape. But I *can* deny my connections, break them, and become a fragment. Then I am wretched.

What we want is to destroy our false, inorganic connections, especially those related to money, and re-establish the living organic connections, with the cosmos, the sun and earth, with mankind and nation and family. Start with the sun, and the rest will slowly, slowly happen.

During the last few months of his life Lawrence grew weaker daily, and often spent the mornings in bed, reading or writing. This is the report of Earl Brewster, whose daughter typed *Apocalypse* when she came to Bandol from her school in England for the Christmas holidays.

Brewster says Lawrence told him that he no longer objected to the word God and that he felt he "must establish a conscious relation with God." Sometimes he tried to trace the causes of his illness; he firmly believed that psychic troubles produced physical disturbances. Tapping his chest, he told Brewster, "The hatred which my books have aroused comes back at me and gets me here." He felt that there was an evil spirit in his body: "If I get the better of it in one place it goes to another." Brewster says that in the last months, Lawrence was gaining in tranquillity; Mrs. Brewster's reference to Lawrence's poems on death would seem to place their composition after the beginning of the year 1930. These include "The Ship of Death" and the items which follow it in *Last Poems*. Aldington seems to believe that "Prayer" in the "More Pansies" section of the *Last Poems* volume was perhaps Lawrence's final creative effort; Aldington quotes the first two lines as "the last broken utterance . . . written by a dying hand":

> Give me the moon at my feet,
> Put my feet upon the crescent, like a Lord!

On February 6 Lawrence made a difficult journey to a sanatorium at Vence, in the mountains above Nice: he left his Bandol villa, named Beau Soleil, for a place called Ad Astra. He had wanted to go to New Mexico, but had known he was too ill to make the journey. At the sanatorium he could sit in the sunlight on his balcony and see the coastline far below, and the distant city of Cannes. Frieda stayed at a nearby hotel—she had been joined by her daughter Barbara—now and then remaining with Lawrence during the distressing nights. Earl Brewster and the Huxleys were frequent visitors, and H. G. Wells, the Aga Kahn, and Jo Davidson ("made a clay head of me—made me tired") also came to see Lawrence during that February. He wrote a few letters, which tell mostly of his miserable nights: coughing and pain, inflammation of the liver and stomach, and trouble with the heart. Yet now and then there was an expression of hope—"I'm feeling more chirpy. . . . I wish I could sail away to somewhere really thrilling"—or an appreciation of the spring: "The mimosa is all out, in clouds—like Austria, and the almond blossoms very lovely."

On the first of March, St. David's Day, Lawrence moved to a house in Vence, the Villa Robermond, now the Villa Aurella; and the next night he died there. He was buried on the fourth of March, in a grave next to the wall in the local cemetery; there was no burial service, and only a dozen friends made up the funeral procession. Later he was given a nameless gravestone with the phoenix designed on it in colored pebbles.

Back in the Midlands, Lawrence's elder brother George woke up and leapt out of bed and said to his wife, "Bert's here." He says that his brother had died at exactly that moment. And Jessie Chambers had been "seeing" Lawrence, according to the previously mentioned letter she wrote to Helen Corke in 1933. She had not even known Lawrence was ill, but toward the end of his life she "felt acutely drawn to him at times." On the day he died, she heard his voice saying distinctly: "Can you remember only the pain and none of the joy?" and asking, "What has it all been about?" The next day she saw him, she says, as she "had known him in early days, with the little cap on the back of his head." A day later she was shocked when the papers carried the delayed announcement of his death. Her visions of him, not mentioned in her later memoir, were quite real to her, she told Helen Corke: "I don't think it was self-suggestion, because I didn't know he was ill. . . . You see that in essentials my feeling for him has not changed in spite of other deep affection. What he said about the indestructibility of love is quite true, on a particular plane."

Several years after his death, Lawrence's body was cremated, and the ashes were taken to his New Mexican ranch, in the Sangre de Cristo mountains. Outside the tomb, unfortunately

called a "shrine" on the roadside marker pointing to the ranch,
Frieda (who after Lawrence's death became the wife of Angelo
Ravagli) is buried; she outlived Lawrence by some twenty-six
years, dying on August 11, 1956, her seventy-seventh birthday.

The final version of Lawrence's last important poem, "The
Ship of Death," reads in part:

Now it is autumn and the falling fruit
and the long journey towards oblivion.

•   •   •

Have you built your ship of death, O have you?
O build your ship of death, for you will need it.

The grim frost is at hand, when the apples will fall
thick, almost thunderous, on the hardened earth.

And death is on the air like a smell of ashes!

•   •   •

Now launch the small ship, now as the body dies
and life departs, launch out, the fragile soul
in the fragile ship of courage, the ark of faith
with its store of food and little cooking pans
and change of clothes,
upon the flood's black waste
upon the waters of the end
upon the sea of death, where still we sail
darkly, for we cannot steer, and have no port.

•   •   •

The flood subsides, and the body, like a worn sea-shell
emerges strange and lovely.
And the little ship wings home, faltering and lapsing
on the pink flood,
and the frail soul steps out, into the house again
filling the heart with peace.

Swings the heart renewed with peace
even of oblivion.

Oh build your ship of death. Oh build it!
for you will need it.
For the voyage of oblivion awaits you.

SOME CONCLUSIONS

ALTHOUGH D. H. LAWRENCE WROTE POEMS, travel books, plays, and philosophical essays, he thought of himself as primarily a novelist. "And being a novelist, I consider myself superior to the saint, the scientist, the philosopher, and the poet"—men who may be "great masters of the different bits of the man alive," but never of the whole man. "The novel is the one bright book of life. Books are not life. They are tremulations on the ether. But the novel as a tremulation can make the whole man alive tremble. Which is more than poetry, philosophy, science, or any other book-tremulations can do."

Lawrence was not a creative philosopher. He had a few central thoughts, not precisely new thoughts, that he continually tried to convey to his reader. Sometimes he dramatized them effectively, sometimes he let them hamper his stories. Often his ideas were common sense given exalted utterance, often they were downright foolish, and often they were muddled in his own brand of mysticism.

Essentially Lawrence was trying to say one thing all his life. He had been saying it even before he was altogether aware of what it was, though he formulated it fairly early in his career: "My great religion is a belief in the blood, the flesh, as being wiser than the intellect. We can go wrong in our minds. But what our blood feels and believes and says, is always true."

Virtually all statements he made on all topics, and virtually

271

all stories he told, were elaborations of that idea: his Figure in the Carpet. His hatred of middle-class standards ("How beastly the bourgeois is") comes from his hatred of civilization, which tramples on instinctual ("blood") values. And many of Lawrence's other oppositions—to money-worship, to censorship, to machines, to literature bowdlerized at conception—stemmed from this blood-versus-mind doctrine, which determined the outcome of his fictional efforts and the behavior of his characters. And of course it was this philosophy that motivated Lawrence to write so fully about sexual matters, that made the sexual battlefield his principal base of operations.

It is necessary to explain again that Lawrence did not advocate "sheer animalism" or the destruction of the mind. He felt that the intuitional and the intellectual had fallen into imbalance on the side of the intellectual: he repeatedly explained that in emphasizing our need to revive the emotional values, he was trying to restore the balance.

We might understand the prophetic aspect of Lawrence more readily if we consider it in terms of that brilliant book on Tolstoy by Sir Isaiah Berlin, *The Hedgehog and The Fox*, which looks at novelists and poets in terms of the statement of Archilochus: "The fox knows many things, but the hedgehog knows one big thing." Lawrence, for all his identification with a fox in his story "The Fox," was essentially a hedgehog. What is important in his work is the power with which he expressed "one big thing" and its contingencies.

In Lawrence there is, as we have seen, an abundance of poetry to enjoy, not only in the lyrics but also in the novels and stories, for in vision and language Lawrence was always essentially a poet. As a writer of verse, he produced few outstanding single lyrics; there are hundreds of poems he wrote that, taken separately, do not seem to have particular distinction. The total effect, however, is of a passionate and important experience.

There is always flux in Lawrence, always transition, always struggle, always renewal; the life of his people is never undynamic. And with these people, through their "advanced" consciousness—heightened by their conflict and suffering—Lawrence presents another type of character not always obviously similar to the "realistic" literary kind most readers are used to. But as we look beyond the luminous flesh of these characters, to their beating consciousness, we find that they are not "unreal," not mere mock-ups for the points of philosophy the author wants to put across. If Lawrence sometimes fails—as in the case of Sir Clifford Chatterley, whose crippling somewhat cripples the story—it is not on the side of "character," of livingness, that he errs, but on the side of plot. For the people, even Sir Clifford, do live in their stories. There they do not necessarily dominate—except in those last tales written when the colors had faded out of nature for Lawrence—but have a dynamic relationship with natural forces outside them, as when the landscape is a pervasive and compelling influence. Lawrence had tended toward this kind of writing from the first—his landscapes were always *charged*—but he proved in story after story that he could skillfully handle characters and situations in the traditional manner; and it was not until after he had displayed his powers in one of the finest traditional-type British novels—*Sons and Lovers*—that he developed an interest in matters beyond characterization. But when he did, he did not thereafter fill his novels with dummies and corpses. Rather he illuminated fiction in a new way, and in dealing with ultrasensitive people on the edges rather than in centers of life, he was giving his readers a new vision of existence.

While Lawrence belonged to no group, he had much in common with the *symboliste* writers of the foremost literary movement of recent times. In many of his poems, and particularly in such novels as *The Rainbow* and *Women in Love*, he used "dynamic" symbols to convey inward states not ordinarily expressible in denotative language. Even his "blood-knowledge" ideas, whatever their moral status, were intuitional expressions of a *symboliste* kind. In all ways Lawrence was ahead of his time: today's readers can evaluate and be tolerant of his mistakes, for they are greatly outweighed by the good he has to offer.

Literature is the autobiography of humanity. Imaginative literature focuses, as nothing else can, the important elements that comprise the life of man. This is what Lawrence meant when he called the novelist superior to saint, scientist, philosopher, and poet; they cannot reach the whole man as the novelist can. The important writer, the truly creative man who works from internal compulsion, comprehends in his vision the elements that make up the different departments of life, and in expressing them and their impact upon mankind, he uses the medium of fable. Whether the fable takes the form of the epic, the drama, or the novel will depend on which of these is the living form of the age, as the novel is of ours. The important thing is that the fable presents experience in the fullest and richest way. When we read a great fable of the past, it shows us what the people of another time were like, the ancestors who moulded us, and it illuminates the enduring human themes. What has happened to people in great literature is what has happened to our past selves, is what is happening to us now. Writers of the recent past, or of the present, may lack the sanctification of accepted immortality, but they can tell us much that is valuable if they offer us more than we are given by all the little tickling authors who possess the top of our minds for one moment and are forgotten the next. The important writer invades large areas of our minds and our emotions, and shows us—often by jarring us unpleasantly—what the world about us is really like. By revealing to us a chapter of the autobiography of the present world, which is our own autobiography too, he gives us a heightened sense of values and increases the fullness of our response to life.

This is what a good contemporary writer, or a good writer of the recent past—and there are always few enough of either—can do for us. It is a different thing from what the hallowed classic writer, with his quality guaranteed by long survival, does for us, and the contemporary achievement is often considered of a lower order of importance. But it is important; and Lawrence is one of the few twentieth-century authors who can give us the vital intensification of our own world. And now that enough years have passed, since his death, to cool the anger into which he shocked so many of his own generation, an increasing number of readers is discovering him. In the wonder of his writing they are finding, whether they are in agreement or disagreement with all that he says, that Lawrence is one of the richest reading experiences of our time.

APPENDIX A

BOOKS ABOUT D. H. LAWRENCE
And Some Notes on the History of his Reputation

Of making many books about D. H. Lawrence there seems no end. During his lifetime, Lawrence had a certain notoriety but was rarely taken seriously in an age that celebrated the now forgotten John Galsworthys and Louis Bromfields. But, soon after Lawrence's death, a number of volumes about him appeared, chiefly the memoirs of campfollowers who put forth their competing views of the Master. These squabbling disciples didn't of course create a widespread interest in Lawrence's own writings; on the contrary, they tended to make the man they were variously in love with seem a preposterous eccentric who couldn't have written significant works.

The War of the Books was preceded by the Battle of the Obituaries. Rarely has the death of a man brought up such venom as filled the London journals in the spring of 1930. But the most vicious obituary came from an American source, the must-be-sophisticated *New Yorker*, in whose files the startled reader of today will find a report to the effect that Lawrence "had, among other eccentricities, a fancy for removing his clothes and climbing mulberry trees." This *canard* about a man who had just died was the handiwork of one "Genêt" (Janet Flanner), who still contributes impressions to the *New Yorker* from Paris, though it is difficult to believe that the anti-Vichy French can be happy over her wartime writings in praise of Pétain.

Her nastiness about Lawrence was equalled in 1930 only by that of a man of the type so often elected to the United States Senate: Senator Reed Smoot, who just at the time of Lawrence's death had read *Lady Chatterley's Lover* and roared to his

275

astounded colleagues in the senate chamber that the man who
had written such a book had a soul so black that it would be a
shining light in hell. Well, times have changed: Lawrence as a
human being has now a far better reputation than the ridiculous
statement by "Genêt" would have allowed him, and whatever
the color of his soul in the afterlife, his best-known novel has
been sold legally in America since 1959 and in England since
1960.

The uniquely bitter obituaries by J. C. Squire and others in
the British and American press were answered by a number
defending Lawrence, including those by Catherine Carswell,
Richard Aldington, and Lady Ottoline Morrell. Rebecca West's
"Elegy" was later printed as a book. E. M. Forster disagreed
with many of his Bloomsbury friends and declared, in the *Nation
and Athenaeum*, "Now he is dead, and the lowbrows whom he
scandalized have united with the highbrows whom he bored to
ignore his greatness. This cannot be helped; no one who alienates
both Mrs. Grundy and Aspasia can hope for a good obituary
Press. All that we can do . . . is to say straight out that he
was the greatest imaginative novelist of our generation"—a judg-
ment magnanimous and daring at the time, but one with which
the world has subsequently come to concur.

Meanwhile, in 1930, Stephen Potter's pioneer volume, subtitled
A First Study, paid serious critical attention to Lawrence. The
following year, John Middleton Murry's *Son of Woman*, a psychological portrait of Lawrence and his work, appeared to do
its quota of damage. (It must be noted that, before his death
in 1957, Murry had a far higher opinion of Lawrence, as represented for example by his essay in *A D. H. Lawrence Miscellany*, 1959.) In the year following that in which Murry's *Son
of Woman* was published, 1931, the zaniest of all the memoirs
appeared, Mabel Dodge Luhan's *Lorenzo in Taos*, which frenet-
ically told of Mrs. Luhan's unsuccessful attempts to take Lawrence into camp. Then in 1932, Catherine Carswell attempted a
corrective with her generous biography, *The Savage Pilgrimage*,
and Lawrence's sister, Mrs. Ada Clarke, wrote calmly of his
childhood and youth (in collaboration with G. Stuart Gelder)
in *Young Lorenzo: Early Life of D. H. Lawrence*. This was also
the year of Aldous Huxley's edition of the *Letters*, in which

Lawrence was allowed to speak for himself. It was high time: after Mrs. Luhan's account of the brouhaha in New Mexico, the reader could only shake his head sadly and repeat Matthew Arnold's words about the Shelley circle: "What a set! What a world!" Huxley prefaced the *Letters* with a fine essay which coolly helped to destroy at least part of the "Genêt"-Mabel Luhan image of the crazy Lawrence, which the letters themselves further helped to destroy.

In 1933, the Hon. Dorothy Brett's *Lawrence and Brett: A Friendship* appeared, written in the historical present and in a second-person style addressed directly to Lawrence; the book was friendly and worshipful, but didn't offer the reader a frenzied hero. In that same year, Murry supplied *Reminiscences of D. H. Lawrence*, which enroute attempted to refute a good deal of what Catherine Carswell had said. And 1933 also saw the first appearance of one of the Lawrencean critical landmarks, Horace Gregory's *Pilgrim of the Apocalypse*, fortunately still available and still emphatically excellent. In the following year, 1934, two more valuable books of memoirs appeared. One of them was *D. H. Lawrence: Reminiscences and Correspondence*, by Earl and Achsah Brewster, containing valuably selfless recollections and important letters; the other was Frieda Lawrence's *Not I, But the Wind.* . . . In this biography, Lawrence's widow told with childlike frankness of her life with Lawrence, of the happy occasions and of the quarrels—as time passed, Frieda tried more and more to sanctify her late husband, until the point was reached at which she wouldn't let anyone even suggest that there had been any quarrels. But her book remains an important memoir; it records not only the quarrels but also matters of greater importance.

The original of Miriam, the farm girl in *Sons and Lovers*, Mrs. John Wood (née Jessie Chambers), launched her self-defense in *D. H. Lawrence: A Personal Record*, in 1935, a book which cast much valuable information on Lawrence's youth but was partly an attempt to answer what can't be answered, a novel; she spent a lifetime of injured bewilderment after Lawrence had, in *Sons and Lovers*, portrayed her with the artist's combination of sympathetic understanding and cruel detachment.

In 1938, Knud Merrild's memoir, *A Poet and Two Painters*, told of the winter which Merrild and a fellow-Dane spent with the Lawrences on the mountains above Taos. This adds little to the Lawrence story; a good part of the book is made up of passages excerpted from Lawrence—written at and concerned with other occasions and places—and crammed in as conversations with Merrild or as what Lawrence might be assumed to be thinking at a certain time. Hugh Kingsmill, who specialized in books about other authors' ineptitudes, prepared a pastiche of the Lawrence disciples' memoirs which he brought out in 1938 as *The Life of D. H. Lawrence*. The *New Republic's* review of the book noted its distortions, but found one bit of hope in it: "Kingsmill's skeptical attitude will have a corrective value, however, if it discourages the Lorenzophiliacs who try too literally to worship the master. . . . At least Kingsmill serves as a low bridge to knock off those who try to ride on top of the train." This last was a reference to the cultists who were a phenomenon of the time, made fun of in 1939 in William York Tindall's *D. H. Lawrence and Susan His Cow*, which offered some serious and important scholarship on Lawrence as well as some jibes and jabs at his vulnerable side and at the cultists. Professor Tindall, now one of the world's leading Joyce scholars, has recently come to respect Lawrence more than he did in the past. And, oddly enough, it is the Joyceans who are now the cultists, with anniversary meetings at the Gotham Book Mart at which sacramental wine is drunk; there are also the pilgrimages to Dublin which so many of us who study, teach, and write about Joyce feel piously inclined to make.

Cults or no cults, Lawrence's reputation, judging by books and articles about him, was at its lowest during the Second World War. William White's *D. H. Lawrence: A Checklist, 1931-1950* (supplementing E. D. McDonald's valuable earlier bibliographical volumes of 1925 and 1931), pointed out in 1950 that the number of books and articles about Lawrence throughout the world had "dwindled to virtually nothing in 1942." Two years earlier, the editorial in the *Saturday Review* (written by the author of the present volume) which appeared on March 2, 1940, exactly ten years after Lawrence's death, had spoken of him as "The Great Unread," but had predicted that the condition would change.

Those who wanted to read about the proletariat in the 1930s failed to perceive that Lawrence had written some of the greatest of all fiction about the working class, and those who were preoccupied with the war in the 1940s had similarly not seen what Middleton Murry subsequently stated (in his previously mentioned *Lawrence Miscellany* essay): "Lawrence was alone in the depth of his prescience of the crisis of humanity which has developed since his death." But after the war, the attitude began to change, as in the case of William York Tindall, who in *Forces in Modern British Literature*, first published in 1947, took a modified post-Hiroshima look at Lawrence, whose crusade against science, "preached by allegory and symbol, seems less absurd today than it used to seem. . . . About to be decomposed, we can turn with understanding," Professor Tindall suggested, to such prophets as Lawrence and can perhaps even accept some of their religious pronouncements.

In 1950, Anthony West's small volume in "the English Novelists Series" made a valuable addition to Lawrence criticism. In that same year, one of Lawrence's old friends and most consistent defenders, Richard Aldington, brought out a biography of him that was somewhat disappointing in that it contained little that was new; but it was a sympathetic portrait, painted in dry wit, and altogether a pleasant book to read. In the following year, 1951, the first edition of *The Life and Works of D. H. Lawrence* appeared; the reader has the evidence in hand to form his own opinion about this volume. In that same year, Martin Jarrett-Kerr's *D. H. Lawrence and Human Existence* was first published as by "Father Tiverton" (the revised edition of 1961 correctly ascribes the authorship to Father Jarrett-Kerr); now that the book can be seen in perspective it is possible to state that it is by far the finest all-inclusive critical interpretation of Lawrence.

A book of a quite different kind also came out in 1951, Witter Bynner's *Journey With Genius*, which evoked the atmosphere of the essentially anti-Lawrence reminiscences of the 1930s. Lawrence had prophetically called Bynner "a belated sort of mosquito." His delayed sting was accompanied by a great deal of self-glorification: the careful reader of the book will see that Bynner spends a large amount of space in telling about the occasions on which he got the better of Lawrence.

The "Lorenzo" memoirs in general were given a masterful lampooning by James Thurber in his hilarious sketch, "My Memories of D. H. Lawrence," reprinted in *The Achievement of D. H. Lawrence* in 1953 by Frederick J. Hoffman and Harry T. Moore, who collaborated in editing a collection of critical essays by T. S. Eliot, F. R. Leavis, Richard Ellmann, Mark Schorer, Aldous Huxley, Horace Gregory, Edmund Wilson, and others, a volume showing that Lawrence criticism was coming of age. Another 1951 book, published in Ceylon, was Martin Wickramasinghe's *The Mysticism of D. H. Lawrence*, the first study of this author's occultism to be made by an Easterner versed in such matters (Martin Wickramasinghe is a Sinhalese novelist). He discusses Mme. Blavatsky and others who had an influence on D. H. Lawrence, and he criticizes Middleton Murry and others for their inadequate understanding of the roots of Lawrence's mysticism; he unfortunately doesn't seem to have read W. Y. Tindall's examination of the matter in *D. H. Lawrence and Susan His Cow*. The most useful parts of the Wickramasinghe book are the suggestions of parallels between Lawrence's doctrines and those of the Tantricists, who celebrate a kind of sexual mysticism.

By 1955, the revival was fully on—revivalistic in the case of F. R. Leavis, with his belligerently dogmatic *D. H. Lawrence: Novelist*, which provides some fine insights when not attacking Mr. Leavis's pet peeves, such as T. S. Eliot, who has been acclaimed by the readers of this century even if some of the age's most scrupulous scrutinizers have been persecuted by neglect. There was an ironic note in Mr. Leavis's shrillness, for by this time Lawrence himself was no longer being neglected, and those who had adopted the persona of the worst side of him—the angry, sick man of the last years—could afford to cast it off, if their own sickness had not reached a stage of no return.

The kind of criticism Lawrence now needed was not the Leavisian *folie de grandeur* (to cite the phrase William Gerhardi has used in connection with Mr. Leavis), but reasonable assessments of the kind found in Mark Spilka's *The Love Ethic of D. H. Lawrence*, also in 1955; Mr. Spilka was sometimes given to oversimplifying his points, but he often made those points very neatly, and in any event called attention to a perhaps unconscious pattern of organization in Lawrence's work. Another volume of 1955 contains so excellent an essay on Lawrence that it cries out for the breaking of the rule to the effect that only books entirely devoted to Lawrence be mentioned in the present appendix: Leone Vivante's *A Philosophy of Potentiality*. Signor Vivante makes an extremely fine and rewarding investigation of Lawrence's spontaneity, and in so doing comes closer to the "secret" of this author than most critics who see him purely as a literary figure or than most interpreters who view him chiefly as a socio-religious prophet.

In that same year of 1955, the most comprehensive biography of Lawrence appeared, *The Intelligent Heart*, by Harry T. Moore, followed the next year by this author's *Poste Restante: A Lawrence Travel Calendar*, which was prefaced by Mark Schorer's brilliant essay on Lawrence and the spirit of place (reprinted three years later in the *Lawrence Miscellany*). In 1956, Graham Hough's *The Dark Sun: A Study of D. H. Lawrence* presented a competent interpretation which summed up a good deal of the public knowledge about Lawrence; the book presented no strikingly imaginative insights.

John Middleton Murry had, with the passing of time, taken an improved view of Lawrence, and in 1957, the year in which Murry died, his *Love, Freedom and Society* appeared, subtitled *An Analytic Comparison of D. H. Lawrence and Albert Schweitzer*. Murry thought that although these men were in many ways opposites, they had certain beliefs in common, namely: that Christian civilization was coming to an end, that salvation "depends upon opening up new sources of love," that they reject traditional Christianity, "although both are deeply religious men . . . . dedicated to a revolution of the religious consciousness." Murry felt that Lawrence "failed" because he put his faith in what he called "blood knowledge," and that Schweitzer, on the other hand, has been too rational. "They forgot that love was there at the beginning: it was the cause of their despair." Murry's friend Sir Richard Rees published, in

1958, a comparison of a different kind, *Brave Men: A Study of D. H. Lawrence and Simone Weil.* Lawrence had said that "brave men are for ever born, and nothing else is worth having"; Rees finds that these two compassionate writers, both of whom profoundly disliked industrial civilization, were in many ways antipodal but were alike in being ahead of everyone else of our time in their reverence for life.

Biographical studies of Lawrence were given a forceful impetus by Edward Nehls's *D. H. Lawrence: A Composite Biography* whose three volumes appeared respectively in 1957, 1958, and 1959. These expertly edited books put together the various memoirs about Lawrence, to which the compiler added fresh ones he had induced former acquaintances of Lawrence to write. Except for a bit of extraneous matter in the third volume, the *Composite Biography* is a magnificent achievement, and those interested in Lawrence's life and his writings are greatly in Edward Nehls's debt.

Armin Arnold, a Swiss student of Lawrence, in 1958 judiciously assembled much critical material for his *D. H. Lawrence in America*, which he followed four years later with *The Symbolic Meaning.* This book valuably presented the "uncollected" or earlier versions of Lawrence's *Studies in Classic American Literature*, with which Armin Arnold's volume may be interestingly compared. Whether, as the editor claims, the earlier versions of the essays are better than the later is a highly debatable point; nevertheless, *The Symbolic Meaning* is an important contribution to Lawrence scholarship.

The Lawrence number of *Modern Fiction Studies* (Spring 1959) had the effect of a book. It contained excellent essays by Kingsley Widmer and others, and a full checklist of Lawrence criticism compiled by Maurice Beebe, editor of the journal, and Anthony Tomasi. In the fall of that year, *A D. H. Lawrence Miscellany* appeared, edited by Harry T. Moore, with essays and articles by, among others, Marvin Mudrick, Angelo Bertocci, Richard Aldington, Frederick R. Karl, Raymond Williams, and Karl Shapiro. The publication of the book by the Southern Illinois University Press was commemorated at that school by a symposium on Lawrence and Joyce and an exhibition of their books and manuscripts. The participants in the symposium included Richard Ellmann, David Garnett, Horace Gregory, Frederick J. Hoffman, Marvin Magalaner (who had edited a *Joyce Miscellany* also published by the Press there), William York Tindall, and Lionel Trilling. In the following year, 1960, the seventy-fifth anniversary of Lawrence's birth and the thirtieth of his death, the University of Nottingham sponsored, under the direction of Professor V. de Sola Pinto, the largest Lawrence exhibit ever held, and a lecture series devoted to Lawrence.

That year was also marked by an excellent critical interpretation of Lawrence's work, or at least of part of it: Eliseo Vivas's *D. H. Lawrence: The Failure and Triumph of Art*, which discussed Lawrence's principal novels out of chronological order. First, Mr. Vivas dealt with those he considered failures or half-successes, even if like *Lady Chatterley's Lover* they belong amid the later work, and then he discussed those he regarded as triumphs: such comparatively early volumes as *The Rainbow* and *Women in Love*. In these books Lawrence is seen as effectively dramatizing his material; in them, the ideas don't get in the way of the story. One of the interesting points of Mr. Vivas's book is its author's application of what he calls "the constitutive symbol," which he finds in Lawrence's better work.

In contradistinction to the early 1940s, books about Lawrence flourished in the early 1960s, and the magazines were full of references to him and articles about him. Indeed, Lawrence himself had a small magazine devoted to him, the *D. H. Lawrence News and Notes*, edited now and then by Dexter Martin of the State University of California, Pennsylvania. The *News and Notes*, at times a bit too much on the *enfant-terrible* side of Lawrence, is in any event always lively and informative.

As Lawrence criticism continued to thrive in the 1960s, Anthony Beal, who in 1956 had edited a volume of Lawrence's *Selected Literary Criticism*, brought out a small but comprehensive manual, *D. H. Lawrence* (1961). As the present revised edition of *The Life and Works of D. H. Lawrence* goes to print, a number of critical studies of Lawrence have appeared: *The Utopian Vision of D. H. Lawrence*, by Eugene Goodheart; *The Deed of Life*, by Julian Moynihan; *Oedipus in Nottingham*, by Daniel Weiss, and *The Art of Perversity: D. H. Lawrence's*

Shorter Fictions, by Kingsley Widmer. Mark Spilka's *D. H. Lawrence* is an anthology of critical essays in a series of such collections. There is also the comprehensive, accurate, and immensely useful new volume, *A Bibliography of D. H. Lawrence*, by Warren Roberts, who is also collaborating with Harry T. Moore on a pictorial biography of Lawrence. The articles devoted to this author continue to increase, and of making many books about Lawrence there still seems no end.

APPENDIX B

THE GENESIS OF SONS AND LOVERS

as revealed in the Miriam Papers

When Lawrence was writing *Sons and Lovers* he showed parts of the manuscript to Jessie Chambers, who made some emendations upon them. She also wrote several episodes which Lawrence incorporated into the final version of the novel. The documents containing the material she wrote—examined for the first time in the following pages—will hereinafter be referred to as The Miriam Papers. They are now located at the Humanities Research Center of the University of Texas. (It is interesting to note that the final manuscript version of *Sons and Lovers*, given by Frieda Lawrence to Mabel Luhan and "missing" for many years, was purchased in 1963 by the University of California.)

Jessie Chambers is identified elsewhere in this book as the Miriam of *Sons and Lovers*. Jessie Chambers, who in 1915 had become Mrs. John R. Wood, died in March 1944 at the age of fifty-seven. A year younger than Lawrence, she had outlived him by fourteen years.

The Miriam Papers, which date from 1911 and probably 1912, fall into two parts. One of these parts comprises three manuscript sections in Jessie Chambers' own hand; the second part of The Miriam Papers consists of two sections; one is a twenty-three-page fragment of manuscript in Lawrence's hand, with Jessie's interlinear comments and protests; the other is a separate four pages of comments in her hand.

The description and analysis of these documents will follow the order in which they are mentioned above. In the first part—passages of *Sons and Lovers* originally written by Jessie—one fragment is on ruled white paper, seven and seven-eighths inches

285

by nine inches, and the two other fragments are on ruled white paper seven and three-quarters by ten and a half inches; all the writing on these sheets is in ink. The first of these items was possibly cut, along its left margin, out of a composition book (British, "exercise book"); the other two are composed of apparently independent leaves, although they might have been in a writing tablet whose pages tore off easily at the top.

The first item consists of two full pages and one-third of another that has four lines of writing which end the episode, for above the place where the sheet is cut off, a wavy line indicates the end of the preceding text. The text itself provides the basis for the episode which occurs in Chapter VII—"Lad-And-Girl Love"—and describes one of Paul's arrivals at Willey Farm and an encounter with Miriam and her sister Agatha.

Lawrence took the outline of the episode from Jessie Chambers, and then used some of her sentences, but he greatly expanded the material—and illuminated it. Her effort is a commonplace account of an incident, the kind of writing almost any literate person could provide. Lawrence in adapting it does not produce a "great" passage, but he transmutes the material creatively and makes the episode one of the many living bits that contribute to the total effectiveness of *Sons and Lovers*.

In Jessie Chambers' version of this "Saturday Afternoon" fragment, Miriam and Agatha are dressing when they hear the "characteristic, click of the chain" as Paul flings open the gate and pushes his bicycle into the yard. Lawrence in *Sons and Lovers* sets the scene more fully; he does not merely have the girls "upstairs dressing," but describes the bedroom, which is above the stable: the Veronese reproduction on the wall, and the view from the windows. Lawrence "characterizes" the girls somewhat, contrasting not only their appearances but their ideas of values. In both Jessie's version and Lawrence's, the dialogue is identical when the girls briefly discuss the arrival of Paul, and in both accounts "Agatha was dressed first, and ran downstairs," but Lawrence's adaptation differs in many details. It is interesting to note that the comma before "and" in the sentence just quoted, technically incorrect in modern English, was omitted in Jessie's manuscript; a comma with the double predicate was habitual with Lawrence, probably because of his familiarity with the King James Bible, in which the use of commas in this construction is common. Jessie Chambers in her "Saturday Afternoon" fragment has Paul make no further appearance until Miriam descends and sees him in the parlor, where he is talking to Agatha. But in *Sons and Lovers* Lawrence, while keeping the focus on Miriam in this sequence, also keeps Paul within range: Miriam hears him talking in Midlands dialect to the "seedy" old horse in the yard below. Miriam also—in Lawrence's version—hears her sister gaily greeting Paul downstairs. In both versions, Miriam prays at this point, asking the Lord to keep her from loving Paul if it is not right for her to love him; Lawrence throughout the prayer sequence writes more skillfully than the girl who was here providing a part of her own autobiography, though now and then he takes over phrases and even whole sentences from her manuscript. He omits, however, Jessie's extravagant comparison between Miriam's plight and Gethsemane; at the end of the prayer he describes her as she kneels by the bed, "her black hair against the red squares of the patchwork-quilt." After she finishes her prayer, she gets up and goes to meet Paul:

When she went downstairs Paul was lying back in an armchair, holding forth with much vehemence to Agatha, who was scorning a little painting he had brought to show her. Miriam glanced at the two, and avoided their levity. She went into the parlour to be alone.

It was teatime before she was able to speak to Paul, and then her manner was so distant he thought he had offended her.

These two paragraphs are taken over almost verbatim from Jessie's narrative. The only difference in the first sentence, besides Lawrence's omission of the comma Jessie put after the opening adverbial clause and his altering of "the arm-chair" to "an arm-chair," is in Lawrence's slight improvement of the expression "talking in an animated way to Agatha." In the second sentence Miriam, in Jessie's version, "glanced at them, half afraid of their levity, and went into the parlour." Lawrence makes a separate paragraph, of the next sentence, which is precisely as Jessie wrote it, with the very minor exception of Lawrence's making "teatime" one word instead of using Jessie's hyphenation.

In her manuscript the episode ends with Paul wondering whether Miriam has been offended; it is below this sentence that the wavy line is drawn and that the rest of the page is torn off. In *Sons and Lovers* another sequence begins immediately, one that again draws upon material supplied, as will be shown, by Jessie Chambers.

At this point, however, an examination of some of the background facts of the material is in order. Jessie Chambers—in her *D. H. Lawrence: A Personal Record* (1935), for whose ascription of authorship she used the pseudonymous initials E. T.—said that when she gave Lawrence her reactions to the first draft of *Sons and Lovers*, he "asked me to write what I could remember of our early days, because, as he truthfully said, my recollection of those days was so much clearer than his." She suggested that his request was made in the autumn of 1911; she was wrong, however, in stating that Lawrence began the novel in that year, for in a letter to Sydney Pawling of Heinemann's on October 18, 1910, Lawrence speaks of the book—then entitled *Paul Morel*—as being one-eighth completed.

The contents of the early version of this novel, as outlined by Jessie Chambers in her book, and by Lawrence Clark Powell in *The Manuscripts of D. H. Lawrence* (1937), have been mentioned in the section of the present volume dealing with *Sons and Lovers;* the various stages in the composition of the book were also discussed there. The Miriam Papers apparently are concerned with improving the first version of the novel, the version which was begun in 1910 but not shown to Jessie Chambers until the autumn of the following year. This version will be referred to hereinafter as *Paul Morel A.*

Lawrence was violently ill by the end of that autumn of 1911, and was convalescent through most of the ensuing winter. At this time he was working on *The Trespasser*, which he completed in early February, for publication in May. In a letter to Edward Garnett on February 24, 1912, Lawrence spoke of his "third novel," which was obviously *Paul Morel*. He expected to complete it by May: he had not expected to meet Frieda.

Jessie Chambers said that Lawrence wrote *Sons and Lovers* in a frenzy, in about six weeks. This was probably the second draft, and it was doubtless this version of the manuscript he wrote of as practically completed, in May 1912, when he was alone in the Rhineland after he and Frieda had gone to the Continent and had temporarily separated. This version of the book that was to be *Sons and Lovers* will subsequently be referred to as *Paul Morel B*. Early in June Lawrence mailed the finished product to England; late in July he had received it back and by the middle of November had finished it in Italy—the *Sons and Lovers* that was published the following May.

It is necessary to point out once again that Jessie Chambers' contribution of various episodes to the novel was doubtless an attempt to improve the *first draft*, or *Paul Morel A*. Two more of these contributions remain to be discussed: they might be called "Easter Monday" and "Flower Sequence."

These are, as previously explained, on larger-size paper than the section previously analyzed. "Easter Monday," which carries that title at the beginning, is a complete unit on four pages. Lawrence does not use this sequence in the "Lad-And-Girl Love" chapter, but in the second chapter afterward, "Defeat of Miriam."

Once again Lawrence takes a narrative outline from Jessie, using the same incidents and occasionally the same language, but once again the result is vastly different: her prose is lead, his quicksilver.

In "Easter Monday," Paul walks through the fields with Miriam, her mother, and two of the smaller children. At tea, Paul complains about a sermon he had heard on Good Friday. Later, he and Miriam sit under a haystack, and he reads from *Jane Eyre*. Then he and the girl discuss their status. When they go back indoors, Miriam's mother says that Paul is pale and that she is sure he has caught cold. He leaves, and two days later he sends Miriam a copy of *The Mill on the Floss*.

All this is familiar to readers of *Sons and Lovers*, where Lawrence scrambled the material somewhat, however; the mockery of the sermon Paul had heard in the Primitive Methodist Chapel comes early in the chapter, during Paul's visit to the farm on

Easter Sunday. Jessie's "Easter Monday" sequence he gives to the following *Sunday*.

Once again, where Jessie Chambers provided the barest outline, Lawrence filled it in with living details. In her first "Easter Monday" paragraph, for instance, Paul finds a thrush's nest, and after carefully breaking away the thorns he holds the "eggs reverently in the hollowed palm of his hand." Then Jessie's narrative abruptly switches to Paul's later discussion of the sermon, at tea. But in *Sons and Lovers* Lawrence brings the whole scene alive, using it to develop story and character. The mother thrush has been frightened away by the approach of the human beings, and the eggs are still warm; Miriam's mother speaks sympathetically of the bird, and Miriam is compelled to touch the eggs, as well as Paul's hand, which "cradled them so well." She says it is a strange warmth, and he tells her it is blood heat. She watches him as he reaches through the thorns of the hedge, putting the eggs back, his hands carefully folded over them. "He was concentrated on the act. Seeing him so, she loved him; he seemed so simple and sufficient to himself. And she could not get to him."

Later, when Paul and Miriam have been reading by the haystack, he asks "Do you think—if I didn't come up so much—you might get to like somebody else—another man?" This is almost exactly as Jessie wrote it, and for two pages Lawrence closely follows her version of the conversation, ocasionally changing a word or a phrase, adding "he blurted," or noting that "Miriam wanted to cry. And she was angry, too," and making similar additions.

When Paul and Miriam go back indoors, Miriam's mother exclaims, as previously mentioned, that Paul looks pale; in Lawrence's version, instead of merely stating that Paul has probably caught cold, she keeps the balance between all the characters by asking whether he does not feel that he has caught cold; Paul, kept in focus, laughs and says "Oh no!" Lawrence adds that Paul did, however, feel "done up," worn out by "the conflict in himself."

In Jessie Chambers' account, "While it was quite early and not yet dark, Paul rose to go. The family exclaimed at his going so soon. Miriam, sitting in the rocking-chair, near the wall of the stairs, was silent." In *Sons and Lovers* Lawrence breaks this paragraph up, intensifies the situation. Paul starts to leave while it is "quite early," and Miriam's mother "anxiously" asks "You're not going home, are you?" He replies that he had promised to be home early; he is "very awkward." Miriam's father steps into the little contest: "But this *is* early." Miriam sits in her chair; Paul hesitates beside it, expecting her as usual to walk out to the barn with him when he goes after his bicycle. When she does not join him, he is "at a loss," and he departs. In Jessie's story, as he passes the window he looks "at her with so much reproach that she" goes to the doorway to wave farewell to him. Lawrence is not content to have Paul merely look at Miriam with "much reproach": in *Sons and Lovers*, Miriam sees Paul "pale, his brows knit slightly in a way that had become constant with him, his eyes dark with pain."

The third section of the first part of the Miriam Papers is less interesting than the other two; it is a two-page fragment out of context, called "Flower Sequence" here.

Lawrence took over virtually all the material in this fragment, spreading it over three pages of *Sons and Lovers* in the "Lad-and-Girl Love" chapter. This "Flower Sequence" describes an episode in the Morels' garden, where Paul picks some sweet peas and pins them on Miriam's dress, saying "Don't let mother know." Miriam tells Paul that she will no longer call for him at his house on the Thursday evenings when she comes into town to the library; if Paul wants to be with her at the library he can meet her at some place in town; because he will not do this, the Thursday evenings at the library are "dropped." Paul's attitude in regard to "the glances and remarks of acquaintances is that such manifestations are unimportant: 'Let them talk.'"

Lawrence in *Sons and Lovers* again makes the situation more effective by dramatizing the material Jessie has provided, by adding opposing statements, and by swinging his camera around to catch peripheral but significant details. Instead of statements about Paul and Miriam arriving at decisions, Lawrence shows them in discussion, using tense, brief sentences. And where Jessie merely says that "the Thursday evenings at the library were dropped," Lawrence intensifies the situation by addition, deepening it particularly by introducing Paul's mother at the end of the paragraph: "So the Thursday evenings, which had been so precious to her, and to him, were dropped. He worked instead. Mrs. Morel sniffed with satisfaction at this arrangement."

Lawrence, however, took over a good deal of Jessie's text in this sequence. He even assimilates some of the descriptions and color: Jessie's sentence, "The sky behind the church was orange-red with sunset: the garden was flooded with a strange warm light that lifted every leaf into significance," goes into *Sons and Lovers* almost exactly as she wrote it.

The foregoing discussion of the first part of the Miriam Papers proves the truth of Jessie Chambers' assertion that she wrote what she modestly called "notes" to help Lawrence with the composition of *Sons and Lovers*. The comparison of her text with that of the published novel indicates that Lawrence advantageously used the material, greatly improving it in the process. It might be pointed out that Jessie Chambers was not trying to write a novel, that she was merely providing "notes," but actually she did use the narrative form, and there can be little doubt that her effort represents the best that she could do at the time: her *Personal Record*, written years later in direct autobiographical form, is superior in composition to her *Paul Morel* "notes." (She wrote an autobiographical novel, *Eunice Temple*, which she destroyed; the name character furnished the initials, E.T., which she used to signify the authorship of her later *Personal Record* of Lawrence.)

The questions remain, how much credit should she be given for collaboration on *Sons and Lovers*, and how far did her collaboration actually extend?

So far as credit for collaboration is concerned, Jessie Chambers in her essential modesty never put in a claim for any: her principal contention in regard to *Sons and Lovers* was that the book "betrayed" the beauty of her early relationship with Lawrence; she continually makes it clear that she cannot distinguish between biographical fact and the necessary fiction required for the novel-form. So far as the question of combined authorship is concerned, the situation is certainly different from that of Lawrence's collaboration with M. L. Skinner, whose entire novel *The House of Ellis* was rewritten by Lawrence as *The Boy in the Bush*. It is doubtful that Jessie Chambers' contributions were much more extensive than the sections already surveyed. That Lawrence was an extremely resourceful, richly inventive writer cannot be gainsaid: occasionally he drew upon the recollections or reactions of others in order that parts of his writing not dealing with himself, or not dealing exclusively with himself, might have some of the immediacy of his purely objective passages. It has been mentioned in the body of the present book that Lawrence's wife says that he kept asking her, when he was writing about his mother in *Sons and Lovers*, what a woman would feel at certain times, in certain situations—and Frieda says that she wrote several passages of *Sons and Lovers*. Lawrence's reworking of Miss Skinner's book did not represent his only attempt at large-scale collaboration with women in the writing of novels: he wanted Mabel Luhan to work with him on a story about her life, and Catherine Carswell includes in *The Savage Pilgrimage* a vivid synopsis Lawrence prepared of a Scottish novel for which Mrs. Carswell was to supply the Caledonian background and the character of the heroine. In *Sons and Lovers*, however, Lawrence went far beyond the range of what Jessie Chambers could have supplied, or what Frieda might have provided as a description of the mother's feelings; indeed, Jessie was irritated because he went too far beyond her own ideas of reality and propriety in introducing Clara Dawes into the story and in giving the mother "the laurels of victory" in the conflict with Miriam.

Lawrence's originality can be defended easily: the re-creation of his own family background, for example, reveals a gift of selection by artistic principle, of inventiveness in which imagination dominates fact, and of sustained narrative intensity, all present in a high degree. Throughout the novel, the descriptions of the life of the coal miners, of the workers in an artificial-limb factory, of young people from Midlands farms and towns, all presented in a rich fullness, are testimony to Lawrence's surpassing ability to transmute fact into what might be called the imaginative reality of first-rate fiction. If Jessie Chambers provided him with some details about life at Haggs Farm, and even with some memories of the time she and Lawrence were living through their unhappy relationship, these raw materials were used by him in the same way as his own observations and remembered experiences.

It may be said, then, that while Jessie Chambers supplied a number of reminiscental passages which Lawrence assimilated into *Sons and Lovers,* she was in no true sense a collaborator. Her innate modesty did not merely prevent her from making such a claim: there is no hint in her book on Lawrence that she even remotely considered doing so. She was, indeed, as previously pointed out, hostile to *Sons and Lovers.* But in discussing the book, she mentions merely that she provided some notes and suggestions. That is what she did, and no more. Her material had an ancillary value; Lawrence's gift was the primary one, and he used the material creatively.

So far, Jessie Chambers' positive contributions have been considered; her appearances in the second part of the Miriam Papers are chiefly negative.

As previously pointed out, this second portion of the Miriam Papers comprises twenty-three pages of Lawrence's manuscript with comments by Jessie Chambers, plus her four-page critique of that section of the manuscript. It is quite possible, as will be shown later, that this part of Lawrence's manuscript was based on papers of Jessie's that are now missing.

Lawrence's twenty-three holograph sheets are numbered pp. 204-226. The first page begins with two words (". . . knock it.") ending a paragraph; p. 226, which apparently concludes a section, contains only five lines of writing. The paper, nine and seven-eighths by seven and seven-eighths inches, is obviously torn from a tablet bound at the top; the paper is thin, the ruled lines are dim and on one side only, and the ink of the handwriting is grey. Jessie's comments are in pencil.

The material covered in this segment of manuscript corresponds for the most part to incidents in the "Lad-And-Girl Love" chapter (Chapter VII) of the final version; judging from Miriam's notations, this was Chapter IX in the earlier version, and entitled "Young Love." This manuscript evidently represents a fragment of the second stage of composition of *Sons and Lovers;* as previously noted, the entire second *Paul Morel* manuscript will be designated hereafter as *Paul Morel B.* The manuscript described by Dr. Powell in *The Manuscripts of D. H. Lawrence*—the crude early *Paul Morel* in which the father is jailed for accidentally killing one of his sons—would then properly become *Paul Morel A*, as also previously noted. This *Paul Morel A* was the product of 1910-1911. *Paul Morel B* was evidently written in the spring of 1912, completed in Germany about the beginning of June. Between July and November, in Germany, Austria, and Italy, Lawrence wrote what might be designated as *Paul Morel C*, the actual manuscript of *Sons and Lovers* as published. The segment of manuscript discussed here as comprising the first section of the second part of the Miriam Papers is apparently a section of *Paul Morel B*; it is probably a variant, for Lawrence doubtless rewrote this chapter and

	Sequence	Ms. pages
1.	Paul, Miriam, and the swing	204
2.	Paul discusses art	204-207
3.	Paul teaches algebra	207-208
4.	Paul and his mother	208-209
5.	Paul walks with Miriam	211-214
6.	Paul talks with his mother	214-216
7.	The Good Friday hike	216-221
8.	The broken umbrella	218-219
9.	Easter Monday excursion	221-226
10.	The blowing skirt	223

placed the revised version in the complete manuscript of *Paul Morel B*, retaining the part under discussion and putting it away with the other Miriam Papers, among which they were found after his death. On the strength of this speculation, this holograph text of twenty-three pages will, in further references to it here, be called *Paul Morel B*[1].

The table indicates the disposition of the principal sequences—episodes and narrative statements—of this part of *Paul Morel*; that is, of *Paul Morel B*[1]. The pages on which the material appears in the manuscript are indicated in the column. The table is of course a simplification, but it must serve until such time as the material concerned is published in full. The table cannot indicate transitions between sequences, which are often made by means of minor narrative statements. In the ensuing discussion, these sequences will be referred to by the numbers in the left-hand column of the table which designate their order of appearance. One fact for the reader to keep continually in mind throughout this part of the Miriam Papers is that Jessie Chambers was completely unable to see Paul and Miriam as fictional characters. Everything must be according to fact. And twenty years later she still regarded *Sons and Lovers* in the same way: it was "bad" when it introduced imaginative elements.

Discussion of Sequences

1. Since this manuscript fragment begins with the tail end of a sentence, the swinging episode, of which that sentence is a part, cannot be fully compared with the later version in the published *Sons and Lovers*. The existing evidence, however, indicates that the earlier version is less intense: in *Sons and Lovers*, Miriam's ecstatic fear of the swinging seems rather sexual—the dread and excitation of sex felt by a Victorian girl inclined to virginity. In the *Paul Morel* manuscript of the second compositional stage, she is merely nervous. She notices that Paul enjoys swinging, and therefore she lets him have longer turns; this helps establish a sense of harmony between them. Jessie Chambers struck a line through the last thought and substituted a statement to the effect that the swinging incident showed her how deeply Paul could become absorbed in activities that interested him, an idea Lawrence took over in *Sons and Lovers* and intensified: Paul becomes himself "swinging stuff," and "every particle of him" is involved.

2. In this B^1 version of *Paul Morel*, Paul tries to explain his painting to Miriam's brother Edgar, who mocks at him. In *Sons and Lovers* Edgar's comments are omitted; Paul makes a revised version of some of his explanations, to Miriam; she accepts them without mockery.

3. The algebra lessons are presented in somewhat more detail in *Paul Morel* B^1 than in *Sons and Lovers*. In the published novel, the account of the lessons is more general: Paul is described as

storming at Miriam and becoming furious and abusive. In the earlier version, the sequence is presented chiefly in dialogue: Paul shouts at her such names as duffer, fathead, and donkey. In the *Paul Morel B*[1] manuscript, Paul's "wrath, overcharged, would burst like a bubble. Then he would be very gentle, and she would want to cry. Once, in a real passion, he threw the soft covered algebra book full in her face." If this passage is compared with its improved version in *Sons and Lovers*, the superiority of the later text becomes evident at once. In *Sons and Lovers* Paul's anger still bursts like a bubble, and he throws a pencil rather than a book in Miriam's face; but the whole incident is made more vivid by the addition of details—significant, not irrelevant—and by intensification of emotion and concentration of focus. In the later version, for example, there is more concrete motive for one of Paul's spurts of anger than the mere statement that he was "in a real passion"; part of a single sentence will show how the material has been vivified: "When he saw her eager, silent, as it were, blind face, he wanted to throw the pencil in it; and still, when he saw her hand trembling and her mouth parted with suffering, his heart was scalded with pain for her." (In another passage he does, as previously mentioned, throw the pencil in her face.) Jessie Chambers wrote a suggestion on the manuscript of the original to the effect that the algebra sequence should be modified or left out; she had no personal objections to it, but she thought that readers might find it unintelligible or dull. And in a later paragraph she objected to Lawrence's saying that Paul and Miriam, at seventeen and sixteen, read Schopenhauer and Spencer and Nietzsche, "authors who," Lawrence wrote, "hurt her inexpressibly, and delighted him"; Lawrence subsequently omitted the reference to those authors.

4. A discussion between Paul and his mother about his frequent visits to Willey Farm stands out prominently in the *Paul Morel B*[1] manuscript. There are some general statements about Paul's attitude to his mother, including one that strikingly suggests the "blood-knowledge" doctrines Lawrence was to develop later: "Their connection was subconscious, physical, of the blood." (After Lawrence read Freud he stopped using the term *subconscious* and instead used Freud's term *unconscious*.) This

particular mother-son sequence is not found in *Sons and Lovers*, though various thoughts and phrases from it are applied or suggested throughout the book.

5. Paul's walk with Miriam on a summer evening is one of the romantic high points of *Sons and Lovers*. Like the other material taken over from *Paul Morel B*[1], it is greatly improved in the rewriting. The incidents are similar in both versions, but the treatment of the second is, once again, more vivid, intense, and living. For example, the sentence, "It was early June, and the red of sunset was being spun down behind the Derbyshire hills, as Paul and Miriam went between the young wheat on the high lands," becomes: "There was a yellow glow over the mowing-grass, and the sorrel-heads burned crimson. Gradually, as they walked along the high land, the gold in the west sank down to red, the red to crimson, and then the chill blue crept up against the glow." The landscapes throughout this sequence are touched up in this way, though occasionally a bit of the earlier picture is taken over without change, such as "the high road to Alfreton, which ran white between the darkening fields," the second "the" being the only addition to the later version. This version is not only enriched in the matter of landscape descriptions, but also in regard to the relationship of Miriam and Paul, which is considerably more intensified in *Sons and Lovers*. This sequence is particularly remarkable because it is one of the first successful large-scale attempts by Lawrence to fuse character and landscape. In the earlier version, Lawrence had included an erotic passage; in it, Miriam is so excited by "her" flowering rose-tree that she wants Paul to kiss her, "almost for the first time." But Paul feels that passion is sealed in him, his mood is "abstract, purely religious." Touching Miriam's lips would cause him great agony of spirit; he cannot give her "cool kisses." But Miriam, who "had made it impossible for him to kiss her," now wants his mouth. She wants him "to clasp her body," but it is her tragedy that she has "purified his love too much"; it is painful for him even to touch her. Jessie Chambers drew pencil marks across this passage and noted at the end that Lawrence in writing it had been guilty of an amazing misconception, for Miriam at sixteen was "as pure and fierce in virginity as Paul." Lawrence omitted the passage from *Sons and Lovers*.

6. Paul's talk with his mother after he gets back home on that summer evening is, like most of the other assimilated passages, expanded in *Sons and Lovers*. The dialogue at the beginning of the scene is almost the same in both texts—the mother sarcastically remarks that Miriam must be "wonderfully fascinating," she speaks against "boy-and-girl courtship," she insists she has nothing against Miriam, she angers Paul by referring persistently to courtship—but in *Sons and Lovers* Lawrence gives the episode more breadth by introducing references to Paul's sister Annie's "keeping company" with a young man. In the manuscript, Paul ends the scene by flinging his boots down, kissing his mother hastily "on the brow," and leaving; in the published novel, Paul exhibits more sympathy for his mother, who looks weary; she has not been strong since the death of Paul's older brother, "and her eyes hurt her." Paul stays with her for a while, trying to make peace, and as he kisses her forehead he notices the wrinkles on it, the greying hair, and "the proud setting of the temples." His hand lingers on her shoulder—he has forgotten Miriam. This ends the sequence in the book, where the transition passage to the Good Friday hike is different from the one in the manuscript. In the latter, Miriam is irritated because Paul is "at the beck and call of everybody." Jessie Chambers questioned this passage in a note at the bottom of the page, in which she protested that "Miriam revered Paul's love for his mother." She added that both Paul and Miriam were at this time "unconscious," not desiring "even love." Lawrence's statement that Paul was at this time a child, "just an unmanageable, tiresome child," was crossed out by Jessie Chambers, who noted: "Not until twenty-one."

7. Lawrence in *Sons and Lovers* makes Paul older in the Good-Friday-hike sequence than in *Paul Morel B*[1]; in the latter, the hike takes place when Paul is eighteen, but in *Sons and Lovers* he is a year older—perhaps Lawrence was weary of Jessie's marginal notes to the effect that Paul and Miriam were too young to have certain feelings. In the transition passage preceding the hike episode, Lawrence in *Sons and Lovers* has a long paragraph about Miriam's hypersensitiveness to the physical facts of life: grossness of any kind upsets her, and the men around the farm must be careful what they say in her presence; they cannot

even mention that the mare is in foal. The Good Friday hike itself is essentially the same in both manuscript and book; the latter is, as usual, more detailed and vivid. The sequence ends, in both accounts, with a discussion between Paul and Miriam; this is the "love begets love" dialogue that takes up about half a page in *Sons and Lovers*. This was a longer scene in *Paul Morel B¹*, but Jessie Chambers scratched out a good deal of it and pencilled in extensive comments. Lawrence did not use anything she had objected to here. He had originally cast the scene into "another day" (from the day of the hike), but Jessie wrote in "the same" above "another"—Lawrence put "another evening" into *Sons and Lovers*. In both cases, Paul and Miriam are walking under the trees at Nether Green; in *Sons and Lovers*, before he speaks about love's being necessarily reciprocal, he has been "talking to her fretfully," as if "struggling to convince himself." In the earlier text, Miriam has wanted Paul to acknowledge his love; she was sure of his love but desired to have him acknowledge it. Jessie Chambers drew pencil marks through this passage and wrote above it: "Oh dear no: the conversation was Paul's." Later she noted that Paul's remarks in this scene were self-justification; he was coming under the spell of "the second self that watches things." She wrote further that Miriam was at this time the stronger of the two because her love for Paul had not yet grown beyond control; the denial of it became terrible later, when "it became invested with holiness like religion and had behind it the whole force of the will to live."

8. The broken-umbrella sequence stands out importantly in *Sons and Lovers* and in Jessie Chambers' comments upon it. The scene is presented so vividly from Miriam's point of view in *Paul Morel B¹* that it suggests that this manuscript was in part based on passages originally prepared by Jessie Chambers, as in the first part of the Miriam Papers—or that Jessie had perhaps mentioned emphatically to Lawrence how deeply she had been impressed by the incident when it actually occurred. She wrote of it in her *D. H. Lawrence: A Personal Record*, more than twenty years after the publication of *Sons and Lovers* and more than thirty years after the probable date of the incident itself. In her memoir she gives it the position of climax at the end of her first chapter: a party of young people had been walk-

ing, and she had strayed away from the others. Suddenly she saw Lawrence, a figure apart from the rest, bending over an umbrella. "His stooping figure had a look of intensity, almost of anguish," and he became to her "a symbolic figure"; she dates their "awareness of sympathy for one another from that moment." The situation in the previously mentioned passage in *Paul Morel B*[1] is the same; in both accounts, the young man explains that he is concerned because the umbrella belonged to the older brother who had died, and the mother will be grieved if it is broken. In *Sons and Lovers* the episode is, like all the others assimilated into that work, greatly improved. Again, the correct details are added to provide the most effective background and to sharpen the action in the foreground. The positions of the figures concerned are made clearer—there is no vague or merely half-defined wandering, but a distinct geographic placing of the characters involved. And Lawrence in his final version of the incident lifts it into poetry: Miriam sees Paul "in dark relief" against "one rift of rich gold in that colourless grey evening." He is "slender and firm, as if the setting sun had given him to her." He tells her why he is upset about the broken umbrella: Lawrence in this version deepens the emotional texture of the scene by explaining that Miriam realizes with shame that the umbrella had been damaged not by Paul but by her brother Geoffrey. In *Paul Morel B*[1], Lawrence wrote a paragraph about Miriam's later reflections, in which she was aware of Paul's essential loneliness; Jessie Chambers crossed out several of his sentences in this passage, particularly statements trying to interpret her feelings about him, such as her inability to understand his sadness. In *Sons and Lovers* Lawrence omitted all further reference to the incident except one sentence stating that Miriam "always regarded that sudden coming upon him as a revelation."

9. In the transition passage between the Good Friday and Easter Monday excursions, Lawrence in *Paul Morel B*[1] has Paul from time to time outrage "the family feeling at Willey Farm," by becoming suddenly angry at one of Miriam's brothers, and Miriam ("much distressed") take Paul's part against the family. Jessie pencilled out this entire passage and wrote at the end of it, "This was not my meaning," indicating once again that *Paul*

Morel B[1] was possibly based on passages originally written by Jessie Chambers, such as those in the first part of the Miriam Papers. Lawrence included this passage, only slightly modified, in *Sons and Lovers;* this is one of the few times he overruled Jessie's objections. The descriptions of Miriam's dreams, which he wedges into the "family feeling" paragraph in *Sons and Lovers,* he incorporates with little change—it was a separate paragraph in *Paul Morel B*[1]—but he omits the original last sentence, which had stated that Miriam "knew she and Paul were woven together unconsciously"; Jessie noted that Miriam did not realize this "until Paul insisted upon it." She also makes several changes in the account of Easter Monday excursion which, nevertheless, is taken into *Sons and Lovers* very much as it stood in *Paul Morel B*[1]. As usual, the material is enriched in the later version. One of the passages Jessie Chambers crossed out occurred at the end of the paragraph which describes Paul putting his hand over Miriam's hand as she carries her bag by its strings. In *Paul Morel B*[1], Lawrence remarks that Paul rarely touched her, and that she failed to understand how she could so intensify "his already fierce virginity." Jessie Chambers wrote above these lines she had crossed out that there was no question of Paul's touching her "at that time." Lawrence, as usual, omitted the passages Jessie had crossed out. Her other significant comments on this sequence occur toward the end of it, when Paul is tired at the end of the day; in *Sons and Lovers* Lawrence merely indicates that Miriam understands his fatigue and is gentle with him. In *Paul Morel B*[1], Lawrence had written that Miriam did not dare speak to Paul, who might have spoken sharply to her. Jessie Chambers drew pencil marks through this passage and added that such a statement was not true as applied "to that time"—she was "not yet unbalanced" by the strife that later caused her to be thrown "into extravaganza etc." This Easter Monday sequence, incidentally, is different from the "Easter Monday" fragment in the first part of the Miriam Papers; they are Easter Mondays of different years, occurring in different chapters in *Sons and Lovers*. The one just discussed is chronologically earlier and occurs in Chapter VII of the published novel, the other in Chapter IX of the novel.

10. The passage describing the blowing of Miriam's skirt is a

part of the narrative of the Easter Monday excursion. As Miriam climbs the stone stairway to the ruin of Wingfield Manor, the wind blows her skirt up, so that she is "ashamed"; Paul takes hold of the hem of her dress, holding it down, "chattering naturally all the while." Jessie Chambers, in striking out the last phrase, wrote that "there was no need" for Paul "to chat" while committing this "act of the purest intimacy." She cautioned him: "Do not degrade it." In *Sons and Lovers* this scene stands out, like that of the broken umbrella, as one of the important "human touches" in the book; there are many of them, and they are among the elements that contribute to the book's power. In the novel, Lawrence tells of Paul's catching the hem of Miriam's dress and holding it down, and he ends the passage with telling effectiveness: "He did it perfectly simply, as he would have picked up her glove. She remembered this always."

One more document remains to be examined: the last section of these Miriam Papers is a four-page commentary, in pencil, entitled "Chapter IX." This commentary is on ruled paper, seven and seven-eighths inches by nine, possibly cut out of a composition book; it is apparently of the same type as the one on whose pages the "Saturday Afternoon" sequence was written in the first part of the Miriam Papers; both the "Saturday Afternoon" and the "Chapter IX" notes may, of course, be from the same "exercise" book—even if they are, however, they may have been written at different times. The "Chapter IX" section refers chiefly to what became Chapter VII in *Paul Morel C*, the final draft of *Sons and Lovers;* as previously pointed out, Jessie Chambers refers to this chapter, in her "Chapter IX" section, as "First Love," corresponding to the "Lad-And-Girl Love" title of Chapter VII of *Sons and Lovers.* This chapter begins with an account of Paul's frequent visits to Miriam's farm which, Lawrence explains, had been a laborer's cottage. The kitchen is "irregular" and quite small, but Paul loves it, even the "old and battered furniture." Jessie Chambers' first note in her "Chapter IX" comments is a protest against Lawrence's "cruel and unnecessary" description of the furniture and of the family mealtimes; since the first part of Lawrence's holograph of *Paul Morel B*[1] is missing, we cannot tell how much he may have modified his "unnecessary cruelty" in the final draft.

Jessie accused Lawrence, in these comments, of writing the chapter "from the standpoint of twenty-six instead of that of seventeen." Her questioning of his passage about Nietzsche, Schopenhauer, and Spencer has already been mentioned; here she complains that a boy of seventeen and a girl of sixteen would find these authors "hard stuff." Another hand has scrawled something below this which may be a large NO: it is apparently the same hand (Lawrence's) that wrote a number of such NO's on a manuscript Bertrand Russell sent Lawrence (see the facsimile facing p. 88 of *D. H. Lawrence's Letters to Bertrand Russell*).

Another commentary by Jessie Chambers concerns the episode of the rose tree in Sequence 7 of the *Paul Morel B*[1] fragment; Jessie Chambers reiterated that there was no sexual instinct awake in either Miriam or Paul at that time, and that to suggest that such an instinct was awake in Miriam "destroys the purity of the whole incident," which was as spiritual to her as it was to him. She spoke again of the broken-umbrella episode as "a spiritual awakening" that revealed Paul's inner quality to her and "set her wondering and eternally seeking."

Jessie Chambers protested against p. 220 of Lawrence's holograph; this page has already been discussed in reference to Sequence 7, the Good Friday excursion—Lawrence had written that Miriam knew Paul loved her, but wanted him to acknowledge this, and that Paul had spoken of love engendering love; Jessie had written over this passage that Miriam had been the stronger of the two then, before her love for Paul got beyond control. In her "Chapter IX" commentary she complained that Paul tries to stand aloof in the passage just mentioned, but that in life he (Lawrence) was a part of the situation. Jessie explained that their relationship had been "of the spirit of God, as I lived it and as I gave it to you in my writing"—another indication that all of the *Paul Morel B*[1] chapter was possibly drafted from original manuscripts Jessie Chambers wrote after reading *Paul Morel A*. She asked, in her comments on p. 20 of the *B*[1] holograph, if what she felt for Lawrence could have lasted "till now" had it not been "a fine rare robust thing." Jessie wrote this before she heard of Frieda; possibly just before, rather than after, Lawrence had met Frieda.

Jessie Chambers concluded her notes with a critique of the entire chapter, which she felt was inadequately and unsympathetically conceived; it contained facts but lacked interpretation. Miriam, Jessie felt, should have been more impersonally presented (it might be pointed out that Jessie's presentation of the girl's case is at the remotest extreme from the impersonal). She told Lawrence, in further comment, that since love is so great a miracle, Miriam's "complete" love for Paul should have been treated as something more than a weakness, to be "laughed at a little." She pointed out that Miriam and Paul were in unconscious sympathy at this stage, with no thought of distinguishing between body and spirit "because each was perfectly pure" ("each" probably refers to Paul and Miriam rather than body or soul). Jessie insisted that the idea of purity should dominate the chapter, for Miriam had no thought of kisses; she was proud and delighted that there was between her and Paul "no constraint of sex"; Paul could not have been more virginal than the girl—and this assertion is underlined. The chapter should be "white," she said, unsmudged by sex, which at seventeen would "be rather smudgy." And "all that" (the smudginess of sex?) came largely from the Lawrence family's strife; "my own folk were generous to a fault." The misery and the constraint in Lawrence's and Jessie's relationship came from "interference from outside: with all the inexplicable things of sex dragged in train." Her comments end with the statement that the chapter "First Love" must stand or fall "on Miriam's absolute purity of motive."

All this is the cry of a broken heart—and of a broken Victorian heart. And despite the fact that Jessie Chambers felt betrayed because "in *Sons and Lovers* Lawrence handed his mother the laurels of victory," we must once again remember that Lawrence was writing fiction, not biography; that despite his personal involvement in the subject matter he saw it with the eye of the artist. And at the last he wrote without sentimentalism or self-pity, but with tenderness and with artistic truth.

APPENDIX C

The Lawrence Country

A Guide to the Map

In an essay written shortly before his death, "Nottingham and the Mining Countryside" (published in *Phoenix*), Lawrence described what might be called the Lawrence Country:

I was born nearly forty-four years ago, in Eastwood, a mining village of some three thousand souls, about eight miles from Nottingham, and one mile from the small stream, the Erewash, which divides Nottinghamshire from Derbyshire. It is hilly country, looking west to Crich and towards Matlock, sixteen miles away, and east and north-east towards Mansfield and the Sherwood Forest district. To me it seemed, and still seems, an extremely beautiful countryside, just between the red sandstone and the oak-trees of Nottingham, and the cold limestone, the ash-trees, the stone fences of Derbyshire. To me, as a child and a young man, it was still the old England of the forest and agricultural past; there were no motor-cars, the mines were, in a sense, an accident in the landscape, and Robin Hood and his merry men were not very far away.

This was the landscape of Lawrence's early novels, stories and poems, and he returned to it in some of his later books, such as *Lady Chatterley's Lover* and *The Virgin and the Gipsy*. Ada Lawrence and G. Stuart Gelder have a note on the Lawrence Country in *Young Lorenzo: Early Life of D. H. Lawrence*. They explain that many readers are confused because Lawrence sometimes described one part of the Notts-Derby region and called it by the name of another; Strelley Mill in *The White Peacock*, for example, was actually Felley Mill; Strelley is a village located several miles away, and it does not

306

figure in the story. Lawrence did not disguise the name of the Ram Inn in that same novel, although he changed Moorgreen reservoir to Nethermere and the residence of the colliery owner, Lamb Close, to Highclose; the name of the mining company, Barber, Walker, and Company, became Tempest, Warrall, and Company in the story.

The authors of *Young Lorenzo* further explain that the Bestwood of *Sons and Lovers* is Lawrence's native Eastwood, though there is a nearby village and colliery actually called Bestwood. Moorgreen reservoir in this novel became Minton, while the name of the mining company was changed to Carson, Waite, and Company. Willey Farm was The Haggs farm where Miriam (Jessie Chambers) lived. "Nuttall is Underwood and has nothing to do with the picturesque village, now being rapidly spoilt by building speculators, which lies on the Nottingham-Eastwood main road."

In *The Rainbow*, Lawrence changed the name of the village of Cossall to Cossethay: Marsh Farm actually lies near the canal bank there, and the Brangwens' cottage stands near the village church. Lawrence took the town of Quorn, Leicestershire, as his model for Beldover. The authors of *Young Lorenzo* do not discuss the background of *Women in Love*, in which many of the place names used in *Sons and Lovers* and *The Rainbow* are repeated; but Lamb Close house becomes Shortlands in that book, and Eastwood is Willey Green. The authors make several identifications, however, in relation to *The Lost Girl*, in which Eastwood became Woodhouse. The cinema at Lumley in the story was actually at Langley Mill, adjoining Eastwood, and the Klondyke Brickyard was at New Eastwood. Extreme reticence is observed by the authors in connection with *Lady Chatterley's Lover*, the book with which Lawrence in later years returned imaginatively to the Midlands. But although Ada Lawrence Clarke and G. Stuart Gelder do not make any identifications in connection with this novel, it is well known that the Sitwell family, which has an estate in Derbyshire, felt victimized by *Lady Chatterley's Lover*. Frieda Lawrence, however, denied in her memoir that the Sitwells were involved, and Lawrence in one of his humorous little "Last" poems scoffed at the idea. He had once again used Lamb Close house; those who know it and the area will easily recognize them in *Lady Chatterley's Lover*.

Lawrence twice in his correspondence referred to his fictional use of this region. In one of the *Letters* he wrote:

The scene of my Nottingham-Derby novels all centres round Eastwood, Notts (where I was born): and whoever stands on Walker Street, Eastwood, will see the whole landscape of *Sons and Lovers* before him: Underwood in front, the hills of Derbyshire on the left, the woods and hills of Annesley on the right. The road from Nottingham by Watnall, Moorgreen, up to Underwood and on to Annesley (Byron's Annesley)—gives you all the landscape of *The White Peacock*, Miriam's farm in *Sons and Lovers*, and the home of the Crich family, and Willey Water, in *Women in Love*.

The Rainbow is Ilkeston and Cossall, near Ilkeston, moving to Eastwood. And Hermione, in *Women in Love*, is supposed to live not far from Cromford. The short stories are Ripley, Wirksworth, Stoney Middleton, Via Gellia ("The Wintry Peacock"). *The Lost Girl* begins in Eastwood—the cinematograph show being in Langley Mill.

And in another of the *Letters*, one more personal in tone, he said:

How well I can see Hucknall Torkard and the miners! Didn't you go into the church to see the tablet, where Byron's heart is buried? My father used to sing in the Newstead Abbey choir, as a boy. But I've gone many times down Hucknall Long Lane to Watnall—and I like Watnall Park—it's a great Sunday morning walk. Some of my happiest days I've spent in the fields just opposite the S. side of Greasley church—bottom of Watnall Hill—adjoining the vicarage: Miriam's father hired those fields. If you're in those parts again, go to Eastwood, where I was born, and lived for my first 21 years. Go to Walker St.—and stand in front of the third house—and look across at Crich on the left, Underwood in front—High Park woods and Annesley on the right: I lived in that house from the age of 6 to 18, and I know that view better than any in the world. Then walk down the fields to the Breach, and in the corner house facing the stile I lived from 1 to 6. And walk up Engine Lane, over the level-crossing at Moorgreen pit, along till you come to the highway (the Alfreton Rd.)—turn to the left, towards Underwood, and go till you come to the lodge gate by the reservoir—go through the gate, and up the drive to the next gate, and continue on the *footpath* just below the drive on the left—on through the wood to Felley Mill (the *White Peacock* farm). When you've crossed the brook, turn to the right through Felley Mill gate, and go up the footpath to Annesley. Or better still, turn to the right, uphill, *before* you descend to the brook, and go on uphill, up the rough deserted pasture—on past Annesley Kennels—long empty—on to Annesley again. That's the country of my heart. From the hills, if you look across at Underwood wood, you'll see a tiny red farm on the edge of the wood. That was Miriam's farm—where I got my first incentive to write.

BIBLIOGRAPHY

BOOKS BY D. H. LAWRENCE

Listed According to Genre

[*Note*. Many authors dislike the bibliographical studies and the first-edition mongering of their books; Ernest Hemingway, for instance, said in the introduction to a bibliography of his work that he thought such books were "all balls." Lawrence, in his preface to E. D. McDonald's first Lawrence bibliography, sounds more tolerant; he said that "to every man who struggles with his own soul in mystery, a book that is a book flowers once, and seeds, and is gone. First editions or forty-first are only the husks of it," but "if it amuses a man to save the husks of the flower that opened once for the first time, one can understand that too. It is like the costumes that men and women used to wear in their youth, years ago, and which now stand up rather faded in museums. . . ." The list of Lawrence first editions which follows is meant to be an informational supplement to the present volume, but enough bibliographical data are provided to be of positive assistance to readers who wish to start collecting Lawrence "firsts." The list gives the title, place, publisher, date, and number of pages of every important Lawrence first edition; additional information is occasionally supplied, as in the case of a pseudonym (Lawrence H. Davison, *Movements in European History*), a collaboration (M. L. Skinner and D. H.

311

Lawrence wrote *The Boy in The Bush*), or an important introduction (such as the one by Robinson Jeffers to the volume of
Lawrence's poetry called *Fire*). Dr. McDonald's two volumes
(1925 and 1931) are the principal source, with some information
drawn from Gilbert H. Fabes (1933), who relied extensively on
McDonald, from the checklists by William White in the *Bul-
letin of Bibliography* (1948-49), and from *A Bibliography of D.
H. Lawrence* by Warren Roberts (1963). McDonald is of the
school which believes that primacy of date establishes the true
first edition. Some bibliographers, however, believe that first
editions "follow the flag," and that any work of an author published in his home country takes precedence over editions of the
same work published elsewhere within that year. For example,
R. L. Mégroz in his chronological list of Lawrence "firsts" at
the end of his *Five Novelist Poets of Today* lists the Martin
Secker publication of *Aaron's Rod* in London in 1922 as the
proper "first," though McDonald credits Thomas Seltzer of
New York, who brought the book out in April, two months
before Secker. McDonald, however, lists William Heinemann's
London edition of *The White Peacock* as the true first, though
Duffield in New York had brought it out a day earlier, on
January 20, 1911. McDonald, the authority for these dates, probably thought it wiser not to state that the first edition of Lawrence's first book was the American edition, particularly when
only one day's difference was involved; McDonald is usually on
the side of common sense, and when there is a discrepancy of
several months between editions, as in the case of *Aaron's Rod*,
he has good reason to label the earlier edition as the proper first.
The following checklist will, as previously indicated, follow the
McDonald adjudications. Various small pamphlets are listed here
as "firsts," though obviously their value is slight in comparison
with first editions of such books as *Sons and Lovers* and *The
Rainbow*. The author of this volume agrees with Dr. McDonald
that the pamphlet *Dirty Words* (c. 1931) is spurious. And he
hopes that the following list is, within its limits, authentic and
correct. For completeness, the reader is referred to *A Bibliography of D. H. Lawrence, by* Warren Roberts (1963), though the
present compiler doesn't always agree with the adjudications of
his good friend Dr. Roberts.]

NOVELS

The White Peacock. London: William Heinemann, 1911 (copyright 1910). pp. iv, 496.

The Trespasser. London: Duckworth and Co., 1912. pp. iv, 292.

Sons and Lovers. London: Duckworth and Co., 1913, pp. viii, 424.

The Rainbow. London: Methuen and Co., Ltd., 1915. pp. viii, 468.

Women in Love. New York: Privately Printed for Subscribers Only [Thomas Seltzer], 1920. pp. iv, 540.

The Lost Girl. London: Martin Secker, 1920. pp. 372.

Aaron's Rod. New York: Thomas Seltzer, 1922. pp. 348.

Kangaroo. London: Martin Secker, 1923. pp. vi, 408.

The Boy in the Bush, "with M. L. Skinner." London: Martin Secker, 1924. pp. vi, 376.

The Plumed Serpent. London: Martin Secker, 1926. pp. 480.

Lady Chatterley's Lover. Florence: Privately Printed, 1928. pp. iv, 368.

The Virgin and the Gipsy. Florence: G. Orioli, 1930. pp. 220.

Lady Chatterley's Lover. London: Martin Secker, 1932. pp. 327. (First authorized British edition, abridged.)

The First Lady Chatterley. New York: Dial Press, 1944. pp. xviii, 320.

STORIES AND SHORT NOVELS

The Prussian Officer and Other Stories. London: Duckworth and Co., 1914. pp. viii, 312.

England, My England and Other Stories. New York: Thomas Seltzer, 1922. pp. vi, 274.

The Ladybird: The Fox, The Captain's Doll. London: Martin Secker, 1923. pp. 256.

St. Mawr: Together with the Princess. London: Martin Secker, 1925. pp. 240.

Sun. London: E. Archer, 1926. pp. ii, 22.

Glad Ghosts. London: Ernest Benn Ltd., 1926. pp. iv, 80.

Rawdon's Roof. London: Elkin Mathews and Marrot, 1928. pp. 32.

The Woman Who Rode Away and Other Stories. London: Martin Secker, 1928. pp. 296.

Sun. Paris: The Black Sun Press, 1928. pp. viii, 46. (Authorized unexpurgated edition.)

The Escaped Cock. Paris: The Black Sun Press, 1929. pp. xii, 104.

Love Among The Haystacks and Other Pieces. With a Reminiscence by David Garnett. London: The Nonesuch Press, 1930. pp. xiv, 98.

The Lovely Lady and Other Stories. London: Martin Secker, 1933. pp. 246.

A Modern Lover. London: Martin Secker, 1934. pp. 312.

The Tales of D. H. Lawrence. London: Martin Secker, 1934. pp. 1138.

Prelude: With an Explanatory Foreword . . . by P. Beaumont Wadsworth. Thames Ditton, Surrey: The Merle Press, 1949. pp. 48.

POEMS

Love Poems and Others. London: Duckworth and Co., 1913. pp. vi, 64.

Amores. London: Duckworth and Co., 1916. pp. viii, 140.

Look! We Have Come Through! London: Chatto and Windus, 1917. pp. 168.

New Poems. London: Martin Secker, 1918. pp. 64.

Bay: A Book of Poems. London, 1919. pp. 48. [The Beaumont Press.]

Tortoises. New York: Thomas Seltzer, 1921. pp. 50.

Birds, Beasts and Flowers. New York: Thomas Seltzer, 1923. pp. 208.

The Collected Poems of D. H. Lawrence. 2 vols. London: Martin Secker, 1928. pp. 232; 304.

Pansies. London: Martin Secker, 1929. pp. 160.

Pansies. London, 1929. pp. xiv, 126. (Privately printed for Subscribers only, "printed complete, following the original manuscript," subsequent to trade edition.)

Nettles. London: Faber and Faber Ltd., 1930. pp. ii, 30.

The Triumph of the Machine. London: Faber and Faber Ltd., 1930. pp. 8.

Last Poems. Edited by Richard Aldington and Giuseppe Orioli. Florence: G. Orioli, 1932. pp. xxii, 320.

Fire and Other Poems. With a Foreword by Robinson Jeffers. San Francisco, 1940. pp. xiv, 46. ("Printed at the Grabhorn Press for the Book Club of California.")

Look! We Have Come Through! With an Introduction by Frieda Lawrence. Marazion: The Ark Press, 1958. pp. 109. (First complete edition.)

ESSAYS AND STUDIES

Movements in European History ("by Lawrence H. Davison"). London: Oxford University Press, 1921. pp. x, 306.

Psychoanalysis and the Unconscious. New York: Thomas Seltzer, 1921. pp. 120.

Fantasia of the Unconscious. New York: Thomas Seltzer, 1922. pp. 176.

Studies in Classic American Literature. New York: Thomas Seltzer, 1923. pp. x, 266.

Reflections on the Death of a Porcupine and Other Essays. Philadelphia: The Centaur Press, 1925. pp. x, 246.

Sex Locked Out. London, 1928. pp. 12. ("Reprinted, December 1928, from the Sunday Dispatch, London, November 25, 1928"; a pamphlet apparently printed without Lawrence's authorization or knowledge.)

My Skirmish with Jolly Roger. New York: Random House, 1929. pp. 12.

Pornography and Obscenity. London: Faber and Faber Ltd., 1929. pp. 32.

A Propos of Lady Chatterley's Lover. London: Mandrake Press, 1930. pp. 64.

Assorted Articles. London: Martin Secker, 1930. pp. 216.

Apocalypse. Florence: G. Orioli, 1931. pp. 308.

We Need One Another. New York: Equinox Cooperative Press, 1933. pp. 68.

The Universe and Me. New York: H. Taylor, 1935. pp. 6. [Privately printed: Powgen Press.]

Foreword to Women in Love. San Francisco: Gelber, Lilienthal, Inc., 1936. pp. 11.

Phoenix: The Posthumous Papers of D. H. Lawrence. Edited by E. D. McDonald. London: William Heinemann Ltd., 1936. p. xxvii, 852.

The Symbolic Meaning: The uncollected versions of *Studies in Classic American Literature.* Edited by Armin Arnold. Fontwell: Centaur Press Ltd., 1962. pp. 264.

TRAVEL

Twilight in Italy. London: Duckworth and Co., 1916. pp. viii, 312.

Sea and Sardinia. New York: Thomas Seltzer, 1921. pp. 356.

Mornings in Mexico. London: Martin Secker, 1927. pp. 180.

Etruscan Places. London: Martin Secker, 1932. pp. 202.

PLAYS

The Widowing of Mrs. Holroyd. New York: Mitchell Kennerley, 1914. pp. x, 94.

Touch and Go. London: C. W. Daniel, Ltd., 1920. pp. 96.

David. London: Martin Secker, 1926. pp. 128.

The Plays of D. H. Lawrence. London: Martin Secker, 1933. pp. 312.

A Collier's Friday Night. London: Martin Secker, 1934. pp. vii, 87.

[Note. Several other plays by D. H. Lawrence have been published in magazines, generally as supplements or as entire issues. *Keeping Barbara,* usually known as *The Fight For Barbara,* appeared in *Argosy,* December 1933. The *Laughing Horse,* Summer 1938, contained *Altitude;* the *Virginia Quarterly Review* printed *The Married Man* in the Autumn 1940 issue and *Merry-Go-Round* in the Winter 1941 issue. Walter Greenwood's *My Son's My Son,* a Lawrence manuscript of an unfinished play completed by Greenwood—as yet unpublished—was produced in London in 1936. One of Lawrence's *England, My England* stories, "You Touched Me," was dramatized by Tennessee Williams and Donald Windham and presented on Broadway in 1945, with Edmund Gwenn and Montgomery Clift featured in the production; the play was first published in Boston by the Walter H. Baker Company, 1946.]

LETTERS

A Letter From Cornwall (January 5, 1916). San Francisco: Yerba Buena Press, 1931. pp. 12.

The Letters of D. H. Lawrence. Edited by Aldous Huxley. London: William Heinemann Ltd., 1932. pp. xxxiv, 889.

D. H. Lawrence's Letter to "The Laughing Horse." Privately printed, 1936. pp. 14. [San Francisco: Yerba Press.]

D. H. Lawrence's Letters to Bertrand Russell. Edited by Harry T. Moore. New York: The Gotham Book Mart, 1948. pp. 111.

Eight Letters by D. H. Lawrence to Rachel Annand Taylor. With a Foreword by Majl Ewing. Pasadena: Castle Press, 1956. pp. 16.

The Collected Letters of D. H. Lawrence. Edited by Harry T. Moore. 2 vols. London: William Heinemann Ltd., 1962. pp. 1,307.

TRANSLATIONS

Shestov, Leo. *All Things Are Possible.* Authorized translation by S. S. Koteliansky. With a Foreword by D. H. Lawrence. London: Martin Secker, 1920. pp. 248. (According to a statement by the late S. S. Koteliansky, his translation was revised by Lawrence, who thus became co-translator of the book.)

Bunin, Ivan. *The Gentleman From San Francisco and Other Stories.* Translated from the Russian by S. S. Koteliansky and Leonard Woolf. London: The Hogarth Press, 1922. pp. vi, 88. (A tipped-in title-page erratum note says "The first story in this book . . . is translated by D. H. Lawrence and S. S. Koteliansky. Owing to a mistake Mr. Lawrence's name has been omitted from the title-page.")

Verga, Giovanni. *Mastro-don Gesualdo*. Translated by D. H.
   Lawrence. New York: Thomas Seltzer, 1923. pp. xii, 465.
Verga, Giovanni. *Little Novels of Sicily*. Translated by D. H.
   Lawrence. New York: Thomas Seltzer, 1925. pp. 228.
Verga, Giovanni. *Cavalleria Rusticana and Other Stories*. Trans-
   lated by D. H. Lawrence. London: Jonathan Cape, 1928.
   pp. 224.
Lasca, Il. *The Story of Doctor Manente: Being the Tenth and
   Last Story from the Suppers of A. F. Grazzini Called Il
   Lasca*. Translation and Introduction by D. H. Lawrence.
   Florence: G. Orioli, 1929. pp. xxiv, 122.

PAINTINGS

The Paintings of D. H. Lawrence. London: The Mandrake
   Press, 1929. pp. 148. (Introduction by Lawrence.)
[Lawrence's paintings—not only those from the Mandrake Press
edition, but others from all over the world—will be reproduced
in a forthcoming volume to be issued in England by Cory,
Adams and Mackay, Ltd., under the editorship of Anthony
Adams of that firm, of Mervyn Levy of *Studio*, and of Jack
Lindsay, who was instrumental in getting the Mandrake volume
published. Basic Books is reported to be planning a somewhat
similar volume in the United States.]

INDEX

319